D0372235

EDIZIONI
MV
MUSEI VATICANI

sillabe

back cover:
Address of his holiness Benedict XVI
to the staff of the Vatican Museums
Thursday, 23 November 2006
© Libreria Editrice Vaticana

ISBN 978-88-8271-032-3

© Edizioni Musei Vaticani
www.museivaticani.va

First edition 2010

Texts: *Susanna Bertoldi*

Coordination: *Maria Serlupi Crescenzi* (Educational Division of the
Vatican Museums)

published by
s i l l a b e s.r.l.
www.sillabe.it
ISBN 978-88-8347-521-4

Managing editor: *Maddalena Paola Winspeare*
Graphic design: *Laura Belforte*
Italian editing and iconographic research: *Barbara Galla,
Nicola Bianchini*
English editing: *Giulia Bastianelli*
Translation: *Catherine Burnett*

Photo credits
Archivio fotografico Musei Vaticani
*selection: Rosanna Di Pinto, photos: A. Bracchetti, L. Giordano,
D. Pivato, P. Zigrossi; A. Angeli, Berri, F.M.R.-G. Ricci,
A. Maranzano, G. Nimatallah, T. Okamura, M. Sarri, G. Vasari;*
Archivio Casa Buonarroti, *Florence;* Archivio Sillabe, *Livorno;*
Biblioteca dell'Istituto Nazionale di Archeologia e Storia
dell'Arte, *Rome*

The Vatican Museums

discover
the history
the works of art
the collections

EDIZIONI MUSEI VATICANI

sillabe

BENEDICTVS ·XIV· P· M·
AD AVGENDVM VRBIS SPLENDOREM
ET ASSERENDAM RELIGIONIS VERITATEM
SACRIS CHRISTIANORVM MONIMENTIS
MVSEI CARPINEI BONARROTII VICTORII
ALIISQVE PLVRIMIS VNDIQVE CONQVISITIS
ET AB INTERITV VINDICATIS
NOVVM MVSEVM
ADORNAVIT INSTRVXIT PERFECIT
ANNO MDCCLVI

'*Ad* *ugendum Urbis splendorem et asserendam religionis veritatem*'. The epigraph of Benedict XIV Lambertini over the entrance to the Christian Museum effectively summarises the history and the destiny of the pope's art collections.

Pope Benedict XIV understood everything, all the treasures and history visitors encounter as they walk through the areas full of famous names (Michelangelo in the Sistine Chapel and Raphael in the *Stanze*, Caravaggio and Leonardo in the Pinacoteca, the *Laocoon* in the Octagonal Courtyard and the *Ariadne* in the Pius-Clementine Museum, the Gallery of Maps, Fra Angelico in the Chapel of Nicholas V, Matisse and Rouault in the Modern Religious Art collection, the Etruscan and Egyptian works collected under the name of Gregory XVI, the African masks and customary Papuan pirogues in the Missionary Ethnological Museum). All this and more was created, collected and preserved to add glory and splendour to the city of Rome and, by extension, to the greatest city of all – the world – entrusted to the magisterium of the universal Church.

The treasures and history of the Vatican Museums also serve '*ad sserendam religionis veritatem*' ('to affirm the truth of the Christian religion'). In this regard the pope's collections are an immense marvel rooted in catechesis and the history of the Church. On the subject of catechesis, we can behold the Sistine Chapel where the Quattrocentists under Sixtus IV (Botticelli, Perugino, Ghirlandaio and Signorelli), and then Michelangelo, recount the "historia salutis" from the Law of Moses and the Law of Christ ranging from the creation of the world to the Last Judgement. We can admire the Chapel of Nicholas V dedicated to the deacon saints Lawrence and Stephan, where Fra Angelico illustrated the virtues of charity, pureness of heart and self sacrifice to the point of martyrdom. We can also look at the Room of the Signature, where Raphael drew the destiny of Man set between knowledge and revelation, the observance of the Law and the consolation of beauty, or the Room of Heliodorus, where the artist transformed God's providential incursions in history into figures.

Along with the catechesis embodied in great art, the two thousand year history of the Church as well as its ideological, cultural and "political" choices can also be seen in the Vatican Museums, when, for example, Early Christianity took on the naturalistic and illusionistic style of the Greeks and the Romans and used it to give form to its messages. Hence, we can recognize Christ the Saviour's face in Orpheus or Phoebus Apollo and in nude Hercules and indomitable Daniel in the lions' den.

Later on, during the age of Humanism, the Renaissance and the Baroque period, the Church took a great chance on a comparison with truth (the truth of nature but also an emotive and psychological truth) through the work of Melozzo, Leonardo, Caravaggio, Guercino and Bernini. At the same time it "Christianised" the ancient by filling its galleries with vast collections of classical sculptures (the Chiaramonti Museum, the New Wing etc...).

Later still, in the dramatic twentieth century of Pius XI, Pius XII, John XXIII and Paul VI, a respectful homage to extra-European cultures emerged (the Ethnological Missionary Museum), while an attempt to reconstruct the painful rupture between art and the Church produced by the modern age took shape with the birth of the Museum of Modern Religious Art.

The Vatican Museums are referred to in the plural as there many different collections (from Greco-Roman sculpture to Symbolists, from Egyptian mummies to the ivory works of the Early Middle Ages, from Renaissance painting to Burri and Bacon and from ethnographical furnishings to Etruscan bronzes); there was not an aspect of human creativity which the Church did not wish to recognise, preserve and honour.

Whoever tackles the collections and history that the Museums of the Pope conserve, with a scientific method and an aim to reach a large audience, cannot but consider the specificity I have tried to summarise above.

Religious, catechetic and apologetic values lay on one side while the history and destiny of the Roman Catholic Church lay on the other and, in the middle, we can find many decades of world-renowned places, works, and artists, which deserve a special mention and due attention.

These are, in short, the Museums of the Pope. The difficult task of describing them and conveying their essence has been undertaken by Susanna Bertoldi in this book, which the publisher Sillabe edited and printed under the coordination of Maria Serlupi Crescenzi, Head of the Educational Division of the Vatican Museums. This is a book full of information, effectively laid out in a graphic design by Laura Belforte and accompanied by a rich iconographic selection provided by the Photographic archive of the Museums directed by Rosanna Di Pinto.

This is a book which arises from the educational experience and daily work in our museums of Susanna Bertoldi and Maria Serlupi Crescenzi. It has been conceived for students in secondary education and, even more so, for their teachers.

It can be used as a guide but it is much more than a guide. It goes over the history of the collections, it dwells upon the works and the foremost artists, it separates certain thematic subjects (Portraits, Still Life, the Gregorian Calendar), it deciphers iconography, explains traditions, hierarchies and rites and it intertwines literature, poetry and history. It has been conceived for those who want to master a basic lexicon of the values and meanings on which the magnificent framework of the Vatican Museums stands; values and meanings which have grown through additions and stratifications in symbiosis with the history of the Church over the five centuries since their symbolic foundation.

I felt strongly about publishing this book. Actually, I am convinced that the first responsibility of every director of the Museums, immediately after the conservation of the patrimony which has been entrusted to him, is the awareness and divulgation of said patrimony to as many people as possible. I therefore accepted the challenge willingly.

The Vatican Museums are a difficult complex of museums visited each year by almost four and a half million visitors, people from all walks of life and all types of cultures, religions or even people of no religion. My hope is that this small book, conceived, developed and written with extraordinary care, passion and competence and translated into the main languages, will be a success. I would like everyone to understand and appreciate Benedict XVI's message of 23rd November 2006 – printed here on the cover – a message we hold most dear.

Antonio Paolucci
Director General of the Vatican Museums

View of the original entrance to the Museums

The history

Near the entrance to the Museum's offices there is a mosaic in the form of a medallion, a modern work depicting the well-known episode of young Ganymede's abduction in the sky to become the divine cup bearer by an eagle sent by Zeus, or by the god himself in eagle form. Every time we cross the threshold of a Museum are we not swept up into the sky like Ganymede to contemplate fragments of eternal truths?

Carlo Albacini,
*Ganymede abducted by
the eagle*, mosaic, 1812,
Vatican Museums

The Belvedere Garden

The idea of creating the Vatican Museums came about at the beginning of the 16th century when Cardinal Giuliano della Rovere became Pope, taking the name Julius II (1503–1513), and had important classical statues such as the *Apollo* and the *Laocoon* transferred to the Vatican and placed in the Belvedere Palace garden, which had been transformed into a courtyard.

The courtyard was designed by Donato Bramante, who had drawn inspiration from literary descriptions and the remains of villas and ancient palaces to recreate a natural environment with the ancient marble statues placed amongst orange, lemon, myrtle and bay trees accompanied by a continuous flow of water from the fountains. The classical statues were harmoniously positioned along the walls of the courtyard in niches and in the centre as part of the fountain. This environment edified and delighted the men of letters and artists who came to Rome as guests of the Pope to study classical antiquities.

The Belvedere Palace was built in the 15th century for Innocent VIII (Cybo, 1484–1492) as a papal summer residence. The view over the Roman countryside must have been spectacular, though it has now been replaced by the sight of the city's Prati and Trionfale areas. For the most part the original architecture has been retained, although the Palace was altered in the 18th century. We can still reconstruct its original appearance thanks to a series of drawings, engravings, maps and elevations from the sixteenth and seventeenth centuries. The main façade was dominated by a loggia with two avant-corps at the far ends and a crown of merlons running all the way around building.

The Palace was actually part of a much larger complex, as this engraving by Mario Cartaro clearly shows. It can be seen on the right, to the north, with the Garden holding Julius II's statues and its view over the roman countryside. On the opposite side to the south we can see the complex of the Papal Palace, first built by order of Pope Nicholas III (Orsini, 1277–

Mario Cartaro, *True drawing of the magnificent buildings, gardens, woods, fountains and wonderful things of the Belvedere in Rome*, Rome, Library of the National Institute of Archaeology and History of Art

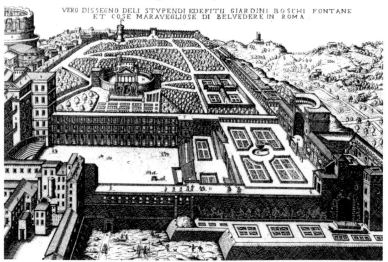

Reconstruction of Innocent VIII's Palace, from D. Redig de Campos, *The Vatican Palaces*, ed. Bologna 1967

1280) who took into consideration the potential of the Vatican in becoming the fixed papal residence, fully aware of the importance of living in proximity to Peter's tomb. The former papal residence was the Lateran and it was only after the Avignon Exile (1305–1377) that the Pope lived permanently at the Vatican. This illustration also shows the connecting courtyard designed by Donato Bramante. Bramante and Julius II were able to come to a unique understanding as their intentions converged to satisfy one in his search for a universal architectural language and the other in his plan to recover the splendour of ancient Rome, brought to life again in a Christian setting. In this case Bramante's study and reintroduction of classical architecture in the expression of a universal language was operative in Julius II's plans to reorganise the Papal Palace. Among the various renovation projects, the architect designed the Belvedere Courtyard to link the summer Palace with the Papal Palace

Tournament in the Belvedere Courtyard, 1565, from A. Lafréry, *Speculum Romanae Magnificentiae*, 1575

13

View of the Vatican Museums
and Gardens

through two very long, straight and parallel wings on three levels. He also designed a series of shelves at various heights in the large interior areas, which could be accessed by monumental ladders. These wings had flat roofs so they could be used as paths by people on foot, in sedan chairs or even on horseback.

In the large Belvedere Courtyard displays featuring knights took place based on life at the Papal court. Unavoidably, these displays were very similar to the presentations held at secular courts. The illustration on page 13 shows one of the tournaments with great scenographic effect which took place in 1565 for the wedding of Ortensia Borromeo, the niece of Pius IV (Medici, 1560–1565), to Giacomo Altemps.

The tournament and the joust

In the joust two knights at a time with their lances at rest galloped towards each other trying to unseat their opponent. The tournament on the other hand, was a simulated battle between two groups of knights, each fighting to overpower the other and become masters of the battlefield. These tests originated in France and appeared in Italy from the 12th century onwards. The tournaments were held to celebrate victories, peace, alliances, marriages, religious festivals and important political events. Originally they hardly differed from real battles to the point where, at the end of the day, it was not unusual for many participants to suffer injuries or even death. Over time, and after numerous outcries, the games became less and less violent and took on the form of grand festivals in which participants used blunted weapons without their sharp points or covered them with a shield. It was not until the 17th century, however, that the displays definitively shed their primitive nature involving the representation of a battle and became contests of grace and agility, often choreographed with music, floats and fireworks.

After the *Apollo* and the *Laocoon* had been positioned on site, the so-called *Venus Felix* came to the Belvedere Garden. The three statues originally stood in the niches of the main wall of the courtyard, the one visitors would see in front of them as they came into the Garden from the "Lumaca" (snail), another name for Bramante's spiral staircase commissioned by Julius II as one of the entrances to the Palace. Soon after, other antiquities arrived to

Hendrick van Cleve III, *Belvedere Romanum*, from
A. Lefréry, *Speculum Romane Magnificentiae*, 1575

occupy the niches and the courtyard. While Julius II was still in office two statues joined the others: *Hercules with Baby Telephus*, the latter famous for both his fight against the Greeks advancing on Troy and the wounds he suffered at the hands of Achilles, and the fragmented *Hercules and Antaeus*, the giant killed by Hercules during one of his famous "labours".

Besides the sculptures in the niches other statues were reused as ornaments for the fountains. Under the papacy of Leo X (Medici, 1513–1521), Julius II's successor, a new discovery was added to the pontifical collection: the colossal statues of the *Nile* and the *Tiber*. These were placed in the centre of the courtyard among the orange trees on high plinths with the Medici coat of arms, the *Nile* with its back to the *Laocoon* and the *Tiber* opposite. During Julius II's reign two other statues were added and used as fountains. The *Ariadne* was positioned in the corner of the courtyard above a sarcophagus held up by dolphins which served as a basin, and an ancient statue of a river thought to be the *Tigris* or the *Arno* was placed in the niche at the other end of the same wall, it too being reduced to a fountain on a sarcophagus supported by turtles. The last additions were the world-famous *Torso*, particularly admired by Michelangelo who declared himself to be a 'disciple of the Belvedere Torso', placed near the fragment of *Hercules and Antaeus* and a statue identified as *Hermes* standing in the niche next to the Palace's entrance. The walls of the courtyard also held marble masks which were thought to have come from the Pantheon. This collection of sculptures transformed the Vatican into an ideal Parnassus – the hill of the Muses which inspired the creative process in all its forms – the very one which Raphael painted at around the same time on one of the walls of Julius II's apartment on the third floor of the Papal Palace with the intention of recapturing and studying the work of classical civilisations, a practice which was considered to be very important during the Renaissance.

The testimony of an anonymous ambassador from the Veneto region, who saw the Belvedere Garden when he made his visit of allegiance to the new Pope Adrian VI (Florensz, 1522–1523), is very effective in providing a description of the area. He recounts a beautiful garden with lush grass, laurels, a magnificent orange tree and more particularly the ancient statues of the *Tiber* and the *Nile* which gushed with water, the *Apollo*, the *Laocoon* and finally the exquisite *Venus*.

What is a museum?

According to the International Council of Museums (ICoM) "a museum is a non-profit, permanent institution in the service of society and its development, open to the public, which acquires, conserves, researches, communicates and exhibits the tangible and intangible heritage of humanity and its environment for the purposes of education, study and enjoyment."

Why a museum?

Every time we enter a museum and walk through the various rooms we make an ideal journey, a sort of itinerary of the soul which allows us to return to the origins of Man and consequently to piece together the collective identity of the whole of humanity on its voyage through history. During this eternally unique and fascinating journey, however, we must keep in mind that we are faced with a fragmented situation, incomplete in the partial and fragmented display of each work of art and of each object which can nevertheless restore traces of truth to us, like the fragments of a mirror.

The origin of the word

Where does the word "museum" come from? The term has ancient Greek origins stemming from the noun *museion* or rather "temple, shrine, or seat of the Muses" – the goddesses who, according to ancient mythology, inspired creative thought in all its shapes and forms. They were the supreme inspirers of Man's intellectual activities such as poetry, oratory, music, history, mathematics and astronomy. Originally the seat of the Muses was probably meant to be on a hill or in a wood and not in a building.

The noun *museion*, referring to a building, was used to indicate the *Great Museum of Alexandria in Egypt,* a religious institution in which study and research were placed under the protection of the Muses. This museum was built in the 3rd century BC and included lodgings for the academic community of men of letters and scientists, rooms and porticoes for reading, studying and conversing, various works of art and more especially the great cultural institution of the famous library. Both these institutions were founded on the initiative of the ruling Ptolemy dynasty and represented a cultural reference point for the whole of the Mediterranean at the time, containing specially dedicated areas and a building for teaching and research under the auspices of the Muses. Plato and Aristotle also organised their schools, the *Academy* and the *Lyceum* respectively, as places conceived for the cult of the Muses.

The birth of the museum as an institution

The museum as an institution has deeply-rooted and distant origins and was founded thanks to our inclination for gathering together and collecting all kinds of objects at risk of being damaged over time.

The first collections of art had religious connotations both in ancient Egypt and in Greece, for example the objects of worship in the temples and grave goods. In Roman times the practice of secular collecting arose after great military conquests and the arrival of the spoils of war in Rome. Noble houses and villas, temples and porticoes were filled with works of art, especially of Greek origin. This is supported by historical sources and by archaeological findings. Pliny, for example, in his *Naturalis Historia* lists a series of Greek statues and paintings in the so-called *Portico of Octavia*, and findings at Pompeii and Herculaneum like the series of bronze portrait sculptures of philosophers in the library of the Pisoni family villa. In the Middle Ages the Church, and therefore all places of worship, became the favoured destination for commissions and collections of works of art as educational and religious messages could be communicated through them, for example the frescoes or the mosaics depicting the episodes of the Old and New Testaments or the lives of saints along the churches' naves, which were aimed at bringing worshippers and pilgrims closer to the great themes of faith (*Biblia pauperum*, the Bible of the Poor) using a simple and immediate means of communication.

In the 15th century and then during the Renaissance with the renewed interest in the study of classical antiquity, the spread of humanistic culture and the reconsideration of works of art from an independent aesthetical point of view, there was not a court in Italy which did not also become a home for ancient works of art and a source of commissions for contemporary craftsmen. Milan, Mantua, Ferrara, Urbino and Florence came to house splendid collections and the very same artists and humanists became collectors. With Humanism collecting became a method of investigation and the collector became a philosopher, a theologian who would search for the order of the world in his collections. Collections began to blossom with *naturalia*, *artificialia* and *mirabilia* which included antiquities (Egyptian, Greek, Roman and Christian), gems, coins, marble objects, scientific and musical instruments, portraits of illustrious men, fossils, minerals, coral, various other objects (talismans, lamps, ethnographic findings from far away continents, stones), rare animals (crocodiles, shells) and plants (exotic fruits). Essentially these collections did not just include man-made objects (*artificialia*), they also included natural discoveries (*naturalia*) and items which excited admiration (*mirabilia*). For the humanists from Petrarch and Poggio Bracciolini to Pietro Bembo at the beginning of the 16th century, a paradigm of all this was

Inscription of
Benedict XIV,
entrance to the
Christian Museum

the "study", a place where books joined all the various antiquities constituting a local variation on the European model of the so-called "Wunderkammer" or "cabinets of curiosities", embryos of the Museum as we recognise it today, a laboratory of history and knowledge of the world.

The penetration of Humanism in Rome was at the root of the Papal collections and their usage by scholars and artists, as well as the collections on display in the large houses and courtyards of the great families. These collections revealed refined cultural awareness and they became tools for orchestrating agendas and political plans. Julius II's plans for the statue garden, for example, can be interpreted in this light. He gathered together sculptures which called to mind the protagonists of the Trojan War such as the *Laocoon*, the *Apollo* and the *Venus Felix* reminiscent of Aphrodite, and the group of *Hercules and Telephus* reminiscent of Aeneas with his son Ascanius. The Pope wanted to create a real Virgilian theme which would link the statues together to communicate a precisely-conceived political agenda. Just as Virgil celebrated the origins of Rome through the Trojan War and Aeneus' adventures in the *Aeneid* in accordance with Augustus' political agenda to exalt the city's centrality and the imperial family, Julius II used his "Virgilian" statues and played on his own name *Iulius* to put himself in the direct line of the *Gens Iiulia*, Caesar and Augustus' family, with the aim of heralding a new golden age for recently-established Christian Rome.

There was also a public dimension to collecting in Rome which became more marked after Sixtus IV's (della Rovere, 1471–1481) "donation" to the Roman people of large bronzes with great symbolic value. They were transported from the Lateran to Capitol Hill and became the nucleus of the future Capitoline Museums.

However, it was during the 18th century, the Age of Enlightenment, that the modern concept of the Museum took shape, that is to say a public institution open to everyone aiming to safeguard cultural heritage and promote its understanding. This institution was therefore a creature of the Enlightenment in Europe; it was during this era that an architectural space was designed for the first time to give a universally recognisable form to the museums. Previously, works of art had been simple decorative elements in the large houses and villas which received them. Now a new awareness arose which underlined the importance of making the cultural heritage formerly restricted to the enjoyment of a limited and elite circle accessible to everyone. It also exposed the necessity of designing a building, a home for the works to be collected; a container conceived especially for its contents. This century, therefore, witnessed the birth of the great museums and after various expansion works and changes to the organisation of the collections, Clement XII (Corsini, 1730–1740) decreed the opening of the Capitoline Museums.

The Vatican Museums in the sixteenth and seventeenth centuries

During the Counter-Reformation in the middle of the 16th century the tradition of collecting was opposed and expurgated with harsh words; in reference to the ancient sculptures collected in the Vatican, St. Pius V (Ghislieri, 1566–1572) declared: 'sunt idola profana' ('these are profane idols'). Furthermore, the great new construction site of St. Peter's required unprecedented effort and attention so the Popes of the 17th century had to concentrate on the colossal project, indirectly imposing a lull in the growth of the future museums. The ancient Basilica of St. Peter was erected by the emperor Constantine but then demolished at the beginning of the 16th century by Julius II, who, according to celebratory medals, laid the first stone of the new church designed by Donato Bramante in 1506.

The experimental exhibition set up in the Vatican by Paul V (Borghese, 1605–1621) at the beginning of the 17th century is noteworthy both for its historical and cultural value. As the construction work went on the moment came to demolish the old façade of St. Peter's, the last surviving element of the Constantinian basilica. In the Vatican Grottoes the sculpture fragments, paintings and mosaics which were able to be saved from the demolition were exhibited with captions in Latin. Furthermore, a series of frescoes done especially for the occasion documented the appearance of the demolished basilica in detail.

The Vatican Library

The Vatican had to wait until the early 18th century for collecting to blossom again and for artistic heritage to take on a new role. The first key events during this period of new awakening for the museums were strongly linked to another great cultural institution, the Vatican Library and its Museums, whose first collections were gathered together thanks to the great Pope Nicholas V (Parentucelli, 1447–1455). Pope Nicholas V was a highly-cultured humanist who surrounded himself with artists and men of letters such as Marsilio Ficino, Leon Battista Alberti and Fra Angelico. After the Avignon Exile, Rome became the fulcrum of fervent cultural and political exchanges once again, the prelude to a new period of magnificence and the destination of artists, architects, philosophers, poets, musicians, orators and scholars. The Pope also implemented a vast programme of urban reorganisation and restoration of monuments and buildings. In particular, he began to enlarge the mediaeval Papal Palace, erecting a building with three floors facing the Belvedere Courtyard.

Melozzo da Forlì, *Sixtus IV and Platina* (detail), Pinacoteca, Room IV

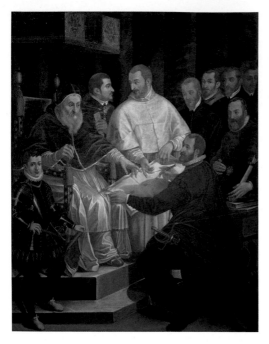

Pietro Facchetti, *Sixtus V approves the project for the Sistine Salon presented by Domenico Fontana*, Vatican Apostolic Library, Sistine Salon

There on the ground floor, formerly the Pope's granary, he set up the first seat of the Vatican Library, largely constituted from what was left of the rich Library of Constantinople after it fell into the hands of the Turks in the middle of the 15th century.

Here, Sixtus IV (della Rovere, 1471–1484) furthered expansion work on the new Library. The task of creating a suitable place for the safe-keeping and conservation of the collections, which had grown since Nicholas V's time with a considerable number of Greek and Latin manuscripts, was entrusted to Bartolomeo Sacchi, known as Platina, the first prefect of the Vatican Library. In short, Nicholas V founded the Library and Sixtus IV institutionalised it. The building was divided into three sections dedicated respectively to the conservation of Latin, Greek and Papal codices. The rooms were decorated by famous painters such as Melozzo da Forlì, the creator of the famous fresco celebrating the Library's foundation in which Sixtus IV is portrayed consigning the decree of appointment of the Vatican Library's first custodian to Bartolomeo Platina, depicted kneeling before him. The fresco was detached in the 19th century for conservation reasons and is currently on display in the Vatican Pinacoteca.

The rooms on the ground floor, however, soon turned out to be too dark and humid, posing a serious threat to the conservation of the precious manuscripts. Furthermore, thanks to progress made in printing techniques, the library's collections were growing with acquisitions from the most prolific centres of book production of the time so the rooms quickly became too small. The Vatican had picked up on the importance of printing as a means of spreading artistic ideas and recognised the necessity of printing books and finding new more suitable premises for both the various phases of production and for the storage of the resulting volumes.

Sixtus V (Peretti, 1585–1590) entrusted the construction of a new three-storey building for the Library to his architect, Domenico Fontana. It was decided that the new construction site would be set up in the Belvedere Courtyard near the stairs between the two levels. The new building would connect the east and west wings of the Belvedere, cutting the courtyard in two.

The map in the inside cover shows the Belvedere Palace of Innocent VIII to the north (5), inside of which Julius II built a courtyard-garden, the first stepping stone to the future Museums. On the opposite side, to the south, we can see the early Papal Palace built by Nicholas III (1277–1280) on three sides, later enlarged by Nicholas V, who completed the perimeter with a new wing overlooking the Belvedere Courtyard and subsequently created the Parrot Courtyard (Cortile del Pappagallo). The large courtyard designed by Bramante can be seen in the centre of the map forming the wings connecting the Papal Palace and the summer residence, later divided in two by the building for the Vatican Library. Essentially, Bramante reorganised the grounds into three areas which correspond to the present day courtyards of the *Pigna* (Pinecone), the Library and the Belvedere. The two wings were originally open loggias and could be passed through on horseback before they were closed off and used to accommodate works of art.

Illuminations

Much of the literary heritage we possess today, such as the works of Greek and Latin authors, was passed down to us thanks to the efforts of copyist monks, veritable scribes of the Middle Ages who hand-copied ancient texts, thus ensuring their preservation. The medium they used par excellence was vellum. The papyrus scrolls, known as *volumina* in Latin, had defects such as their fragility, the fact that they could only be used on one side and their impracticality in terms of handling. Vellum was obtained from animal skins (sheep, calf or goat) and turned out to be more resistant and longer lasting. It also provided the significant advantage of being able to be used on both sides, as well as the possibility of adding illuminations (small paintings illustrating the manuscript). When the work was finished the sheets were gathered and sewn together to make a *codex*, the ancestor of our modern books. Codices, partly because of the great value of their illuminations, were always considered to be precious objects and as a result they were destined to be enjoyed by a privileged few in elite locations and circles such as abbeys, bishops' palaces, courts and rich families. The costs of producing them were high because of the long and elaborate techniques used to prepare the skins and to acquire the colours (including lapis lazuli and gold leaf) for the illuminations.

Various phases were involved in the composition of an illuminated letter, a border or a scene: first a stylus was used to outline all the parts of the "picture" (text, landscape, figures), then it was passed over with ink before the gold leaf could be applied. The widely-used red colour was obtained from a mixture of minium (a red-orange pigment) and the yolk and white of eggs which gave it a glossy and iridescent effect on the parchment. The term "miniature" (the illustrations on the illuminated manuscript) originates from the use of minium.

The place where the manuscripts were copied, decorated and rebound was called the *scriptorium*; it was usually situated near the monastery library and could be set up in a special room or a series of small, individual cells. Each scribe had a high-backed chair and a book rest and the first task was that of smoothing the vellum sheets with a knife blade or a pumice stone. This process removed stains and rough patches in order to obtain an even surface which would absorb exactly the right quantity of ink. The scribes wrote with a goose feather quill which gave much more calligraphic freedom compared to the rush pens used on papyrus scrolls.

The most important area of the Library is the renowned Sistine Salon, which was used as a reference room up until the 19th century. It is divided into two naves by a row of pillars with a vaulted ceiling and natural light floods in through the great north and south facing windows. Cupboards to hold the manuscripts line the walls. The decorative pictorial cycle portrays the exaltation of books throughout the centuries and the glorification of Sixtus V's papacy.

Each panel, depicting the libraries of antiquity, is divided into two scenes and the cycle begins with the Hebrew Library. In the first scene Moses is consigning the books of the law and seems to symbolise the transition from the oral tradition to books. This is followed by the Library of Babylon, the Library of Athens, the Library of Alexandria and the Library of the Romans. The Library of the Romans is divided into two scenes: on the left we can see the legendary founder of the Library in Rome, Tarquinius Superbus, to whom the Cumaean Sibyl offers her last three books while the others burn on the brazier; on the right Augustus can be seen between Virgil and Horace in the library he founded on Palatine Hill. The series continues with the Library of Jerusalem and the Library of Cesarea then comes to end with the Library of the Apostles and the Library of the Popes, in which we can see Nicholas V, Sixtus IV and Sixtus V, the founders and renovators of the Vatican Library. This cycle aims to underline the Church's commitment as a wise custodian of Christian culture following in the wake of classical tradition.

On the opposite wall of the Salon the frescoes show the great Councils held in the Orient before the Byzantine Schism. Particularly noteworthy

View of the Sistine Salon, Vatican Apostolic Library

▲ *St. Peter's Square adorned for the coronation of Sixtus V,* Sistine Salon, Vatican Apostolic Library

▼ *St. Peter's Square and Basilica in Sixtus V's time with the obelisk,* Sistine Salon, Vatican Apostolic Library

scenes include the Council of Nicaea, accompanied by a panel depicting the burning of the Arian books ordered by Constantine; the First Council of Constantinople before the emperor Theodosius to condemn Macedonius for denying the divinity of the Holy Spirit; and the Council of Ephesus where Nestorius was condemned for denying that Mary was the Mother of God. In the lunettes above the large panels there is a series of episodes illustrating the salient moments of Sixtus V's papacy starting with the Pope's coronation ceremony in St. Peter's Square. The scene shows the façade of the old Basilica as it was at the end of the

23

16th century before the changes took place which brought it to its current state. Consequently this fresco, like the others around it, has great documentary value.

Taking advantage of the ingenuity of the architect Domenico Fontana, Sixtus V decided to move the granite obelisk on the southern side of St. Peter's Basilica to the centre of the level ground in front of the church. The obelisk had been brought to the Vatican from Egypt during the emperor Caligula's reign. It ornamented the private, imperial circus which stood in the area and according to tradition the apostle Peter was martyred here. In the background we can see the old façade of St. Peter's Basilica. Notably, in the centre we can see the three entrances to the ancient portico in front of the church, known as the Portico of Paradise. The monumental bronze fountain in the form of a crown was in the centre; to the right the loggia from which the Pope would look out on formal occasions to bless the faithful; and finally, further towards the right, the main entrance to the Apostolic Palaces under the clock.

Among the construction work ordered by Sixtus V noteworthy projects include the erection of an obelisk in the centre of the level ground overlooking the apse of the Basilica of Santa Maria Maggiore and another in the Piazza del Laterano. In the last fresco we can see the new building also built by Sixtus V to provide a worthy setting for the Holy Stairs and the Chapel of San Lorenzo or the *Sancta Sanctorum*, thus called because it held the most precious relics of the Church of Rome.

After the renovations ordered by Sixtus V the Vatican Library was enriched yet again. Whole sets of manuscripts poured in from the library of Queen Christina of Sweden, the library of Federico da Montefeltro, Duke of Urbino and the collections of the great Roman families such as the Borghese family (the Borghese Collection) and the Barberini family (the Barberini Collection). Steps were taken to house these collections in specially created rooms in the gallery of one of wings Bramante had designed, which were originally open loggias though they soon accommodated the required storage units.

In chronological order:

Sixtus V's Rooms (Sale Sistine): while the Library was being constructed Sixtus V decided to add two new rooms to the new building, putting them in the portico of the west wing of the Belvedere (facing south) **(14d)**.

Paul V's Rooms (Sale Paoline): during the papacy of Paul V (Borghese, 1605–1621), two rooms were built for new acquisitions similar to the Sale Sistine **(14c)**.

Gallery of Urban VIII's (Galleria di Urbano VIII): Pope Urban VIII (Barberini, 1623–1644) built a new gallery and furnished it with cupboards along the walls **(14e)**. For the most part the cupboards held the manuscripts from the library of Heidelberg and the library of Federico di Montefeltro of Urbino.

Alexander VIII's Room (Sala Alessandrina): an extension ordered by Pope Alexander VIII (Ottoboni, 1689–1691) to hold the manuscripts from the library of Queen Christina of Sweden **(14b)**.

Clementine Gallery (Galleria Clementina): under the papacy of Clement XII (Corsini, 1730–1740) the arches of the portico which ran along the western side of the Pinecone Courtyard (Cortile della Pigna) were closed off to create a gallery furnished with storage cupboards **(14a)**. These cupboards became stands for a series of Etruscan vases

View of the Christian Museum, formerly the Vatican Apostolic Library

which remained there until they were moved to the future Gregorian Etruscan Museum (Museo Gregoriano Etrusco).

The pictorial decoration of the Galleries was done using the same methodology as the Sistine Salon. The rooms and galleries the various Popes had added to the original buildings from the seventeenth to the nineteenth centuries were painted with significant episodes from their respective papacies, thus creating a unique ensemble of views of Rome in all the rooms linked to the Vatican Library both on the walls and on the storage cupboards lining the galleries' long corridors.

The Museums of the Vatican Library

While the collections of manuscripts grew, other objects poured into the Vatican which enriched and completed the Library. Benedict XIV (Lambertini, 1740–1758) made the decision to give a definitive order to the various groups of objects which had joined the Vatican Library collections over the first half of the 18th century by creating the "Museo Sacro" ("Sacred Museum"), now the Christian Museum. The museum was set up at the end of the Gallery of Urban VIII **(14e)** and an inscription at the entrance declared that it had been created "ad augendum Urbis splendorem et asserendam religionis veritatem", underlining the fact that the collection was destined to hold documents which substantiated Early Christianity. The objects were placed in precious walnut display cupboards made by the best craftsmen of the time and included early Christian antiquities, examples of decorative arts mostly from the catacombs such as small items made of ivory, silver and bronze, cameos, gems and intaglios, coins and medals, goldsmithery, seals, paintings on wood and engraved and gilded glassware. At a later date the bronze busts by the renowned sculptor Luigi Valadier of the 24 cardinals who held the post of librarian were placed on the cupboards.

The works in the cupboards from archaeological digs were organised according to the topographic order of the consular roads of Rome and their respective cemeteries, from north to south: Salaria, Nomentana,

View of the Profane Museum of the Library, 1780,
Gregorian Etruscan Museum, Lower hemicycle

Tiburtina, Labicana, Latina, Ardeatina, Appia and Portuense; the collection draws to a close with objects from other Italian, African and Oriental archaeological sites. In the horizontal display cases made for Blessed Pius IX in the mid-19th century the works are typologically arranged according to the material they are made of, so here we can see various objects including oil-lamps, gilded glassware, quartz crystal, rings and devotional medals all grouped together.

Upon the suggestion of the librarian Cardinal Alessandro Albani, a great antiques dealer and collector, Benedict XIV's successor Clement XIII (Rezzonico, 1758–1769) founded the Profane Museum (Museo Profano) opposite the Christian Museum (Museo Cristiano) at the far end of the Clementine Gallery **(14a)** to hold the profane antiquities of the Vatican Library. The new museum consisted of a room with four niches holding the busts of "orators" and "philosophers"; cupboards holding items from the pagan world such as bronze statuettes, cameos, coins and medals lined the walls.

By order of Pope John Paul II (Wojtyla, 1978–2005) the Museums of the Vatican Library came under the management of the Vatican Museums.

The origins of the Pius-Clementine Museum

Princes and cardinals belonging to papal families who owned rich collections of art often found themselves obliged to get rid of large quantities of their artistic treasures during economic crises. These sales to sovereigns, princes and great foreign collectors, especially from England, took place through the numerous antique dealers living in eighteenth-century Rome. Although strict laws were already in place governing the exportation of works of art, overseen by the so-called Commissioners for Antiquities, the new Pope Clement XIV (Ganganelli, 1769–1774) was worried about the exodus of so many works of art which would eventually impoverish Rome's heritage. Consequently, he started to buy works which were about to be taken abroad, setting himself the task of gathering them together in a new museum. The Pope was assisted by the Commissioner for Antiquities, Giambattista Visconti, who negotiated with the antique dealers and promoted the donation of privately-owned art works as well as furthering methodical excavation projects. Given the small size of the Library areas and the impossibility of being able to use them effectively, as the first works of art arrived the Pope decided to create a new museum in the Vatican transforming the Belvedere Palace to achieve his purpose.

The Palace was already an essential destination for those who came to Rome to study the ancient vestiges of Julius II's renowned Statue Garden. Under the papacy of Clement XIV the renovation work began: the open loggia of Pope Innocent's Palace was transformed into a statue gallery and the architect Michelangelo Simonetti worked on Julius II's famous courtyard, re-designing it as a conjoining element between the surrounding buildings with a portico running all the way around to allow the masterpieces on display to be seen to their advantage. While the Clementine Museum was under construction, work also progressed on the Museums of the Library: a room was built next to the Sacred Museum to hold the papyrus collection in display cases along the walls; and an *Allegory of History* was depicted on the vault, as seen in the illustration on the following page. *History* can be seen seated in the centre writing down the proceedings in a large book which rests on the wings of *Time*, while *Fame* flies upwards sounding a long trumpet to herald the event. The inscription "Museum

Anton Raphael Mengs, *Allegory of History*, Room of the Papyri

27

▲Bernardino Nocchi (?), *Simonetti Staircase*,
Gregorian Etruscan Museum, Lower hemicycle

▼Simonetti Staircase

Clementium" is visible on the architrave indicating the new entrance, accessible from the so-called Royal Staircase coming from the east wing of the Papal Palace.

Finally, thanks to this Pope, additions were made to the Vatican's collections which included statues, busts, sarcophagi, vases and candelabras, statues of animals, altars, urns, reliefs and inscriptions. The Pope was already contemplating bigger expansion projects when he died, leaving his successor the task of completing them.

Construction work began again under Pius VI (Braschi, 1775–1799), who commissioned Michelangelo Simonetti with the task of building a series of large salons in the Palace, which was then definitively demolished, to recreate the spatial magnificence of classical architecture from an eighteenth-century point of view. The Age of Enlightenment endorsed the right of each and every individual to visit museums as they came to be considered as places of education as well as conservation; their doors,

therefore, were no longer only open to scholars and architects who had come to Rome to study ancient art and architecture or simply as guests of the Pope, they were now open to everyone.

The use of ancient components like columns, capitals, mosaics and reliefs is typical of the architecture in these rooms. In the absence of ancient paintings to decorate the walls, the Pope called upon artists who were sensitive to classical art, those experienced in mythological scenes and those who had been inspired by the works on display in the rooms. The ancient statuary, sarcophagi, altars and mosaics are set out according to tastes of the time. Modern museographical criteria take into account the origins of a work of art or its typology but in the 18th century displays were created for decorative purposes which were rarely thematic.

The Pius-Clementine Museum could be accessed from the Vatican Library through a new entrance in the form of a staircase built for Pius VI,

Stefano Piale, *Pius VI visits the Pius-Clementine Museum*, 1783, Vatican Museums

named the "Simonetti Staircase" after the architect who designed it.

The Simonetti Staircase led into the Greek Cross Vestibule which was reminiscent of Roman thermal baths. The new monumental entrance to the Pius-Clementine Museum was characterised by two "Egyptian telamons" supporting the architrave with the inscription "Museum Pium".

Pius VI inverted the route through the museum by designating this new entrance up the Simonetti Staircase and identified it with the new inscription "Museum Pium". The name "Pius-Clementine Museum" was thus created in recognition of Clement XIV's successor, Pius VI, who finalised the exhibiting arrangements of the antiquities collections.

The newly-founded Pius-Clementine Museum also became a venue for important meetings. When King Gustav III of Sweden, the head of the Swedish Protestant Church, came to visit he did not meet Pius VI in the politically charged rooms of the Quirinal or in St. Peter's, a religious setting; he met him in the rooms of the Pius-Clementine Museum. The meeting was immortalised in paintings and in decorative arts filling and remembered in all the chronicles of the time.

Pius VI shows the Pius-Clementine Museum to Gustav III of Sweden, Alexander VIII's Room, formerly the Vatican Apostolic Library

PIVS.VI.GVSTAVVM.III.REGEM.SVECORVM.IN.MVSEVM. CONVENIT
DE.ARTIVM.BONARVM.INCREMENTO.GRATVLATVM
ANNO.MDCCLXXXIIII.

Pius VI also sought other display areas to expand the antiquities collections. He made use of the great covered loggia on the second floor of the west wing used by the Library, transformed by the architect Simonetti into the Gallery of the Candelabras (Galleria dei Candelabri). After the architect's death the construction work on the Gallery of the Candelabras was completed by Giuseppe Camporese, who also designed the Atrium of the Four Gates (Atrio dei Quattro Cancelli) and the Biga Room (Sala della Biga), a sort of small central-plan temple near the entrance to the Gallery of the Candelabras.

Bound for Paris

The start of the French Revolution marked the beginning of a difficult chapter in the history of the Vatican Museums. The inevitable tension between France and the Papal State culminated in the nomination and the subsequent arrival of a Commission of experts, who were charged with choosing the most valuable works of art from the conquered land to take back to Paris. In order to justify this immense removal the educational role of museums and their function as a public institution was cited by the French authorities more than ever. After a period of long and futile negotiations the works that had been chosen were packed up and sent to France, including the precious codices of the Vatican Library.

It was decided that the arrival of the works in Paris should take place

Departure from Rome of the third convoy of works of art bound for Paris, engraving

in a spectacular fashion to evoke the Triumphs held by the ancient Roman generals as they returned to Rome after great military victories. The Vatican museums had actually not only been enriched by examples of classical art, Pius VI had also decided to create a Gallery for paintings, the nucleus of the future Picture Gallery (Pinacoteca).

Reconstitution and growth: The tenure of Pius VII

The new century opened with the election of Pius VII (Chiaramonti, 1800–1823) in 1800 and an incredible state of affairs emerged before the eyes of those who investigated the collections present in the Vatican Museums. The most famous sculptures were missing, while others had been substituted with casts which the previous Pope had had made in view of their impending removal; numerous paintings were also missing from the gallery Pius VI had founded, with only some empty frames remaining.

Pius VII thus took on the task of reforming the collections through carefully selected acquisitions and the resumption of archaeological

Filippo Agricola, *Allegory of the foundation of the Chiaramonti Museum*, Chiaramonti Museum

MVSEVM · CLARAMONTANVM
PIOCLEMENTINO · ADIECTVM

Engraving of the *Lapidary Gallery*

excavations. One of the first measures he took was to nominate Antonio Canova to the post of Inspector General of Fine Arts. Thanks to the zeal and commitment of the Pope and his collaborators, the gaps in the Pius-Clementine Museum soon began to be filled, so much so that the need arose to create a new museum. This time they chose the east wing of Bramante's courtyard (until then the growing collections had been put in the west wing) and construction work began.

As the collections of art and library heritage expanded, the area facing north which had originally been used as a simple connecting passage between the Papal Palace and the summer residence turned out to be perfect for the Museums' development. Part of the east wing was set up to accommodate the Chiaramonti Museum with Canova's precious contribution including classical antiquities. A flight of stairs connects the Chiaramonti Museum to the Pius-Clementine Museum on the side of the Square Vestibule (Vestibolo Quadrato) where the inscription "Museum Clementium" can be seen.

Further along the east wing the Chiaramonti Museum also holds a lapidary collection which had already been gathered together in Clement XIV's time before being added to by Pius VI and Pius VII.

At around this time, thanks to the decrees emitted after the fall of Napoleon at the Vienna Congress (1814–1815), the restitution of the war booty taken by the French from the conquered States began and Pius VII charged Canova with recovering the works of art taken away from the Vatican. At the same time the Vatican Library also demanded the restitution of its treasures. A lunette in the Chiaramonti Museum painted by Francesco Hayez captures the event: the personification of the Tiber can be seen with his gaze turned towards the convoy of art works returning to Rome with Mount Mario in the background.

CLARIORA · ARTIFICVM · EXCELLENTIVM · OPERA · AD EXTEROS · AVECTA
VRBI · RECVPERATA

Francesco Hayez, *The return of the stolen works of art*, Chiaramonti Museum

After the works had been returned the Pope decided to construct a new wing, called the New Wing, to house the sculptures which could not be displayed in the existing areas. The building, inaugurated in 1818, was constructed from a project by the architect Raffaele Stern who made further use of the Belvedere Courtyard to erect a similar structure connecting its two wings.

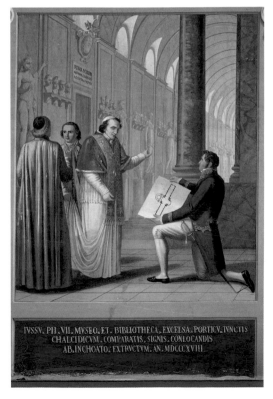

Domenico del Frate, *Pius VII examines the project for the New Wing of the Chiaramonti Museum presented by the architect Raffaele Stern*, Clementine Gallery, formerly the Vatican Apostolic Library

IVSSV. PII . VII. MVSEO. ET . BIBLIOTHECA. EXCELSA. PORTICV. IVNCTIS
CHALCIDICVM . COMPARATIS. SIGNIS. CONLOCANDIS
AB. INCHOATO. EXTRVCTVM. AN. MDCCCXVIII.

The protection of artistic heritage in the Papal State

The regulations which govern the Vatican Museums are the result of a long process of theoretical deliberations and legislative measures aimed at the protection and the conservation of the works of art. The Papal State was actually one of the first states to recognise the necessity of promulgating laws and creating bodies with the sole purpose of conserving the integrity of all its artistic patrimony. During the first half of the 17th century an incredible number of works of art had been amassed in Rome, collected or commissioned by Popes, ecclesiastical dignitaries, great families and religious orders. These riches joined the great number of items from Imperial Rome and the masterpieces of classical art which emerged from under the ground. At the same time as this flurry of activity, the Papal State adopted a series of legislative measures and took concrete steps to regulate the excavations and acquire particularly important collections and single works from the private market.

The Papal proclamation of 1646 which incorporated all these regulations was highly symbolic as it contained, *in nuce*, elements which would later make up the established repertoire of protective measures enforced by all governments aiming to conserve their artistic heritage. The decree was entitled the 'Proclamation on the extraction and digging up of Statues, Figures, Carvings, Medals, marble and various metal inscriptions, Gold, Silver, Gems and similar ancient or modern items'. This proclamation pointed out once again the fact that public servants were allowed to go into "botteghe" ("shops") to 'look at, take and make note of any ancient items in order to impede their eventual exportation. It also required customs officers to block the "said ancient and modern works... of any painted or sculpted material without a licence issued by us...'; furthermore it sanctioned inspections of excavation sites by officials: '...digging can no longer take place without the inspection or assistance of said Commissioner...'.

The procedures for safeguarding heritage were continuously adopted over the next few centuries with the promotion of archaeological digs, the State acquisition of collections put up for sale, the foundation of public museums to accommodate the new acquisitions, and the enforcement of the law requiring owners of the most important private collections to conserve the assets they inherited by passing them down intact in a direct line of succession.

Besides filling in the gaps in previous sets of regulations, Pius VII's enlightened protection policy was implicitly merit-worthy for two reasons: it underlined the historical nature of works of art, or rather the idea that if works of art belonged to a common cultural setting they should be firmly fixed in their original environment, if not they would lose a large part of their historical and artistic value; it also defined works of art as public assets.

Under Pius VII's papacy the Law of 1820 known as the Pacca Edict, after the name of the cardinal who promulgated it, instituted an all-encompassing administrative body for the protection of cultural heritage for the first time, whose workforce was composed of experts.

The Gregorian Museums

Gregory XVI (Cappellari, 1831–1846), like many of his predecessors, contributed to the growth and enlargement of the Vatican Museums. His name is inextricably linked to two new Museums: the Gregorian Etruscan Museum (Museo Gregoriano Etrusco) and the Gregorian Egyptian Museum (Museo Gregoriano Egizio).

The foundation of the Etruscan Museum is linked to the discovery of works of art on the territory of the Papal State, particularly Greek and Etruscan vases in northern Lazio and neighbouring Tuscany and the subsequent need to safeguard this heritage. Making use of the legislation in force (the Pacca Edict), the Papal State succeeded in preventing the removal of the objects found during the excavations and secured them

▲Engraving of the *Entrance and the Room of the Lions of the Gregorian Egyptian Museum*

▼Engraving of the *Room of the Bronzes of the Gregorian Etruscan Museum*

for the Vatican Museums. The Museum was set up in the ancient Belvedere Palace on the second floor, above the Pius-Clementine Museum. The inscription "Museum Gregorianum / ex monumentis hetruscis" was inscribed over the Museum's entrance.

Gregory XVI also linked his name to another creation: the Egyptian Museum. A small collection of Egyptian antiquities had been gathered since Pius VII's time and placed in the great semicircle in the Pinecone Courtyard (Cortile della Pigna), as Canova thought the works should be exhibited separately from the Greco-Roman ones in the neighbouring Pius-Clementine Museum. Consequently, this small collection formed the beginnings of the Gregorian Egyptian Museum.

The necessity of creating a museum in the Vatican dedicated to Egyptian collections stemmed from the great interest in Egyptian antiquities which was widespread in Europe after J. F. Champollion's (1790–1832) breakthrough when he studied the Rosetta Stone and deciphered the hieroglyphics. A series of small rooms with architectural and decorative elements evoking this ancient civilisation were chosen for the new museum. The museum's entrance gate held the inscription "GREGORIVS XVI P. M. AN. IX MVSEVM AEGYPT".

The Lateran Museums

There were three key stages in this new era for the Vatican Museums with the creation of three new museums in the Lateran Palace (Palazzo del Laterano), which would only be transferred to the Vatican much later on. In actual fact they had to solve the problem of where to put the works of art which continued to flow into the Vatican Museums as they were faced with a constant lack of adequate display areas. The Lateran Palace turned out to be a practical solution to their problems. After creating the Egyptian Museum and the Etruscan Museum, Gregory XVI

View of the new building designed to hold the collections of the
ex-Lateran Museums, the Belvedere Palace is visible in the background

Filippo (?) Cretoni, *View of the Pius Christian Museum painted on the door of a cupboard*, 1854, the first of Sixtus V's Rooms, formerly the Vatican Apostolic Library

(Cappellari, 1831–1846) had to solve the problem of where to exhibit the collections of Greco-Roman works of art which continued to grow through acquisitions, donations and excavations; he also had to find room for a great number of modern art paintings. The Pope chose the Lateran Palace, which was reduced to a dilapidated state after being improperly used and long abandoned. The refurbishment work began: the ground floor was destined for sculptures and the three rooms on the first floor were reserved for paintings. The new museum was called the Lateran Profane Museum (Museo Profano Lateranense).

Pius IX (Mastai Ferretti, 1846–1878) succeeded Gregory XVI and came to be at the heart of important events in the Church's history which ended the Popes' temporal power. An important development for the Vatican Museums was the establishment of the Sacred Archaeology Commission (Commissione di Archeologia Sacra, 1852), which was charged with managing the excavations of the catacombs and overseeing their conservation. Amidst this backdrop the Pope also founded the Pius-Christian Museum in the Lateran and the number of objects streaming in was so high that they came to form the largest collection of Palaeo-Christian monuments in existence. The collection was made up of two sections: the first included sarcophagi mostly from churches in Rome and the second held inscriptions transferred both from the churches and the catacombs.

Under papacy of Pius XI (Ratti, 1922–1939), one of the signatories of the famous Lateran Pacts in 1929 which decreed the Reconciliation between the Church and the Italian State and the subsequent creation of the Vatican City State, an important event occurred for the Museums: in 1925, the Jubilee Year, the Vatican Missionary Exhibition (Mostra Missionaria Vaticana) took place and its pavilions filled the courtyards. At the end of the exhibition, Pius XI founded the Lateran Missionary Ethnological Museum (Museo Missionario Etnologico del Laterano). This Museum was set up on the first and second floors of the Lateran building and it held collections and the objects from the Missionary Exhibition of the Holy Year, generously donated to the Pope by curacies, prefectures, dioceses, missionary orders and institutes, indigenous religious communities, scientific societies and private individuals. The objects and collections were divided according to their origin, so everything was sorted into autochthonous objects, examples of local cultural heritage and objects originating from the missionaries' activities, and instances of the evangelical message merging with the local populations and their traditions.

Under the papacy of John XXIII (Roncalli, 1958–1963), the Pope who held the Second Vatican Council, the most important event in the museums' history was the decision to transfer the Lateran Museums (the Gregorian Profane Museum, the Pius Christian Museum and the Missionary Ethnological Museum) to the Vatican: a great accomplishment in which the uniting aim was to show a humanity; a patrimony in which we can find, through each of the objects, a constant search for the truth. Paul VI (Montini, 1963–1978) oversaw the completion of the work on the new location for the former Lateran Museums. The Missionary Ethnological Museum was set up in the basement, the Gregorian Profane Museum on the ground floor, and the Pius Christian Museum on the mezzanine.

The Vatican Pinacoteca (Picture Gallery)

Pius VI (Braschi, 1775–1799) gathered together the beginnings of the future Vatican Pinacoteca in a loggia, which was not closed off at that point, called the Picture Gallery (Galleria dei Quadri), a continuation of the Gallery of the Candelabras (Galleria dei Candelabri) created by Simonetti.

Giacomo Conca, *Allegory of the foundation of Pius VII's Pinacoteca*, Chiaramonti Museum

EXIMIAE · CAMERARVM · PICTVRAE · IN · AEDIBVS · ALEX · VI · DETERSAE
PINACOTHECA · INSTITVTA

View of Gregory XVI's Pinacoteca, from E. Pistolesi, *The Vatican described and illustrated by Erasmo Pistolesi*, 1829, vol. VI

After the works from Paris had been returned, Pius VII (Chiaramonti, 1800–1823) ordered the creation of the new Vatican Pinacoteca. This could no longer be accommodated in the Picture Gallery so it was transferred to the Borgia Apartment and set up in five rooms.

This fresco shows Pius VII's contribution to the development of the Pinacoteca. It is part of a series of lunettes alluding to the Pope's meritorious endeavours in the field of Fine Arts, done at Canova's expense to decorate the Chiaramonti Museum.

However, they soon realised that the Borgia Apartment did not receive enough light so the decision was made to transfer the paintings to the Bologna Room (Sala Bologna) on the third floor of the loggias.

Gregory XVI (Cappellari, 1831-1846) reconstituted the collection of paintings in the gallery now known as the Gallery of Tapestries, a continuation of the Gallery of the Candelabras. This area, however, turned out once again to be inadequate, in spite of the improvements which had been made. As a result the paintings were transferred to the Apartment of St. Pius V in the Papal Palace while Gregory XVI was still in office.

Pius X (Sarto, 1903–1914) founded the great Vatican Pinacoteca which was inaugurated with its newly-arranged collections in the Gallery under the Vatican Library's Sacred Museum (west wing). For the first time the Pinacoteca was housed in well-sized rooms, with an external entrance in the Vatican Gardens. The biggest new development was that they now had the opportunity to organise the gallery according to modern exhibiting criteria, taking into account the chronological order of the works of art. They managed to create nine rooms and the lighting was improved thanks to the large windows overlooking the Belvedere Courtyard. The paintings came from the following collections:

The new Vatican Pinacoteca, 1932

1. The old Vatican Pinacoteca
2. The picture gallery of the Lateran Palace
3. The collection of Byzantine paintings and the so-called "Primitivi" or "Early" paintings which were originally part of the Vatican Library collections
4. Paintings from the apartments and store rooms of the Papal Residence

Pius XI (Ratti, 1922–1939) finally inaugurated the magnificent new building which is the Pinacoteca's current and definitive position. It has 15 large rooms which hold paintings arranged in chronological order following modern exhibiting criteria. Large storerooms and restoration laboratories were created in the basement, while the library and the photographic archives were put on the first floor.

Paul VI: Opening up towards the world of contemporary art

Paul VI (Montini, 1963–1978) initiated a period of great openness in the Vatican towards the world of contemporary art. Previously Pius XII (Pacelli, 1939–1958) had hoped to create a Contemporary Art Area in the Pinacoteca with the help of a special committee and the generosity of artists and donors. The turning point, however, actually came with Paul VI, when he invited the artists to come to the Sistine Chapel on the 7th May 1964 and expressed his wish of re-establishing a friendly relationship between the Church and the artists.

Paul VI therefore created a collection of modern religious art which aimed to provide an overview of contemporary art, revealing its "prodigious capacity to express real human nature as well as the religious, the divine and the Christian", as declared by the Pope at its inauguration on the 23rd June 1973. The new collection was incorporated into the old one and grew thanks to donations from private individuals and national committees; the collection received paintings, sculptures, graphic works and some stained glass windows, set up in the Borgia Apartment on the second floor of the Papal Palace. The original collection, including works by some of the most important artists of the 20th century (Matisse, Rouault, Van Gogh, Chagall, Previati, Fontana, Manzù, Greco, Morandi and Carrà), continued to grow as the Pope's aim was to provide a comprehensive overview of international artistic culture at the time and gather together diverse representations of contemporary spirituality through multiple means of artistic expression. All these developments were well in line with the notion expressed a long time previously at the Second Vatican Ecumenical Council that "the Church has never had its own particular artistic style, but based on the character and the conditions of the people and the requirements of various rites, it has taken in artistic forms from every era, thus creating, over the course of the centuries, an artistic patrimony which must be carefully conserved".

A new door to the world

During Pius XI's papacy the Conciliation Treaty between the Church and the Italian State was signed and the Vatican City State was created (Lateran Pacts). After this the need arose to stop visitors passing indiscriminately through Vatican territory so a new entrance to the Museums from Italian territory had to be created. A gateway was therefore built in the perimeter wall in the form of a spiral graded ramp with two parallel slopes, designed by the architect Giuseppe Momo (1875–1940) and decorated in bas reliefs with the Popes' coats of arms by the sculptor Antonio Maraini (1886–1963).

In order to celebrate the Great Jubilee in the year 2000 the Vatican authorities decided it was time to build a new entrance which would better reflect the Vatican Museums' wish of opening its doors at the beginning of the new millennium, without breaking away from Giuseppe Momo's ancient gateway. John Paul II inaugurated the new door to the world on the 7th February 2000 with a gesture full of symbolic meaning in confirmation of the Church and the Museums' unremitting desire for openness and dialogue. These thoughts and feelings were powerfully expressed by John Paul II himself in his *Letter to the Artists* on the 24th April 1999 in which he underlined, through concrete examples from the history of Christianity from its origins to the modern era, the continuity of the dialogue which had always existed between the Church and the world of art. Two works were commissioned and inaugurated for the occasion: the *Porta Nuova-Attesa (Door of New Expectation)* by Cecco Bonanotte and the sculpture in polychrome marble *Vacare la Soglia (Crossing the Threshold)* by Giuliano Vangi.

The *Porta Nuova-Attesa* by Cecco Bonanotte (p. 44) fits harmoniously in the ancient walls: it is a bronze gateway with square panels divided into two doors which close to form a sort of circular medallion in the centre; there is a web above with John Paul II's coat of arms in the centre, also in bronze, which covers the area up to the travertine bull running over the base of the ramparts. In a barely discernible relief the artist has depicted the human and natural elements which come together in the Museums: a man and a woman move towards the middle in the central medallion while two birds take flight in the higher part of the left-hand door. On the back there is a series of small sculptures depicting the Popes who contributed to the foundation and the expansion of the Vatican Museums, so

Giacomo Manzù, Chapel of Peace

▲Giuseppe Momo, *Spiral Staircase*, 1932   ▼View of the new spiral ramp

we can see the most important Popes in the unique history of the Vatican Museums at a glance. The last Pope depicted is Paul VI, who also laudably initiated a new beginning in the Museums' history.

The sculpture *Vacare la Soglia* by Giuliano Vangi stands meaningfully in the great entrance hall and admirably embodies the spirit of John Paul II's papacy. A relief depicts John Paul II's smiling face as he raises his left hand in a simple yet vigorous gesture which seems to support the figure of Man and the whole of humanity, captured at the very moment it breaks away from the block of marble to take shape and inhabit the surrounding area. As this work has been sculpted in the round visitors can admire it from various angles, while the relief on the other side shows the Pope at prayer, a prayer which guides the course of humanity. The title of this work can be interpreted in three ways, concisely and marvellously expressed in the figure of man, who bursts forth from the stone taking physical shape and form. Firstly it invites us to cross into the Vatican Museums and contemplate the diverse objects reflecting humanity; secondly it invites us to trustfully cross into the third millennium; and thirdly, as we pass through the door, we are "crossing the threshold of hope", which is none other than the title of John Paul II's celebrated book. This sculpture brings this chapter on the history of the Museums to a close and invites us to enter.

View of the entrance hall with Giuliano Vangi,
Varcare la Soglia

Cecco Bonanotte, *La Porta Nuova-Attesa*, 2000

Museums and collections

THE PIUS-CLEMENTINE MUSEUM

The Pius-Clementine Museum takes its name from two Popes: Clement XIV (Ganganelli, 1769–1774), its founder, and Pius VI (Braschi, 1775–1799), who brought it to completion. Clement XIV developed the idea of creating a new museum in Innocent VIII's Belvedere Palace and started the refurbishment work. Pius VI oversaw the completion of the project with the help of the architect Michelangelo Simonetti. The ancient collection of sixteenth-century sculptures was transformed into a real modern museum, even though the lay-out reflected eighteenth-century tastes so we cannot assume that the works would have been organised according to their chronological order or place of origin.

The museum has three main collections of ancient works of art: the statuary and portraits, the works with funerary connotations (sarcophagi and altars), and the mosaics. These collections are supplemented by decorative elements from *thermae* and gardens such as basins and baths. Visitors can see how the rooms intentionally recall great roman architecture with the aim of totally immersing them in antiquity. Here, the great vaults, the niches holding statues and the ancient mosaics set in the paving all constantly evoke an atmosphere similar to one the Ancients would actually have known.

After the great spiral slope up to the new entrance inaugurated by John Paul II in 2000 we come to the Courtyard of the Cuirasses (Cortile delle Corazze). At the end of this Courtyard we can see St. Peter's Basilica and Michelangelo's great dome through a stained glass window and in the centre we can admire the base of Antoninus' Column, part of a monument erected in memory of Emperor Antoninus Pius (138–161 AD) by his successors Marcus Aurelius (161–180 AD) and Lucius Verus (161–169 AD). This monument used to stand in Campus Martius (Campo Marzio) near the current Piazza Montecitorio. It was a red granite, monolithic column supporting a statue of the emperor with a base decorated in relief. On the main side of the base there is a relief with a triumphal scene of the *Godlike emperor with his wife Faustina*. The large winged figure is a personification of Eternal Time (Aion in Greek, different from Chronos, Time in human life), who takes the couple upwards. Lower down on the right we can see the goddess Roma while a personification of Campo Marzio is on the left. A *decury* is depicted on the shorter sides with a parade of figures on horseback followed by foot soldiers. The *decury* was an ancient rite of honour when soldiers on horseback, in this case the Praetorians (the emperor's personal security guards), would circle the place where the emperor's body had been cremated (*ustrinum*) three times. Passing through the Atrium of the Four Gates (Atrio dei Quattro Cancelli), the old entrance to the Museums from the Viale dei Giardini, we come to the Pinecone Courtyard. This Courtyard forms the northern side of the Bramante's great Renaissance courtyard which connected the Papal Palace to the smaller Palace of Innocent VIII (Cybo, 1484–1492) and was subsequently divided into three parts by the construction of Sixtus V's library (Peretti, 1585–1590) and Pius VII's New Wing (Chiaramonti, 1800–1823). The *Pinecone*, dated to the 1st or 2nd century AD, was part of an ancient fountain with water pouring out

Square Vestibule, Pius-Clementine Museum

through holes in its copious scales. It was meant to remain in Campus Martius, in the district which still bears the name *Pigna* (Pinecone) today but in accordance with the common reuse of ancient objects, the *Pinecone* statue was moved to the centre of the entrance atrium of the Constantinian Basilica of St. Peter. It was covered by a splendid baldachin held up by four porphyry columns, decorated with bronze peacocks from the nearby Hadrian's Mausoleum and used as a fountain for the ablutions of pilgrims who went into the Basilica.

THE ANCIENT STATUARY

Pius VI created a new monumental entrance to the Museum which could be accessed from the first flight of the Simonetti Staircase (Scala Simonetti) leading to the Greek Cross Room (Sala a Croce Greca) **(21)**, the first room of the nascent Museum. The staircase was also built to connect the library area to the upper floors, hence a second double flight of stairs was built leading to the antechamber of the Gallery of the Candelabras (Galleria dei Candelabri).

These days visitors cannot go into the Pius-Clementine Museum through Pius VI's entrance as the museum route was modified for logistical reasons. Visitors now reach the Greek Cross Room at the end of the visit, going in through the Museum's former entrance **(1)** constructed for Pope Clement XIV before Pius VI's expansion work began.

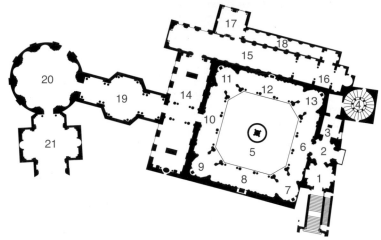

1. Square Vestibule
2. Round Vestibule
3. Apoxyomenos Cabinet
4. Bramante's Staircase
5. Octogonal Courtyard, central area
6. Octogonal Courtyard, East portico
7. Octogonal Courtyard, Apollo Cabinet
8. Octogonal Courtyard, South portico
9. Octogonal Courtyard, Laocoon Cabinet
10. Octogonal Courtyard, West portico
11. Octogonal Courtyard, Hermes Cabinet
12. Octogonal Courtyard, North portico
13. Octogonal Courtyard, Perseus Cabinet
14. Room of the Animals
15. Statue Gallery
16. Gallery of Busts
17. Room of the Masks
18. Open Loggia
19. Room of the Muses
20. Round Room
21. Greek Cross Room

Once we have passed through the Pinecone Courtyard we come to the Square Vetibule **(1)** moving towards the Round Vestibule **(2)**. After the Round Vestibule, designed by Simonetti as a "hinge" in the first part of the Pius-Clementine Museum, and more especially after having admired the wonderful view over Rome from the small portico, we come to a sculpture which forms a perfect beginning to this journey through ancient statuary in the Pius-Clementine Museum.

Apoxyomenos Cabinet (Gabinetto dell'Apoxyomenos)

■ Statue of *Apoxyomenos* **(3)**

The beginning and the highlight of this journey through ancient statuary is the *Apoxyomenos*. This statue was found during the excavation of an imperial era building in the Trastevere area of Rome and it is a Pentelic marble copy from the first century AD of a bronze statue by the Greek sculptor Lysippos around 330 BC. We do not possess any originals by Lysippos, Alexander the Great's favourite, but the identification of this Roman copy of the *Apoxyomenos*, his most well-known work (referred to by Pliny the Elder in his *Naturalis Historia*), has allowed us to create a fixed point of reference in his sculptural activity. The term *apoxyomenos* derives from the Greek verb "to cleanse": the statue represents an athlete scraping his body with a small curved instrument the Romans called a strigil to remove the mixture of oil and sand used by boxers and wrestlers to escape from the clutches of their opponent more easily during the fight in boxing and pankration matches and to wipe off sweat.

Greek artists continued to make progress in their work and Lysippos started using revolutionary new techniques, so this statue does not just represent the height of the artist's personal development, it is also a fixed point of reference in the history of ancient statuary. We have already seen that Greek sculptors revolutionised earlier Eastern traditions and throughout their studies they posed themselves the problem of how to portray figures that could be admired from any angle; whatever the viewing point or perspective the statue had to be fully inserted into three-dimensional space. In the case of Lysippos' statue, the protruding arms emphatically break out of the mould of frontal poses. Furthermore, the distinction between one straight and one bending leg, which had already softened the rigidly frontal pose with two firmly rooted straight legs, was attenuated here by the fact that the weight of the body also falls on the bending leg so the viewer can actually see the moment the balance shifts as the body moves from one position to the other. The statue's skilfully rendered anatomical detail also makes it seem alive. Besides, Lysippos chose not to idealise the athlete and remove him from his everyday life, on the contrary, he captured life as it happened in an ordinary moment and in an almost casual pose.

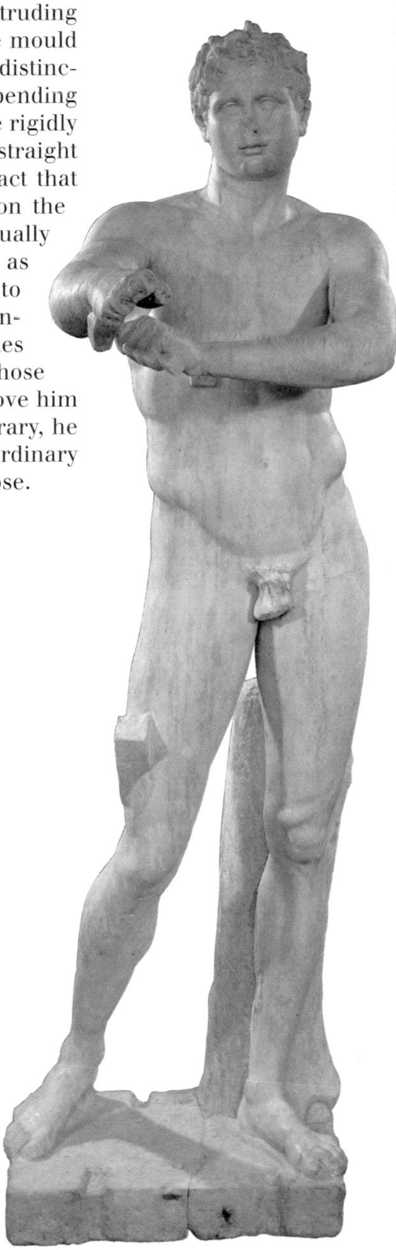

Apoxyomenos,
1st century AD after a
4th-century BC bronze
original, Pius-Clementine
Museum, *Apoxyomenos*
Cabinet

The statuary

The statues and their origins

When we admire masterpieces of classical statuary we have to remember that we are standing before Roman copies of Greek statues. Statues, in Greece, were linked to politics and religion so we must try to imagine them outdoors, in temples, shrines, the Agora, libraries, theatres, gymnasia and as ornaments on tombs.

The military campaigns conducted by the Romans in the Mediterranean afforded various opportunities of coming into direct contact with the thriving centres of Greek civilisation and the inevitable result was that countless Greek works of art – the spoils of war – began to flow into Rome. The first objects came from Syracuse, which was seized and sacked in 212 BC by General Marcus Marcellus. According to the historian Livy the conquest of Syracuse was 'the very beginning of enthusiasm for Greek works of art' (XXV, 40, 1–2), and this was corroborated in Marcellus' biography, written by the Greek Plutarch, in which we can read that the General 'to illustrate his triumph, and adorn the city, carried away with him a great number of the most beautiful ornaments of Syracuse. For, before that, Rome neither had, nor had seen, any of those fine and exquisite rarities; nor was any pleasure taken in graceful and elegant pieces of workmanship.' (*Life of Marcellus*, 21). Seeing as the originals did not satisfy demand, Roman copies began to be made of the Greek originals and entire schools transferred their activities to Rome to work for the buyers. This became one of the main factors in facilitating the mania for private collecting reflecting Catholic tastes which, far from appreciating the shapes and forms of Greek art, concentrated on making the works fit in with their architectural setting.

The materials

The materials chosen to make the statues were extremely diverse: wood, terracotta, bronze, limestone, and marble with a preference for the white varieties, porphyry and granite. The favoured materials were usually the durable ones, partly due to the need to withstand outdoor conditions and atmospheric agents. For the same reasons, as well as for aesthetics, the statues' surfaces were painted, also partly to mitigate the violent effects of the light.

There was a progressive transition from full to partial polychromy, facilitated by the artists' discovery of the marble's beauty. However, the use of colour on the statues never completely disappeared, just as the artists also continued to spread a protective layer of wax on them.

Distinctive colours were also used on the bronzes as well as embellishments in enamel, ivory and mother of pearl for the natural rendering of the eyes and mouth. Unfortunately most of the Greek statues in bronze have been lost as they were melted down in later eras, so the existence of originals is extremely rare and the result of fortuitous circumstances. Luckily the Roman copies in marble from the original Greek bronzes have been mostly well preserved and handed down to us intact. Thanks to these statues, and by studying and comparing various copies of the same model in reliefs, on coins and in glyptics, we can laboriously trace back to the archetypal form of the Greek original.

How can a Roman marble copy be told apart from a Greek bronze original? The presence of supports reveals the works true origins as metal has more elasticity than stone and does not break as easily. The protruding parts of a metal statue do not need to be supported while sculptures in stone need help to stop these parts from cracking away from their main structure. It goes without saying that artists who used bronze had almost unlimited freedom in portraying moving or stretched out figures.

The revolutionary new developments in statuary: the study of anatomy and naturalism

The oriental influence on early Greek statuary is clear. The workmanship, the use of proportion and the poses of the figures are taken from Egypt (which boasted a long tradition in large-scale sculpture) both for the statues depicted standing and seated as well as those in motion. Soon, however, Greek statuary broke away from the earlier traditions and chose a new direction. Egyptian artists portrayed objects irrespective of their position in space following a two-dimensional concept of reality. The unvarying aspects in their execution were therefore the front-facing position of the statues whether seated or standing, their great size (Egyptian statues were colossal), their lack of autonomy from the architecture (the statue could be confused with an architectural element in place of a pillar or column), the lack of anatomical detail and study of a portrait and the preference for durable materials. In ancient Egypt reality was represented as it was thought to be and not how it was actually perceived by the eye. Communicating an idea was considered to be the most important thing, for example the illustration of religious and cosmic principles, rites and cults and the celebration of the Pharaoh's divinity.

In the ancient world traditions generally carried great weight and resistance to innovation was strong, especially in Egypt where some conventions remained practically the same for millennia. The open spirit of the Greeks and their readiness for research and change lessened these traits and although they recognised the value of traditions, followed a code of expression and a system of binding rules, Greek artists made constant advances, moving away from abstraction and drawing nearer to naturalism – statues made their first steps into three-dimensional space. Soon after, Greek sculptors had to deal with problems linked to the representation of the body in motion, its twists and turns, and they realised that it did not necessarily have to stand on the soles of the feet, just as it did not have to face forward.

Another great innovation was the study of anatomy with Man being the absolute centre of attention of Greek artists. The first step in this direction was the need to make statues life-size instead of the colossi of Egyptian descent, and this led to more attention being given to anatomical detail through the careful observation of still and moving bodies; athletes became the pre-eminent source of inspiration. Consequently, attention to anatomical detail manifested itself in a love for the human body, its harmony, beauty and vigour. This led the artists, right up to the Hellenistic era, to avoid portraying the body's declining forms like illness and old age whenever possible. They preferred to depict subjects like gods, heroes, illustrious men, athletes and the deceased, whose likenesses were destined for temples, shrines, porticoes and funerary monuments.

Artists in the ancient world

Artists in the ancient world were considered mostly to be artisans and in the Greek world the distinction was also very subtle. Technical ability was so important for the Greeks that the expression "well made" was the highest compliment an artisan, or a *technites*, could receive. Art was therefore considered to be an ability and the concept of original and independent artistic creation remained beyond ancient ways of thinking. Three factors became important for ancient artists: the material provided by nature, the wisdom provided by traditions and the ability shown in manual activity. Little importance was given to originality as people tended to appreciate the artists' capacity to keep to iconographic traditions which guaranteed universality and continuity. Ancient artists were not even remembered by name, it was only later that we began to find out about lone individuals. The Greek term *techne*, used to indicate "art", was also used to define any practical activity which required ability, specific knowledge and the observation of general rules. Architects, like carpenters, sculptors and weavers were therefore all classified as *technites*.

Bramante's Staircase (Scala di Bramante)

A little further on, after passing through a small vestibule, we come to Bramante's Staircase **(4)**, a spiral flight of stairs enhanced by a granite colonnade made for Julius II (della Rovere, 1503–1513). The graded ramp was built as one of the entrances to the Palace and its structure with wide and low steps made it possible to go up and down easily even on horseback. It is characterised by an elegant colonnade which displays the three architectural orders, Doric, Ionic and Corinthian, changing according to the level you are on as you move upwards from the bottom.

Octogonal Courtyard (Cortile Ottagono)

Moving back, we come to the Octagonal Courtyard **(5)**, the heart and initial location of the Vatican Museums. Originally there was a square, orange tree garden decorated with statues Julius II had built by Bramante. The *Apollo*, the *Laocoon* and the *Venus Felix* were installed in the three *cappellette* (small shrines) along the Courtyard's main wall, the one the Pope's guests would see in front of them as they arrived in the garden from Bramante's Staircase. In the eighteenth century Clement XIV ordered the open area to be closed off by an octagonal portico designed by Simonetti, giving the Courtyard its current appearance. The shorter sides are called Cabinets (Gabinetti), and here we can admire the most important statues adorning Julius II's ancient courtyard.

Donato Bramante's Staircase

▲Vincenzo Feoli, *View of the Octagonal Courtyard*, engraving, Vatican Museums

▼Raphael, *The Parnassus* (detail), Raphael's Rooms, Room of the Signature

Apollo Cabinet (Gabinetto dell'Apollo)

Moving around the portico of the courtyard in a clockwise direction we come to the *Apollo Cabinet*.

■ Statue of *Apollo "del Belvedere"* **(7)**

This statue was brought to the Vatican by Julius II and placed in one of the niches around the courtyard. It was admired by Winckelmann, Goethe and at an even earlier time by Michelangelo. It is a Roman copy from the Hadrian era (2ⁿᵈ century AD) of a bronze original by the sculptor Leochares (4ᵗʰ century BC) which was displayed in the Agora of Athens. It depicts Apollo, who almost seems to appear before the viewer as a sudden apparition in all his divine magnificence. According to ancient mythology Apollo, the god of music and poetry, was represented on the mythical mountain of Parnassus to preside over the Muses, who were thought by the ancients to inspire all the foremost intellectual activities of Man. In this regard, Raphael's representation of Parnassus in Julius II's study on the second floor of the Papal Palace is extraordinary.

Apollo "del Belvedere", 2nd-century AD Roman copy after a 4th-century BC Greek original, Octagonal Courtyard

Apollo was also a warrior god, capable of bringing about a quick death by striking with his bow and arrow. In Homer's *Iliad*, for example, he fights for the Trojans against the Greeks. The statue shows the god dressed as an archer. In his left hand he holds the bow and in his right he grasps the arrow he has just drawn from the quiver. The god's gaze is magnificent as he looks towards an undefined and faraway point in the distance. He has a chlamys, a sort of mantle, thrown over his bow-arm and there is a snake on the tree trunk reminiscent of his victory at Delphi over Python, Gaia's monstrous serpent child. The tripod is also well-known as one of the emblems of Apollo, also a god of divination, on which Pythia, a sort of priestess, sat to deliver her prophecies. A solemn feast was held at Delphi to commemorate Python's death and Apollo's purification.

Although this statue is a copy it displays all the originality and the achievements of Greek sculptors in the 4th century BC giving us the chance to appreciate the statue's movement in three dimensional space.

South portico

■ Statue of *Rivers* (known as *Tigris* or *Arno*) and sarcophagus with *Amazonomachy* (8)

Julius II's "garden" held a series of statues used as parts of fountains, as is the case of this statue of *Rivers*. This fluvial statue is a Roman copy from the Hadrian era (2nd century AD) of a Greek prototype from the Hellenistic era. Alexander's foundation of the Empire was a highly important event for Greek art as it became the figurative language of almost half the known world; at the same time Greek art came into contact and interacted with other cultures. We therefore refer to art from the era following the 5th and 4th centuries BC not as Greek but Hellenistic art, as this name evoked the title given to the empires founded by Alexander's successors in the East, who divided the territory into three great Kingdoms (the Kingdoms of Macedonia, Syria and Egypt). In the high Hellenistic age (from the 3rd century BC) one of the characteristics of the statuary was the variety of figurative themes represented. They did not just portray gods, mythical heroes, illustrious characters and athletes, as artists did in the classical era, they also depicted children, animals, personifications of the natural world, foreigners and barbarians.

This statue of the fluvial deity is known to be the result of a series of restorations, which have allowed the statue to be used to form the higher section of the fountain for the Statue Garden with a basin made of a sarcophagus with an *Amazonomachy*. Which parts have been restored? The first is the right arm holding the water-bearing vase, which is decorated with a ring bearing the Medici coat of arms. This emblem initially caused the work to be identified as a personification of the river Arno, but in actual fact the Medici coat of arms refers to Pope Leo X (Medici, 1513–1521), who probably commissioned the work's first restoration. The second is the magnificent head, which is reminiscent of the Renaissance style and seems similar in terms of expressiveness to the *Moses* sculpted by Michelangelo for Julius II's funerary monument.

The main episodes of the Greek mythological repertoire were often represented on sarcophagi with the protagonists being the gods who meddled in the affairs of men and the heroes who featured prominently in battles and various other undertakings. Naturally the episodes judged to be the most suitable for funerary allegories were chosen. In this case the well-known mythical theme of the *Amazonomachy* was well-suited to become a funerary allegory for soldiers' sarcophagi as it recounts the battle between the Greeks and the Amazons fought both on foot and on horseback, leaving many soldiers dead on the battlefield. This battle took place during the Trojan War when the Amazons, the female warriors descended from the god of war Ares, sent a contingent led by their Queen Penthesilea to help King Priam of Troy. The Amazons were defeated by the Greeks and their Queen was killed by Achilles. The sarcophagus dates back to the 2nd century AD.

Tigris (Arno), 2nd-century AD Roman copy after an Hellenistic prototype, Octagonal Courtyard

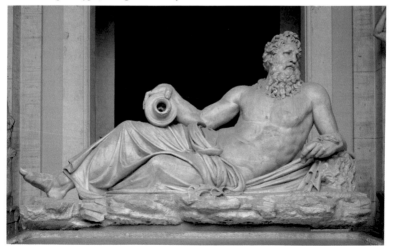

The restoration of the sculptures

The sculptures on display in this area were often fully restored as it was not considered appropriate, according to collecting trends between the sixteenth and eighteenth centuries, to exhibit incomplete or fragmentary works of art. The restorations were generally carried out on the more exposed and fragile parts such as the head, hands, arms and objects which were emblematic of the god or hero depicted. In these cases visitors must be aware that they are in a "museum in a museum", where on one hand they can admire ancient sculptures and on the other they can make out the modern interpolations and additions which arose from sixteenth to eighteenth century tastes for museum displays.

From the sixteenth century onwards classical art was seen as the highest source of inspiration but it was interpreted with contemporary sensibility which occasionally resulted in contradictory actions. On the one hand sculptors felt obliged to use classical styles and forms yet on the other hand, in carrying out restorations they took the risk of transforming an ancient sculpture into a contemporary work of art with additions which were often arbitrary. This led to particularly lively and heated debates on the concept of restoration. The philological approach was the most popular, where people compared similar works of art in order to integrate reconstructions. Problems emerged, however, when the object was an *unicum* and it became virtually impossible to rely on comparisons. The most well-known eighteenth-century sculptors working in the field of restoration were Bartolomeo Cavaceppi, the owner of a large collection housed in his studio on Via del Babuino in the centre of Rome, Gaspare Sibilla, who also worked as a general superintendent for all the Vatican Museums' sculpture restoration work, and Francesco Antonio Franzoni, who studied the art of restoration in the studio of Giovanni Battista Piranesi (the famous architect and engraver who boasted a collection of decorative and architectural works in marble, mostly from the emperor Hadrian's villa near Tivoli).

Laocoon Cabinet (Gabinetto del Laocoonte)

■ Statuary group of the *Laocoon* (9)

As tradition has it, the Trojan priest Laocoon and his two sons were killed by terrible serpents sent from the sea by Athena and Poseidon. The priest had objected to letting the wooden horse into the city of Troy, advising instead to burn it. It had been left as a votive offering to Athena from the Greeks, who in the mean time pretended to go away. When faced with this wondrous sight, however, the Trojans convinced each other to accept the horse with the Greek heroes hidden inside, sealing the city's fate. This group of statues portrays the climactic point in which the monsters coil themselves around the ill-fated heroes' bodies. Thereafter, Laocoon became an emblematic and tragic example of what would happen to those who opposed the inevitable course of events, in this case the events which foretold that Troy should be destroyed and that Aeneas would emerge from the flames to start a new family line with its descendents destined to found the city of Rome. This work of art was found in 1506 on Esquiline Hill in the area where the emperor Nero's *Domus Aurea* formerly stood. It was immediately acquired by Julius II who placed it in the famous garden of the Belvedere Palace, marking the beginning of the formation of the renowned group of statues. As we have seen the *Laocoon* group was full of important symbolic meanings. It is the starting point of a specifically thought-out route which continues with the *Apollo* (who fought on the

Trojans' side), moving on to the *Venus Felix* (Aphrodite-Venus was Aeneas' mother) and the group with *Hercules and Telephus* interpreted as Aeneas and his son Ascanius. Ascanius was the founder of Alba Longa whose descendents included King Numitor and his daughter Rhea Silvia, who would then lie with Mars and give birth to the twins Romulus and Remus, the first of whom would become the founder of Rome. All these statues served in Julius II's plan to emphasise and exalt the origins of Rome, the heir of the great Roman Empire beheld from a Christian point of view.

In his *Naturalis Historia*, Pliny the Elder hands down precious information about works of art he actually saw or heard about and in one passage (*Nat. Hist.*, XXXVI, 37) he mentions the group which then stood in the Palace of Titus (Palazzo di Tito) and bore the names of the sculptors Hagesandros, Athenadoros and Polydoros. The discovery of great sculptural groups by the same artists cited by Pliny in a grotto-nymphaeum near Sperlonga, part of a complex belonging to the emperor Tiberius, has led us to believe that this work is a Roman copy from the early Imperial era for the court of Tiberius (14–37 AD) of an original Hellenistic bronze or marble prototype from the 2nd century BC.

Although this is a copy the artists have infused the group with a strong

---

Laocoön, 1st century AD after a 2nd-century BC
Greek original, Octagonal Courtyard

sense of dynamism through the use of contrasting lines and great narrative pathos, effectively portraying the climactic moment of the event with all the muscles, nerves and facial expressions tense with the strain. Classical Greek artists sought balance and serenity in their work whilst Hellenistic artists did not shy away from showing the human body in the most extreme conditions caused by pain, illness and old age. Laocoon and his sons betray their fear and suffering. Furthermore, the ambition of Hellenistic artists was essentially to reproduce a whole range of feelings from loving passion to rage and from misery to agony, as the composed nature of classical art was no longer present.

Laocoon's right arm was found at the beginning of the twentieth century by the archaeologist Ludwig Pollak (leading to the term "Pollack arm") in the studio of a stonemason and immediately recognised it as part of the well-known sculptural group. On the back of the base we can see the marble arm made by Agostino Cornacchini in imitation of the terracotta one commissioned by Pope Clement VII (1523–1534) from Giovanni Angelo Montorsoli, the result of an interpretation which envisaged the *Laocoon*'s right arm raised almost vertically over his head.

Hermes Cabinet (Gabinetto dell'Hermes)

- Statue of the *"Belvedere Hermes"* (11)

This statue is a roman copy from the Hadrian era (2nd century AD) of a bronze original from the school of the great Greek sculptor Praxiteles (4th century BC), which adorns one of the niches in Julius II's Statue Garden. Hermes was the god of commerce; he guided travellers on the roads and his image was sculpted on pillars at crossroads, with the higher part in the form of a human bust (a sort of herm). Hermes also guided dead souls to the underworld and hence bore the attribute of being a *Psychopomp*, a "conductor of souls", and it is in this role that he is depicted here. Although this work is a copy it evokes great Greek statuary through the softness of its lines, the suppleness of the limbs which create flowing movements and the skilful anatomical analysis. The presence of the support in the form of a palm tree trunk next to the statue further betrays the fact that it is a copy.

North portico

- Statue of *Venus Felix* (12)

This statue was one of the first works to become part of Julius II's collection and it stood, along with the *Apollo* and the *Laocoon*, along the main wall of the Belvedere Garden. As mentioned previously, numerous Roman copies of Greek originals have survived to the present day. Although this statue is not specifically a copy of the work, it is reminiscent of the great masterpiece the *Aphrodite of Cnidus* by Praxiteles, an actual copy of which can be seen in the Room of the Masks (Gabinetto delle Maschere) (17). The *Aphrodite of Cnidus* has been an extremely renowned cult image since antiquity, sculpted in the 4th century BC for the temple of Cnidus. Until then depictions of the female nude in Greek art had been very rare whilst the male nude had always been widespread in all forms of art, but Praxiteles' work marked a turning point. After this numerous statues of female nudes began to appear in the Hellenistic era (3rd century BC), however, unlike male nudes which took the form of gods, athletes and heroes, a considerable amount of time passed before female nudes were portrayed as anything other than goddesses.

The statue known as the *Venus Felix* has a distinctive inscription on the base which indicates its votive purpose. In this case the inscription is thought to attest the fact that the statue was dedicated to Venus Felix by Sallustia, a Roman matron whose portrait can be traced back to the 2nd century AD, and by Helpidus, in all likelihood one of her sons, who stands next to her in the guise of Eros as he hands her an object which could be a mirror. If there was a votive statue dedicated to Venus, there was obviously a temple dedicated to her as well. Venus was also the particular protectress of the city of Rome and consequently had temples dedicated to her. Venus was the Goddess of Love par excellence and granted the Trojans her protection during the Trojan War. Although she could not prevent the fall of Troy, she was able to save the Trojan line by helping her son Aeneas to escape the burning city along with his father Anchises and above all his son Ascanius so they could find a new land to build a home. After Aeneas' well-known wanderings, celebrated in Virgil's *Aeneid*, Ascanius would go on to become the founder of Alba Longa of Latium. This was the reason why the city of Rome developed a special cult in homage to Aphrodite-Venus. She was thought to be the ancestor of the *Iulii* family, the descendents of Ascanius, of Aeneas and hence of the goddess. One of the great members of the *Iulii* family was the emperor Caesar Augustus and Julius II intended to use this connection to attach himself to Aphrodite-Venus. Papal collecting took on the values of Renaissance collecting: the collections on display in the Roman palaces not

"Belvedere Hermes", 2nd-century AD Roman copy after a 4th-century BC Greek original, Octagonal Courtyard

Venus Felix, 2nd-century AD Roman copy after *Aphrodite of Cnidus* by Praxiteles (4th century BC), Octagonal Courtyard

only represented a refined cultural range of works, imbibed with the principles of Humanism, they also formed a code which was used to orchestrate political and moral agendas.

Just as Virgil had celebrated the origins of Rome through the Trojan War and Aeneas' journey in the *Aeneid* to exalt the political plan of Augustus, the heir of *Iulii* family line, Julius II played on his own name *Iulius* to place himself in the direct line of the *Gens Iulia*, Caesar and Augustus' family. He used this connection to proclaim a new golden era for Christian Rome, just as Augustus had done when he too declared the beginning of a new era.

Perseus Cabinet (Gabinetto del Perseo)

- Canova's statue of *Perseus* (13)

Antonio Canova, one of the foremost artists of the neoclassical period, began to sculpt the *Perseus* partly in homage to the original ancient marble statue which had been taken to Paris. At the beginning of the nineteenth century when the *Perseus* was bought by Pope Pius VII Chiaramonti, the Pius-Clementine Museum languished due to the French sackings. The bases of the most famous statues were empty

Antonio Canova, *Perseus, c.* 1800, Octagonal Courtyard

while others held casts instead of the precious originals. Thus, the installation of the *Perseus* in the niche and on the pedestal which had been occupied for almost three centuries by the *Apollo* and Canova's nomination to the post of Inspector of Antiquities and Fine Arts, reaffirmed the Pope's strong resolve to replace the lost works.

Canova captures Perseus, one of the foremost heroes in Greek mythology, just after he has cut off the gorgon Medusa's head with the curved sword given to him by Hermes. The Gorgons were the three monsters who lived in the far west, not far from the Kingdom of the Dead. Their heads were covered in snakes, they had wings which allowed them to fly and with a single glance they could turn anyone who looked at them into stone. Once he finds the monsters' lair, Perseus flies into the sky on his winged sandals and while Athena holds a shield over the Medusa to act as mirror so the hero does not look into her eyes, he beheads the monster. Athena then used the Medusa's head on her shield so her enemies would turn to stone as soon as she appeared. Canova portrays the climactic moment of the violent scene which has just taken place: the hero is holding the Medusa's freshly severed head with its facial expression contracted in pain.

The rediscovery of Antiquity: Neoclassicism

The German scholar Johann Joachim Winckelmann was the foremost theorist of Neoclassicism and the librarian and curator of Cardinal Alessandro Albani's collections of antiquities. He wrote that the only way for us to become great, yes, inimitable, if it is possible, is the imitation of the Greeks, although an imitation was not to be considered as just a sterile copy or a cast of ancient works. In the eighteenth century the past did not only come to light because of the archaeological discoveries of the cities of Pompeii and Herculaneum, it was also taken up again and studied for its ideals, which appeared more than ever to correspond to the need for rationality and civil renovation which animated the most committed scholars of the time. This was the Age of Enlightenment and Neoclassicism reflected the new atmosphere like a mirror, picking up on the renewed tension which would go on to leave its mark on the final decades of the eighteenth century and the first decades of the following century. The most important aspect of this intentional return to the ancient style was the strong influence of Greece and the classical traditions of Roman descent. The first flourish of this new trend was the theoretical definition of the neoclassical concept of beauty. This was seen as being consistent with the concept of truth, or rather nature as well as the concept of reason, and it manifested itself in works of art as noble simplicity of form and purity of lines. More especially, beauty was seen as coinciding with the concept of goodness. Everyone thought that classical references seemed to be the best antidote against Baroque intemperance and its offshoots, namely the Rococo style. To a large extent, opposing the Baroque style meant a refusal to accept the means of expression of a society perceived as free, which should have moved aside for a more conscious world where beauty was not disassociated with virtue. Neoclassicism spread through Europe and involved all areas of artistic production from the major arts to furnishings and fashion. The cultural points of reference, however, did not just come from the Greek and Roman worlds. Artists embraced ideas which sometimes went beyond and differed from the theorists' declarations, reusing Egyptian and Etruscan motifs and traits from the works of remote civilisations.

The marble "zoo"

After the Octagonal Courtyard we come to the Room of the Animals (Sala degli Animali) **(14)** where we can admire a real zoological museum made of marble, that is to say a rich animalistic repertoire which also includes imaginary and exotic animals. Some are ancient while others have been significantly restored or re-sculpted by restorers and sculptors from the eighteenth century. Hellenistic sculptors were open to all kinds of figurative subjects and they particularly focussed on animals, partly due to more advanced scientific knowledge about their appearance and behaviour. The Hellenistic era was characterised by a great interest in the sciences and a predilection for carrying out all kinds of experiments in all fields of knowledge with people studying mathematics, geometry, geography, astronomy, medicine and botany. Moreover, art came to take on the characteristics of a mirror, reflecting new developments. So why create a marble zoo? Its foundation was undoubtedly favoured by eighteenth-century naturalistic interests, in line with the new horizons reached by biological sciences and in light of the new encyclopaedic culture of the Enlightenment. As mentioned previously, some of the works of art here have been heavily restored, so this small museum within a museum can also be studied in terms of the trend for collecting rare and exotic objects as well as for the decorative tastes of the eighteenth century and the history of restoration.

In a small loggia on the right, to the north, there is a magnificent bust of Pius VI contemplating his museum and little marble zoo. At the end of the eighteenth century this room was known by two names, the Room of the Rivers (Stanza dei Fiumi) and the Room of the Animals. Thanks to ancient prints we know that the renowned statues of the *Tiber* and the *Nile* stood here for some time. These personifications suited this environment extremely well as rivers, like animals, were considered to be part of the natural world, in contrast to the world of men, heroes and gods, the main characters in the Pius-Clementine Museum's other rooms. During the French plundering, however, the statues of the *Tiber* and the *Nile* were removed and taken to Paris for the new Louvre Museum, with only the *Nile* later finding its way back to Rome. Deprived of its *Rivers*, the room took on the sole name of the Sala degli Animali.

The tamed animals almost seem to come alive before our eyes, from birds, aquatic creatures, wolves, lynxes, lions and panthers to the group of deer being attacked by dogs and the sculptures of mythical beasts like the centaur, the griffin and the Minotaur. The collection is completed by figures whose names are indissolubly linked with animals, like Meleager, the brilliant hunter from Greek mythology and Mithras killing the bull. There are also two ancient polychrome mosaics set in the paving with still life scenes of flora and fauna. Last but not least, let us not forget that this repertoire of animals before us also holds a wide, though not complete, selection of marble as the sculptors used large quantities of coloured varieties to make the animals seem more lifelike.

This room allows us to understand the Greco-Roman world's rapport with nature seen from a mythological, bucolic, hunting and zoological point of view, with the portrayal of exotic and rare animals extraneous to local wildlife, and also from a geological point of view, thanks to the variety of the stones.

■ Statue of *Meleager*

This hunter-hero is in the niche at the far end of the southern wing of the Room of the Animals and seems to dominate the various animals before him. In keeping with the concept of this area, animals are alternated with people and subjects referring to zoological themes. Meleager, the mythological Greek hunter, is depicted with a dog on his right and the head of the wild boar, his mythical prey, on his left. The wild boar was sent by Artemis, the goddess of hunting, to ravage the region of Calydon in Aetolia as she was enraged that the King of the Aetolians had failed to honour her in his sacrifices to the gods. The foremost Greek heroes participated in the hunt led by Meleager, the son of the King of the Aetolians, who killed the terrible wild beast. This group portrays Meleager at rest, wrapped in a fluttering cloak along with his hunting trophy and his dog, whose gaze is turned towards the hero. This work is a 2nd century AD Roman copy of a 4th century BC Greek bronze original attributed to the famous sculptor Scopas. The hero's left hand should have been leaning on one of his hunting weapons but the copier has inserted elements which do not belong to the original. These elements, the cloak, the dog gazing proudly at his master and the support (further confirming the fact that this sculpture is a copy of a bronze original) can be identified by comparisons and literary descriptions.

Meleager, 2nd-century AD Roman copy after a 4th-century BC Greek original, Room of the Animals

■ *Lion*

Although this sculpture was heavily restored in the eighteenth century, it
is still a noteworthy example of a naturalistic portrayal of an animal. The
use of a brecciated variety of "ancient yellow" marble (*Marmor numidi-
cum*) brings to mind the colour of the animal's fur and its crouching position reveals the dynamic tension of an animal ready to pounce.

■ *Leopard*

The way this African leopard's almost iridescent, spotted coat has been
portrayed is magnificent, thanks to the alabaster (*Lapis Onyx*) and its
circular inlays in "ancient black" filled with "ancient yellow" to create
the spots. This feline is seen in motion and seems to be reacting to an im-
minent threat, roaring with its jaws wide open. Francesco Antonio Franzoni (1734–1818), who held the title of "intagliatore di marmi" ("marble
carver") at the Papal court, heavily restored this animal and it even at-
tracted the attention, from a collector's point of view, of Pius VI during
one of his many visits to the sculptor-restorer's studio. In ancient times
this type of alabaster, with its pale yellow base and large white opaque

◄*Lion*, 17th or 18th-century copy after an ancient prototype, Room of the Animals

◄▼*Leopard*, 18th-century copy after an ancient prototype, Room of the Animals

►*Crab*, 1st or 2nd century AD, Room of the Animals

▼*Sow suckling her piglets*, 1st century AD, Room of the Animals

areas forming a sinuous "wave" pattern, was extracted from sites along the Valley of the Nile, the most well-known of which being situated near a town named after the stone called Alabastron.

■ *Crab*

This Egyptian green porphyry (similar to the Greek "serpentine") has been effectively used here as its olive and dark green hues create iridescent effects to portray the crab, which seems to shine as if it were sitting on a beach bathed in sunlight. This crustacean has been captured in motion with its two large claws at the water's edge searching for food brought in by the retreating wave. The chromatic contrast between the dark colours of the porphyry, the whiteness of the sand and the foam of the surrounding sea bring the scene to life. The original ancient sculpture from the 1st or 2nd century AD was restored in the eighteenth century when, among other additions, the whole base was re-sculpted.

■ *Sow suckling her piglets*

This work dates back to the Augustan era and is thought to be a representation of the mythical sow *Laurentum*, in reference to the episode

recounted by Virgil with the prophecy made to Aeneas that he would land in Latium and see a white sow suckling thirty piglets. Aeneas actually did land on the coast of *Laurentum*, south of the Tiber estuary, after having seen a white sow and thirty piglets. The image of the sow suckling her piglets is related to the origins of Rome as we can interpret the thirty piglets both as the thirty years which would pass before Aeneas' son Ascanius founded Alba Longa, and the thirty generations which would elapse before the birth of Romulus and Remus. All this was particularly well-suited to Augustus' political policies aimed, among other things, at promoting the origins of Rome and the Julio-Claudian dynasty. Sources also mention the existence of a bronze sow which the Augustan marble copy could have been based on, situated in the forum of Lavinium (now called Practica di Mare), the famous town founded by Aeneas. The sculpture is in Parian marble (from the Greek island of Paros) which has a bright white colour and sometimes almost appears to be transparent.

■ *Phoenix bursting into flames*

The Phoenix, according to ancient mythology, is a legendary bird from Arabia, described by Herodotus as an eagle of considerable size whose plumage was decorated with bright colours of flame, red and gold. The legend of the Phoenix is particularly based on the bird's death and rebirth. It is the only one of its species and cannot reproduce like other animals so when the Phoenix feels the end of its existence approaching, it gathers aromatic plants together to make a sort of nest and then sets fire to this fragrant pyre with a new Phoenix rising from its ashes in a cyclical form of regeneration. This sculpture portrays the culminating point of the myth when the bird has started the fire and the flames are licking at its claws. It is an entirely modern work of art, sculpted in the eighteenth century, although it is still emblematic as it develops a theme which the Greco-Roman world held dear. The same is true of the Christian-Medieval world as the scene can be interpreted from a metaphorical point of view highlighting the need for death before rebirth.

■ Group of the *Mithras tauroctony*

This group represents the climax of a crucial event in a religion of Indo-Iranian origin linked to the worship of Mithras, that is to say the creation of life. Creation, according to the Mithraic religion, was made possible by the sacrifice of the bull, a symbol of life force. The bull was slaughtered by the god Mithras, dressed in oriental clothing. Wheat and plant life are said

Phoenix 18th-century copy after an ancient prototype, Room of the Animals

Mithras and the Bull, 2nd century AD, Room of the Animals

Statue Gallery

to have originated from the sacrificed animal's blood. The generative sacrifice, however, is set against the forces of evil, embodied by the scorpion, the snake and the dog, who are trying to stop the blood from falling to the ground, prevent the seed of the bull from fertilising it and impede the animal's soul from rising into the sky. In this sculptural group Mithras is holding back the bull's head and stabbing it with a short sword while all the figures seem to converge on the wound where creation would be generated.

Statue Gallery (Galleria delle Statue)

The Statue Gallery **(15)** is situated in the ancient portico of Innocent VIII's Belvedere Palace. It used to hold a series of landscapes and views painted by Pinturicchio and his helpers on the walls, although only a few of these works can now be seen on the inner wall of the Gallery. At the opposing ends there are two statues: *Ariadne Sleeping* and *Jupiter Verospi*.

- Statue of *Ariadne Sleeping*

In the sixteenth century this statue was in the north-eastern niche of Julius II's famous Garden. The niche had a rocky backdrop decorated with shrubs, and under the statue there was an ancient sarcophagus used as a fountain basin, supported by two dolphins with a shell to collect the water. The fountain was altered in the seventeenth century and then definitively dismantled when the Pius-Clementine Museum was created, although *Ariadne* was moved to a prominent position at the entrance to the Statue Gallery in a niche sculpted especially for her, placed above a sarcophagus with a *Gigantomachy* along the front and the noteworthy *Barberini Candelabras* on either side.

Ariadne was daughter of King Minos of Crete and she helped the Athenian hero Theseus when he went to Crete to defeat the Minotaur. Every year seven young men and seven young women from Athens were sacrificed to the monster, which had the body of a man and the head of a bull. Consequently Theseus went into the Labyrinth, the Minotaur's lair, to kill it. The hero succeeded in his task and managed to escape from the Labyrinth thanks to the ball of string given to him by Ariadne, unwinding it along his

Ariadne Sleeping, 2nd-century AD Roman copy
after a 2nd-century BC original, Statue Gallery

path to make sure he could find his way back. Ariadne ran away with Theseus but she never reached Athens. When they were on the island of Naxos Theseus abandoned her sleeping on the shore and it is in this position that the heroine has always been portrayed in decorative arts throughout the ages. This statue is a 2nd century AD Roman copy of a Hellenistic original from the 2nd century BC, a time when this subject was seen as a sure source of inspiration as sculptors in the Hellenistic era tended to want to reproduce a whole range of feelings and potential human situations.

The sarcophagus with the *Gigantomachy* was used as a base for Ariadne's statue. Giants are related to early deities and they have always been identified with the notion of primitive strength. The giants are the offspring of Uranus (the Sky) and Gaia (the Earth) and their legend is linked to the story of their fight against the so-called Olympian gods, the gods of the Sky, in an attempt to overturn the established order. They are enormous snake-legged beings with invincible strength and a terrifying appearance who threatened the Sky by hurling flaming trees and boulders. When faced with this threat the Olympians, led by Zeus and Athena and followed by Ares, Ephesus, Aphrodite, Poseidon and many others including the mortal hero Heracles, retaliated and won a great victory. On the sarcophagus the Giants are depicted as they try to climb Olympus among the bushes with some fallen, struck down by the gods we can imagine above them. The sarcophagus dates back to the 2nd century AD and for those who worked in plastic arts at that time the theme of the *Gigantomachy* was a favoured subject as it could be interpreted as an allegory of the victory of intellect over brute force.

Completing the scene (set up in the 18th century) we can see the two *Barberini Candelabras* (2nd century AD), which were found in the emperor Hadrian's villa near Tivoli and later passed into the possession of the Barberini family. These two items marked the beginning of Pope Clement XIV's extensive acquisitions campaign which brought about the foundation of the Clementine Museum. An elegant floral motif supports the container for the oil to feed the flame and the bases each have three sides, decorated in relief with effigies of the Olympian gods. These are magnificent figures sculpted in three-quarters, frontal and back poses including Ares, Aphrodite, Athena, Zeus, Hera and Hermes. The *Candelabras* proved to be very popular and were replicated in plaster and in bronze as well as appearing in an engraving by the famous architect and engraver Giovanni Battista Piranesi, who suggested they become models for decorative production.

Room of Busts (Sala dei Busti)

■ Statue of *Jupiter seated* (known as *Jupiter Verospi*) **(16)**

This famous depiction of Jupiter stood in the courtyard of the Palazzo Verospi in Via del Corso until it was sold to the Museums, moving to a new prestigious position in a niche in the area around the Statue Gallery. This position is justified by the importance of the sculpture (even though it is a copy, dated to the 3ˢᵗ century AD), which was based on the famous *Capitoline Jupiter* by the sculptor Apollonius. This colossal cult statue in the great temple on Capitol Hill, dedicated to the Capitoline triad of Jupiter, Juno and Minerva, was in turn inspired by the *Zeus* sitting in the temple of Olympia. According to historical sources the chryselephantine original (a statue with parts made of gold and ivory) was sculpted by Apollonius after a raging fire broke out in the 1ˢᵗ century BC and completely destroyed the temple of Jupiter Optimus Maximus Capitolinus and its ancient cult statue. The copy was restored in the eighteenth century and depicts Jupiter, the god of light, clear skies, lightning and the king of men and gods, enthroned, his right

Jupiter Verospi,
3ʳᵈ- century AD Roman
copy after *Capitoline
Jupiter* by Apollonius
(1ˢᵗ century BC), Gallery
of Busts

hand resting in his lap and grasping a lightning bolt, and his left hand holding up a sceptre.

Three small rooms next to the portico of the Palace **(16)** were assigned to hold a series of busts on shelves, forming a sort of laboratory for the study of portraiture.

Here we can admire examples of portraits related to the funerary world: some are from the late republican era (1st century BC) where the influence of Greco-Hellenistic portraiture, often recognisable due to its idealised nature, combines with uniquely Roman portraits from Italic areas (which reveal the influence of wax masks made for the deceased); some are official portraits of various Roman emperors; some are female figures from the imperial court with characteristic hairstyles which can be dated thanks to comparisons with images on coins; and finally there are various other portrayals which evoke long lost surroundings and ambiences like the head of an actor, a priest (*flamen*), a barber and a young male worshipper of Isis. These portraits do not form a full gallery, although they are still an effective mirror reflecting the Roman world from the 1st century BC to the 4th century AD and in such a "theatre of memory" these characters seem to come alive again.

Portraits

Portraits aim to portray a certain individual and their features, characterising them. Thus the artist does not just reproduce the physical image of the person but he expresses an assessment which judges the individual. The portrait, in this sense of word, first arose in Greece in the early 4th century BC.

Ancient Egypt

In Egyptian, Babylonian and Assyrian art an image was never a portrait but rather the presence of a god or a sovereign, mostly set in a religious context, while statues evoked the presence of the figure represented. The various gods and pharaohs of ancient Egypt depicted standing or seated are implacable and devoid of expression, since they were seen as presences which evoked a religious world and their "being present" linked them to that specific place.

Portaits in ancient Greece: the creation of the "archetype"

In ancient Greece the real forerunner of the portrait was the creation of "archetypes", the young man, the old man, the hero, the servant, the maiden, the athlete, the philosopher, the scholar and so on, identified by fixed attributes just like the images of the gods. An emblematic case was the trial brought against Phidias (5th century BC), superintendent of construction work on the Parthenon, the great temple built on the Acropolis of Athens and dedicated to the protectress of the city, Athena. Besides being accused of stealing part of the treasure from the goddess' shrine, he was also accused of "asebeia", the Greek word for impiety or sacrilege, because people had noticed portraits in the decorative works on two of the vaults. Representations of the artist himself and Pericles, a prominent political figure in Athens at the time, were depicted there. Exhibiting a portrait in a public and sacred place was considered a sacrilege. This incident reveals the opposing current to the emergence of portraiture in early Greek art.

The creation of portraits in the 4th century BC

Greek and Latin sources allude to a turning point which occurred in the 4th century BC with the great sculptors Lysippos and Praxiteles. They did not just depict the outer features of the person, they also captured their inner expression. A portrait of Plato (427–347 BC), many copies of which are known to exist, is considered the first canonically Greek portrait, even though it was made after the philosopher's death and is therefore idealised. So where did the Greeks display portraits? The first portrait-style statues were of an honorary nature for the portrayal of people such as commanders, great political figures, men of letters and philosophers, and they were positioned in porticoes around the Agora, in theatres and in libraries.

Portrait of Alexander the Great

Alexander the Great's portrait signalled a decisive turning point in the history of Greek portraiture. From that point onwards artists did not concentrate so much on the portrayal of archetypes, but rather the representation of a particular physical and spiritual individuality. Furthermore, considering the dates of his life (356–323 BC), Alexander the Great already embodies a turning point in the whole of Greek artistic civilisation. It was thanks to him that previously unheard of horizons became known to the Greek world and contact was established with other foreign worlds. The foundation of the empire, thanks to Alexander, was actually an extremely important event for Greek art as it became the figurative language of almost half the then known world; at the same time Greek art came into contact with a great number of other widely diverse cultures.

The great sculptor Lysippos, the only artist allowed to depict Alexander, created a sort of prototype, of which we unfortunately only have reproductions. This portrait had enormous repercussions on the Hellenistic and Roman worlds. The Romans, for example, from Caesar to the emperors, all considered themselves as the heirs to Alexander's kingdom so they had themselves depicted in a style reminiscent of Alexander the Great's portrait. The most striking advance in Lysippos' creation is that the concept of an inspired commander was expressed for the first time, as if Alexander were in direct contact with the god he seems constantly to look towards.

The religious premises of Roman portraiture

Rome continued the Greek trend with funerary cults furthering advances in portraiture. Sources reveal the practice followed by noble families of making a wax mask of the deceased and placing the image, along with those of other ancestors, in the atria of their houses in special temple-shaped cabinets. During the funeral procession accompanying the deceased's body these masks were worn by actors dressed according to the positions the figures had held during their lives. In this way they created the impression that all the noble family's ancestors were escorting the deceased's soul to the afterlife. Obviously these masks aimed to reproduce the features of the subjects' faces in the most realistic way possible. The existence of these funereal masks therefore had a decisive influence in the development of Roman portraiture. Then, of course, it came into contact with the portraits from the Greco-Hellenistic world.

Hermae and busts

A herm is a sort of small pillar with a head on top, and in its original form it depicted the god Hermes, who guided travellers on their path in his capacity as the custodian of roads. The use of hermae then spread into Roman-era portraiture and adaptations of Greek sculptures.

In Greece, busts did not exist as they involved a form of artistic expression which was typical of Italic areas. Greek portraits consisted of statues placed on bases or columns. How, then, did the Roman bust originate? It is difficult to establish what actually happed but there is an enlightening passage by Cicero (*De Legibus*, II, 26) in which he quotes the funerary laws of Solon and translates the Greek term to indicate the place where the deceased's ashes are held with the word *bustum*. We can therefore hypothesise about a funerary origin, particularly in light of the cinerary urns with human heads present in Etruscan art, although these cinerary urns were not actually real portraits of the deceased but rather the result of an intention to give them human characteristics to the point of transforming their features into a stylised image. Although this may be just a hypothesis, it is true that in the Roman era portrait-busts were extremely widespread, often commercial copies of Greek statues reduced to bust format and produced in large numbers to decorate public places such as porticoes, libraries, theatres and houses.

- Funerary high reliefs: the portraits of the *Gratidii* (known as *Cato and Portia*)

These two portraits were probably part of the decoration of a funerary monument. According to ethical rules and Roman law people were only allowed to bury the dead outside the city walls. As a result there were burial grounds all along the consular roads out of Rome, characterised by various types of funerary monuments and small secondary paths linking them together. One of these cemeteries must have held a tomb with its front characterised by these two portraits. Luckily, although the inscription itself has been lost, a document accompanying the work has survived providing precious information about the names of the two figures who were in fact married: "Graditia Chrite, liberta di Marco, e Marco Gratidio Libano". The man is wearing a toga, a sign of his Roman citizenship, and he seems to be the son of a freedman. His face is furrowed with wrinkles so he appears to be much older than the woman. Roman portraits, aside from their Greek origins, were highly influenced by the custom of making wax masks of the dead. The attention to detail and the lifelike effect made the Roman portraits real mirrors, although

Cato and Portia, end of the 1st century BC,
Gallery of Busts

we can also occasionally observe the existence of idealised portraits. The woman is wrapped in a cloak and her left hand is placed affectionately on the man's shoulder. The couple's heads are turned slightly towards each other and they are holding hands in the typical matrimonial stance of *dextrarum iunctio*. These portraits can be dated to the end of the 1ˢᵗ century BC.

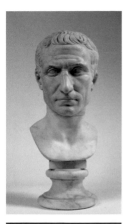

- Head of *Julius Caesar* (known as *Chiaramonti Caesar*)

This portrait of the great dictator displays specific characteristics such as the wrinkles on his forehead and by his eyes and his firm and concentrated facial expression. Thanks to comparisons with other works and sources we can link this work to the portraits done after Caesar died, based on his physical appearance later in life. It can be dated back to the early rule of Augustus (*c.* 30 BC) and is inspired by the semi-idealised portraits of the 3ʳᵈ century BC Hellenistic sovereigns.

- Head crowned with ears of wheat, reworked to depict Augustus

Here we can recognise the familiar facial traits of Augustus (27 BC–14 AD) with the "pincer-like" tufts of his fringe reminiscent of the one from the statue *Augusto di Prima Porta* on display in the New Wing (Braccio Nuovo). As often happened, however, this head was reworked as it had previously been a bust depicting the emperor Domitian (81–96 AD). After an emperor died and received a *damnatio memoriae*, all their images were destroyed or reworked into portraits of other emperors. The crown of ears of wheat around the head was already present in Domitian's portrait and was probably a ritual crown of ears of wheat, a symbol of the religious brotherhood of the "Arval Brethren", the twelve priests devoted to the cult of Dia (later Ceres), the guardian of growing plants. In short, this portrait is an effective image of Augustus' posthumous features.

- Bust of *Antinous*

This portrait probably comes from Emperor Hadrian's villa near Tivoli where the buildings and grounds are reminiscent of the places in the East the Emperor visited in person. The *Canopic jar* in particular brings Egypt to mind. Antinous, Emperor Hadrian's young favourite, unfortunately died during one of Hadrian's voyages to Egypt and he was then deified with the subsequent spread of his cult, as shown by the production of coins, expressly by desire of the

Room of Busts:
Chiaramonti Caesar,
1ˢᵗ century BC

Augustus crowned,
1ˢᵗ century AD

Antinous, 2ⁿᵈ century BC

73

Emperor himself. Antinous is captured here in heroic nudity, a stance often conferred on the deified men who had a cult attributed to them. Consequently, this portrait was made after his death (130 AD).

■Head of *Commodus*

The loricate bust does not belong to the original sculpture but it eloquently evokes the way in which official portraits were presented. Here we can see Commodus (180–192 AD) with a beard and hair characterised by strong chiaroscuro effects and an intense gaze, typical of the philosophical image given to emperors and individuals at the end of the 2nd century AD.

■ Bust of *Caracalla*

This official portrait (211–217 AD) was commissioned by Caracalla after he became the sole sovereign of the Empire (from December 211, after sharing the throne first with his father Septimius Severus and then with his brother Geta). His frowning expression is framed by a low, curly hairline and a short beard. His face turns abruptly to the left and reveals a menacing gaze. This portrait is based on the great portraiture of Alexander the Great and it is characterised by a strong feeling of tension, aimed at inspiring fear and respect.

■ Statue of *Livia at prayer*

Livia Drusilla Claudia, Emperor Augustus's wife, is wearing a tunic covered by a large cloak and she is depicted praying, with her veiled head and the palms of her hands turned upwards. This is perhaps a depiction of Livia as a priestess of the deified Augustus' cult.

■ Bust with portrait thought to be of *Julia of Titus*

This woman has a typical "ad alveare" ("beehive") hairstyle with a diadem (*stephane*) placed on top which can be traced back to the time of the Flavian dynasty, that is to say the dynasty of the emperors Vespasian, Titus and Domitian (69–96 AD). For a long time the portrait was thought to be of Julia Flavia, Emperor Titus' daughter, because of the diadem, but it could also be a portrait, perhaps a funerary one, of any young woman from the Flavian era.

Room of the Muses (Sala delle Muse)

During eighteenth-century excavations at a Roman villa near Tivoli (the so-called Villa di Cassio), seven statues of *Muses* and an *Apollo* cithara player (2nd century AD) were found, which had perhaps adorned the Villa's library. The Room of the Muses **(19)** was built by the architect Michelangelo Simonetti for this sculptural group and evokes an ancient setting. The octagonal layout is marked by columns topped by Corinthian capitals from Hadrian's villa and there is a series of frescoes by Tommaso Conca on the vault. These frescoes depict Apollo and the Muses in the company of eminent poets such as Homer, Aeschylus, Pindar, Virgil, Tasso and Ariosto, reinforcing the subject matter of the classical sculptures displayed along the walls. Herm-portraits of famous people from ancient Greece were positioned between the Muses, which were restored by the sculptor Gaspare Sibilla.

The layout of the Room of the Muses met with great success. Gustav III of Sweden visited the Pius-Clementine Museum with Pius VI and wanted to recreate the Roman group in the Gallery of the Muses in the Royal Palace in Stockholm.

■ Statue of *Apollo Cithara player*

This *Apollo* is depicted in the act of playing the cithara (lyre). Apollo is represented in ancient mythology on Mount Parnassus as god of music and poetry, surrounded by the Muses. He is also the foremost inspirer of soothsayers and poets. This representation of Apollo looks nothing like the *Belvedere Apollo* where he appears as an archer god, ready to strike the dragon Python. Here, we can see his feminine side, draped with a chiton and covered by a cloak linked with pins on his shoulders, crowned with a bay wreath, a musician and an inspirer of beauty in poetic verse. This work is a copy from the Hadrian era (2nd century AD) of a Greek original from the 4th century BC.

■ Statue of the *Muse Calliope* (Muse of Epic Poetry)

During a restoration of this statue the head was reconstructed, thus it did not belong to the original sculpture. It was identified, however, as being Calliope, mainly due to the eighteenth-century additions of a waxed tablet in the form of a diptych on which people wrote and a style (pen-shaped instrument) which was used to engrave the characters. The numerous restorations are justified by comparisons with other statues which depict the Muse seated or in the act of writing on a diptych. This work

preceding page:
◄ *Commodus*, end of the 2nd century AD
◄ *Caracalla*, 3rd century BC
◄ *Livia at prayer*, 1st century AD

▼ *Julia of Titus*, 1st century AD
▼ ▼ *Apollo Cithara player*, Room of the Muses

▲*Muse Calliope*,
2nd-century AD Roman
copy after a 4th-century BC
Greek original, Room of
the Muses

▲▶*Muse Thalia*, 2nd-
century AD Roman copy
after a 4th-century BC
Greek original, Room of
the Muses

▼*Herm of Pericles*,
2nd-century AD Roman
copy after Kresilas
(5th century BC), Room of
the Muses

is a copy from the Hadrian era (2nd century AD)
of a Greek original from the 4th century BC.

■ Statue of the *Muse Thalia* (Muse of Comedy)

This Muse is depicted seated on a rock and was
able to be identified as the Muse of Comedy in
the eighteenth century when her attributes
were added during a restoration, namely a
comic mask, a timbrel (a sort of musical instrument similar to a tambourine), a *pedum*
(the staff carried by shepherds and hunters)
as well as the ancient head crowned with an
ivy wreath which is not an original part of the
statue. These restorations were based on comparisons with other statues of the same type.
This work dates back to the 2nd century AD and
is based on a Greek 4th century BC original.

■ *Herm of Pericles*

'... I, Pericles, return to see the Latin sky, win-
ner over the barbarians, over time and over
destiny'.

These lines are taken from the *Prosopopoeia
of Pericles* which the poet Vincenzo Monti composed and dedicated to Pius VI when a herm
with the portrait of the great Athenian strate-
gist Pericles (495-429 BC) was found at a villa
near Tivoli known as the "Pisoni family" villa.
The entire poem can be read next to the herm
itself. At the same time many other portraits
of illustrious Greeks were also found such as
the seven wise men, philosophers, men of letters, political men and artists, which in all likelihood, according to the custom of decorating
villas and porticoes, all adorned the villa.
On the front of the herm we can see the

following inscription: 'Pericle, [figlio] di Xantippo, ateniese' ('Pericles, [son] of Xanthippus, Athenian'). The work dates back to the Hadrian era (2nd century AD) and is a copy of an original bronze statue near the Acropolis which, according to historical sources (Pliny, *Naturalis Historia*, XXXIV, 74), was done by the Greek sculptor known as Kresilas. A base from the 5th century BC thought to belong to the original statue has been found and bears the artist's signature. Pericles has curly hair and a short beard with his helmet slightly raised, essential for all *strategi* (commanders or leaders of an army).

- The *Belvedere Torso*

'... a magnificent oak that has been felled and stripped of branches and foliage...': Johann Joachim Winckelmann, the foremost theorist of Neoclassicism, wrote these words to express his great emotion in finding himself before this sculpture. Michelangelo was also among the first to have admired it, declaring himself a disciple of the Torso. It is well-known that fifteenth and sixteenth-century artists considered ancient statuary as a primary and inexhaustible source of study. Turning to ancient statuary and the Greco-Roman world signified a return to the roots of art and constituted an indispensable prerequisite for any artistic activity which involved architecture, sculpture or painting. Artists studied this particular sculpture for its anatomical detail and for the great tension expressed in the muscular forms, and its position in the centre of the octagonal room was not unintentional. This work was done in the 1530s and is one of the group of statues in the renowned Statue Garden created by Julius II.

As time went by the male subject of this work became associated with gods, kings and heroes from the Greek world both because of its physical appearance and the presence of the panther skin on the rock it is

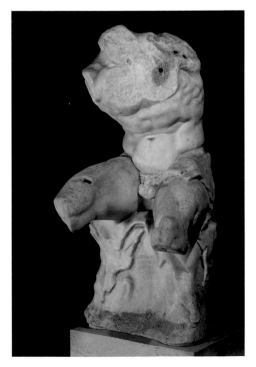

Belvedere Torso,
1st century BC, Room of
the Muses

sitting upon. In particular, for example, the work was identified as Hercules, one of the most eminent gods of the Greek world. On this subject Winckelmann continues his description of the statue and writes: 'A first glance will perhaps allow you to see nothing but an unformed stone; but if you are able to penetrate the secrets of art, then you will see a miracle in it – if you consider this work with a calm eye. Then Heracles will appear to you as if he were in the middle of all his labours, and the hero and the god will simultaneously become visible in this work.'

The most recent theories identify the work as being Telamonian Ajax contemplating suicide. After Achilles' death at the gates of Troy, Telamonian Ajax was considered to be the strongest of the Greek heroes and the natural heir to Achilles' weapons, of which, however, he was deprived after an astute move by Ulysses (Odysseus); mad with rage, Ajax massacres a flock of sheep he believes to be his rivals then, once he comes to his senses and realises what he has done, he kills himself. The hero depicted in the statue is thought to have had his head resting on his right fist, while the elbow of the same arm was leaning on his thigh where the hole for the pin is visible. Comparisons with minor works such as an oil-lamp, a small bronze and some gems can help us identify the statue which should have been completed with the addition of the sword Ajax uses to take his life and a shield. This work dates back to the 1st century BC and holds the sculptor's inscription 'Apollonio, [figlio] di Nestore, ateniese, fece' ('Apollonius, [son] of Nestor, Athenian, did it'). It is a marble copy of a renowned Greek original in bronze from the 2nd century BC and is linked to Emperor Augustus' circle. An evocative hypothesis connects this work to the statue of Ajax in the *heroon*, the place of worship at the tomb thought to belong to the hero, built near the mouth of the Scamander in the Troad. The work became so famous and admired that it was transferred to Egypt by Mark Anthony for his beloved Cleopatra, but after the battle of Actium (31 BC) and his defeat, Octavian Augustus returned it to the *heroon* and may have had a copy made by the artist "Apollonius" written on the inscription precisely for this occasion.

Round Room (Sala Rotonda)

The magnificent Round Room **(20)** with its hemispheric coffered vault and the eye in the centre letting in the light particularly brings to mind great Roman buildings such as baths. The niches around the walls holding the statues, the mosaic and even an ancient utensil such as the large red porphyry cup all complete the effect.

The statues on display here include an emperor and a hero, subjects which filled and decorated indoor and outdoor locations in ancient Rome.

■ Colossal statue of *Claudius portrayed as Jupiter*
This statue comes from the centre of Lanuvium and is thought to have been one of the honorary statues which adorned forums, porticoes and theatres. Here, Emperor Claudius (41–54 AD) is portrayed as Jupiter. In every provincial town or colony, the Roman architects' first task was to erect a *Capitolium* similar to the one in Rome dedicated to the Capitoline triad of Jupiter, Juno and Minerva. Jupiter is the Roman god likened to the Greek figure of Zeus and appears as the god of the sky, the light of day, lightning and thunder; the eagle is the bird which carries Jupiter's lightning bolt so it has become a symbol of strength and power. This is the reason why it became the insignia of every Roman legion and hence

a symbol par excellence of imperial power. Jupiter is the most important god of the Roman pantheon and by having himself portrayed in the guise of such a god, the Emperor wanted to put across a clear message: just as Jupiter reigns over Olympus, the Emperor reigns over his Empire. He is depicted with the eagle at his feet and his head crowned by a wreath of oak leaves, the oak being the tree dedicated to the god. His left hand holds the sceptre and his right holds the *patera*, a sort of plate used for libations. A long cloak partially covers the statue.

▲ Round Room

▶ *Claudius portrayed as Jupiter*, c. 50 AD, Round Room

79

- Colossal bronze statue of *Heracles*

The exceptional nature of this statue lies in its material – bronze. Bronze statues are rarely conserved as people often melted them down in times of metal shortages. This statue was struck by lightning and was buried in the place where it fell (as indicated by the engraved letters '*F[ulgor] C[onditum] S[ummanium]*' on the travertine slab closing off the hole) as it was probably considered inauspicious to melt down a statue struck by a celestial phenomenon. This work is thought to have been a part of the monumental complex of the Theatre of Pompey in Campus Martius, the first brick-built theatre in the city of Rome constructed in the 1st century BC. Campus Martius was further north than the central Roman Forum area and its name reflected the military purpose for which it was mainly used. It was essentially a monumental area of the city; state ownership of the property and the level ground formed the ideal setting for erecting official, public buildings, hence the presence of numerous porticoes, groves, temples and buildings for performances such as theatres and baths. The statue of *Heracles* is thought to have been one of the many statues and decorative items which would have adorned this magnificent plain between the Tiber, the Pincian Hill, the Capitoline Hill and the Quirinal Hill.

Heracles is the most famous hero of all classical mythology and legends linked to him mainly revolve around the *Cycle of the twelve labours*, that is to say the tasks the hero tackled, distinguishing himself for his strength and courage. This bronze *Heracles* is depicted with some of the instantly recognisable attributes which allude to these tasks such as the club, the lion skin and the apples of Hesperides. Heracles' weapon of choice, the club, was carved by the hero himself

Heracles, 2nd century AD,
Round Room

from a wild olivewood branch during the first task. It was this first task which also procured him his other famous attribute, often appearing in depictions on vases or in statues – the skin of the lion he killed and flayed. The golden apples of Hesperides, on the other hand, allude to one of the other famous tasks completed by the hero – the retrieval of the golden apples given to Hera upon her marriage to Zeus. This statue dates back to the end of the 2nd century AD and is based on an original from the 4th century BC. It depicts the hero moving forwards using his right hand to lean on his club while his left hand holds the apples of Hesperides (added during a modern restoration). We can also see the lion skin draped over his left arm. The thick-set structure of the face, however, could place it in the 3rd or even 4th century AD as it is similar to that of the athletes in the Caracalla Baths mosaic dated to the 4th century AD in the Gregorian Profane Museum.

Bronze statuary

When creating statues in metal the preferred material was bronze, an alloy of copper and tin. Before a bronze statue could be created a clay model had to be made providing the opportunity to make corrections and alterations. Very few of the large bronze statues have survived because of the metal shortages from the end of the ancient era throughout the Middle Ages. In terms of metal extraction and sculpting techniques with the subsequent capacity of producing alloys, the Greeks did not make significant progress compared to eastern Mediterranean populations, but they did become experts at creating real masterpieces capable of capturing three-dimensional space. The most complicated aspect of working with the metal was the fact that it could not be directly sculpted, modelled like clay or carved out like stone. It was dependent on a mould made from another material and the technique of fusion. The method favoured by the Greeks was lost-wax casting with clay models:

1 a clay model is made
2 the model is covered by a layer of wax
3 the model is put into a clay mould which can resist the pressure of molten metal
4 the wax melts and leaves a space between the model and the mould
5 the bronze fills the empty space
6 after the bronze has set the mould is removed.

The sculpture would then be finished off with various different techniques. Firstly, in the case of large and medium-sized sculptures, the craftsmen had the arduous task of soldering the separately cast pieces together and disguising the join. Secondly, the more creative finishing touches could be added with various tools:
- a chisel was used to define shapes like the joints of the body and the folds of cloaks
- a burin was used for engraving finer lines like the hair, eyebrows and decorations on clothing
- files, scrapers and punches were also used.

Lastly, inlays made of different materials were added to highlight some parts of the body for a more natural effect. For the eyes, for example, special cavities were left in the bronze and then filled with fragments of white material (marble, ivory) for the whites and coloured stones and glass pastes for the irises and pupils.

Greek Cross Room

A monumental entrance: The Greek Cross Room

Originally the Greek Cross Room (Sala a Croce Greca) **(21)**, created by the architect Michelangelo Simonetti, formed the monumental entrance way to the Museum of classical collections. It was built for Pope Pius VI, who reversed the previous visiting route. In the past people had entered the museum from the other side through the so-called Square Vestibule (with the inscription "MUSEVM CLEMENTINVM" still visible on the architrave) because Pope Clement XIV had considered it to be more practical, directly linked as it was to the Papal Palace through the east wing. When the new construction work began under his successor and more especially when the museum became public, this new monumental entrance was built, marked by the inscription "MUSEVM PIVM".

The great entrance gateway is framed by two gigantic Egyptian-style telamons from Hadrian's villa. The Emperor went on numerous trips to the East, during which he absorbed the culture of the great civilisations, hence, when he constructed his magnificent villa, he wanted the rooms to evoke the symbolic locations and Provinces of the Empire. In one area Hadrian constructed the *Canopus*, a vast space symbolising Egypt with the architecture forming a monumental map of the country with decorative items and Egyptian-style statues including the abovementioned telamons. Telamons were human-shaped pillars and usually portrayed the god Osiris, the guardian of the underworld, so they became also known as "Osiris pillars". These two telamons, crowned by capitals similar to the typical Egyptian capitals in the form of lotus flowers, have a headdress and a short skirt and their rigid and frontal stance is typical of Egyptian statues, blending in with the other architectural elements around them. Similar telamons decorate the great shrine of Isis (the sister/wife of Osiris) and Serapis (the Roman Osiris) in Campus Martius. The "Egyptian-style" trend spread through Rome also touching upon religion. It was not difficult to find cults which had originated in Ancient Egypt in Rome and consequently it was equally common to find shrines linked to their worshipping practices with architecture and adornments which invariably evoked this ancient civilisation.

The mosaic at the entrance to the room is from a *triclinium* (dining room) of a Roman villa and was significantly restored in the eighteenth century. In the centre of the circle there is a bust of Athena, the warrior goddess par excellence, with a crested helmet and an aegis, a sort of cuirass made of goat skin with a *gorgoneion* in the centre, a medal depicting the Medusa's head. According to ancient mythology Athena put the Gorgon's head on her shield after it had been cut off by Perseus, and it had the power of turning anyone who looked at it into stone. The presence of *gorgoneia* in mosaics did not just have an ornamental purpose. The Gorgon's terrible gaze had the power to turn people into stone and, passing from myth to reality, their depiction in the paving of a room warded off ill luck and cautioned guests.

MOSAICS IN THE PIUS-CLEMENTINE MUSEUM

When and how did so many mosaics come to the Vatican? In order to understand the significance of this collection we must first comprehend the historical-archaeological and collecting motives behind this type of production. From the Renaissance onwards the creation of mosaics was not considered to be an independent genre but a type of painting, and consequently it was relegated to the background behind those considered to be major arts (sculpture, painting and architecture). This notion stemmed from the limited importance the Greek and Latin craftsmen themselves gave to this technique. The names of a great number of painters and sculptors have been passed down to us yet we only have the name of one mosaicist. Secondly, from the end of the sixteenth century onwards, a great school of mosaicists flourished due to their work on the new construction site of St. Peter's, which became the largest worksite in Europe. Finally, the discoveries of ancient mosaics were always meagre compared to the quantity of sculptures and frescoes, consequently even a great admirer of antiquity like Winckelmann in the eighteenth century never seemed particularly enthusiastic about this form of artistic expression. More pointed interest in mosaics began in the seventeenth century. In art collections it was not uncommon to find small mosaics which were put on display on walls like paintings and set in elegant frames. In the Vatican one of the most innovative ideas put into practice during the creation of the Pius-Clementine Museum was the use of ancient mosaics set into the paving of the new rooms giving them a prominent position; they were no longer small pieces hung on walls but large works covering a number of square metres. The Pius-Clementine Museum was one of the first instances of a public museum of antiquities constructed for that purpose with the works of art no longer regarded as furnishings in a palace but as focal elements arranged in exhibiting rooms built especially for them.

Mosaic with a bust of Minerva and the phases of the moon, 3rd century AD, Greek Cross Room

The mosaic

The origin of the word

There are various etymological explanations for the word mosaic. One of the possible explanations is that it is a translation from the medieval Latin *musaicus* taken from the Greek word indicating the Muses, goddesses who had grottoes decorated using this technique dedicated to them in Roman gardens.

Production and materials

A mosaic is created by placing small fragments of glass, pebbles, terracotta or marble called tesserae on a prepared surface of fresh plaster made up of marble dust and lime which, once dry, permanently held them secure. While composing the image the mosaicists used painted cartoons to guide them and help them see where to put the tesserae and which colours to choose. The value of the mosaic was determined by the material of the tesserae.

The birth of the mosaic

The first mosaics to appear in Greece (4th century BC) were formed of small, irregular white and black pebbles and were probably inspired by vase ornamentation as the light detail on dark backgrounds was reminiscent of the simple lines of miniaturist drawing used on vases. It was only later, at the beginning of the Hellenistic era (3rd century BC) that the art of the mosaic, thanks to the enrichment of the chromatic range in the use of coloured stones, started to look to great paintings for sources of inspiration. Mosaics were also made using increasingly pre-prepared and squared-off stones so the finished works resembled real "paintings of stone". When mosaicists began to use coloured tesserae it became possible to capture the supple nature of figures accentuated by significant use of shading and the impression of energy, a precursor to perspective. Mosaic works from the 3rd century BC have therefore become one of the most direct means of discovering lost, great Greek painting. Advancements in Hellenistic mosaics were partly made in the choice of subject matter. Instead of simple geometric or floral motifs mosaicists began to make real landscapes with skies and land shaped by the careful study of light and characterised by the minute, almost scientific observation of animals and plants.

Emblems

Progression within the mosaic technique developed the emblem, the "heart" of all mosaics. The word emblem is used to describe a small mosaic featuring a little genre scene or still life, characterised by particularly thin tesserae made separately and then mounted in a central or important position in the main mosaic.

- ■ Mosaic with *Xenia* **(14)**

On this series of compositions framed by a entwined motif we can see some *xenia*, the gifts (mainly foodstuffs) which the *dominus* kept aside for guests as a mark of their hospitality. In particular, looking from left to right and top to bottom, we can see two cornucopias linked together by a tie, a wicker basket full of cuttlefish, two ducks hanging from a hook, a dolphin emerging from the waves, two bunches of grapes, bundles of asparagus, a bowl full of apples, a pheasant, a round shape which may be a pie, three loaves of bread, a duck catching a fish skewered on a cane, and a rabbit coming out of a basket made of canes. This mosaic dates back to the 4th century AD and its theme has Hellenistic origins, particularly based on mosaics with still lifes with naturalistic

Mosaic with *Xenia*, 4th century AD,
Room of the Animals

overtones which were often reproduced from the 3rd century BC onwards. On the northern side of the room we can see some more framed compositions in the same style.

- *Mosaic of the Masks* **(17)**

The mosaic compositions from Emperor Hadrian's villa, originally four separate *emblemata*, were gathered together in the eighteenth century and framed by a frieze with vine-shoots, all encircled by a border with a floral motif festoon. These mosaics can be traced back to the 1st century BC and were used again by Hadrian's craftsmen in the 2nd century AD probably after having been taken from the paving of different late-Republican era villas in the area. Three of these compositions display the theme of the mask; the fourth holds a bucolic landscape.

It is worthwhile focussing on the mosaic *emblem* with masks and a lyre. The references are theatrical: the female mask with flowing hair can be identified as the "young bride" and the mask of the old man with the long beard can be identified as the "old slave". These two masks on the ledge were of Comedy while the one with the "young hero" next to them with the dark skin and the frowning face is a mask of Tragedy.

Mosaic *emblem* with masks and a leogriff (lion-griffin). The theme of this composition is the theatre with a specific reference to Apollo. In Rome the *Ludi Apollinares* (*Apollinarian Games*) was a well-known event, a festival in honour of the god of music and poetry which included circus shows and plays. In ancient theatre music and poetry were closely linked, hence the presence of the lyre in the foreground of the composition and a mask of Apollo crowned with a bay-wreath on a plinth in the background. The scene is completed by a bow and quiver, the god's attributes, and a leogriff, the legendary bird dedicated to Apollo with the body of a lion and powerful wings.

Mosaic *emblem* with masks and a panther. This composition holds indisputable references to Dionysus. During festivals in honour of the gods people celebrated in Athens with various dramatic performances of tragedies and comedies. Dionysus, the god of life, wine and mystical delirium, is often followed by a triumphal procession which came together upon his return from a voyage to India and included a chariot drawn by panthers and the Maenads or Bacchantes, mad women who would abandon all self-control in a violent dance. Objects associated with Bacchus also present in the triumphal procession included

Mosaic of the Masks, 1st century BC, Room of the Masks

a thyrsus (a staff covered with ivy or vine branches), timbrel (a small tambourine played by the Maenads in their frenetic ritual dances), and a crater (a cup in which to mix water and wine). Dionysus was the other great god, like Apollo, linked to the world of the theatre and performances in general. In actual fact it is thought that the very ancient origins of tragedy, comedy and satyr drama stemmed from these tumultuous processions to celebrate the god of wine, in which improvised performances were made by actors with masks evoking the Genii of the earth and fertility. These procession-performances then gave rise to the more "classical" performances of the theatre which, little by little, lost their Dionysian character to grow into the great archetypes of Tragedy and Comedy.

Mosaic *emblem* with a bucolic landscape. This small composition portrays a country shrine in an idyllic rural setting among rocks, a stretch of water, sheep, goats and a thicket with the small chapel dedicated presumably to a rural god. This theme has Hellenistic origins and was frequently depicted in the Roman world which loved to see itself represented in contemplation of the harmony of nature.

SARCOPHAGI AND ALTARS

Through carefully chosen examples of sarcophagi it is possible to illustrate a short story about this important branch of craftsmanship with many specialised workshops and artisans who refined the art of producing coffins in relief and were able to create real masterpieces. The materials they used ranged from peperino and tuff before Roman conquests in the East, to the magnificent varieties of white marble used for sarcophagi from the 2nd and 3rd century AD, as well as the red porphyry which, thanks to its hardness and preciousness, was used for emperors and the imperial family. The coffins sculpted in relief, with widely diverse themes, were always a sign that the buyer possessed a private fortune.

Monuments and funerary customs in Roman times

According to ethical standards and Roman law cemeteries had be outside the city walls along the consular roads leading away from the city such as, in Rome, the famous Appian Way, the Via Ostiensis and the Via Trionfale. As a result countless burial grounds sprang up over time, characterised by various types of funerary monuments and ornaments. Naturally the rule applied to all the colonies and municipalities of the Italian peninsula and all the countries which were once part of the Roman Empire. As the topic of Roman funerary monuments covers such a large geographical area and a long period of time, the following descriptions will be based on specific examples and follow general themes focussing on Rome.

Those who belonged to a certain social class and had the financial means necessary had funerary monuments built for themselves or their families. The vast necropoli outside Roman cities demonstrate how widespread the desire was to have an enclosed and permanent burial ground. Most of the population, of course, had to be satisfied with more modest arrangements. The deceased would simply be placed in an urn if they had been cremated or in the ground if they wished to be buried and covered with a plain slab. We can therefore picture the burial grounds as a combination of monumental structures and simpler, much less obvious graves.

The various types of funerary monuments

The term funerary monument is used to describe any commemorative construction which, aside from the grave, serves as a form of self-representation and perpetuates the memory of the deceased and their family. We must remember that these structures were not just built above ground; magnificent family mausoleums were also constructed underground, designed as large rooms dug out of the rock. Incidentally funerary structures of this kind had been around in Italy since very ancient times (just think of the Etruscan tombs) and these rocky rooms were among the first kinds of funerary monuments to appear in the Roman era. The most well-known example is the Scipioni tomb on the Appian Way, whose origins can be traced back to the early 3rd century BC. Only members of the ruling classes were buried in these tombs. A traveller approaching Rome in the 3rd century BC, however, went past burial grounds in which there were few monuments for members of the ruling classes; a great number of graves were modestly hidden below ground and at most they were marked by a simple sign.

In the Imperial era from the 2nd century AD onwards a different type of funerary structure became particularly popular: the "house tombs". This kind of tomb looked like an actual small house from the outside with simple brick and mortar masonry, small windows to let in light and air and a modest entrance. The sarcophagi of the deceased were set inside in the arcosolia (arched niches in the walls), while the containers for the ashes of the dead were placed in niches around the middle section of the walls. Two examples of necropoli in this house-tomb style can be seen under the central nave of St. Peter's Basilica and near the ancient Via Trionfale, also in Vatican territory.

The furnishings: sarcophagi, altars, urns

As we have seen, funerary traditions in the Roman world were divided into two main categories: cremation and burial. In the first instance the deceased's body would be cremated on a pyre and their ashes collected in an urn in the shape of a vase or a small rectangular altar (made from various materials such as glass, metal or marble), then this container would be buried or placed in a funerary monument. In the second instance the poorer people would be buried directly in the ground under simple pit tombs covered by a tiled canopy (capuchin tombs), while the more affluent classes were able to afford to be buried in richly sculpted sarcophagi placed inside funerary monuments. During the Republican era, people in Rome tended to prefer cremation, a trend which continued until the 1st century AD. From the 2nd century AD onwards burials instead of cremations became more and more popular among the affluent classes. This led to marble sarcophagi decorated with reliefs becoming increasingly widespread, and the formation of specialised workshops. Finally, many tombs constructed during the first two centuries of the imperial era also held furnishings such as funerary altars, placed inside or in front of sepulchral buildings and used as actual cinerary urns. The name of the deceased and the dedicator, often a family member, were inscribed on these containers, with the hollow space for the ashes above. The sides held sculpted reliefs with a small jug and a sort of little plate (*pàtera*) representing the items people used to worship the dead.

A detailed analysis of the sarcophagi reveals the fact that they were produced in workshops in Rome and that they were only decorated on three sides with the other deliberately left smooth because it would then be placed next to the wall of the tomb; in contrast, sarcophagi imported from Greece and Asia Minor had all four of their sides decorated as the eastern regions did not generally use chamber tombs but tended to prefer tombs in the form of a temple (*heroon*), which required the sarcophagus to be placed in the centre of the sepulchral structure.

What type of scene did the craftsman sculpt on the sarcophagi? Some held simple marble garlands with fruit and flowers, alluding to the fresh garlands offered to the deceased during commemorative festivities. There were also heraldic compositions with winged victories or personifications of seasons holding up a portrait of the deceased in a clypeus (a sort of small shield), while others held narrative scenes generally taken from mythological sources or from the public or private life of the deceased. The mythological scenes were often allegories of death and the afterlife (for example the myth of Alcestis was frequently represented; this was the story of the bride who chose to die in the place of her husband and was then brought back to the world of the living by Heracles, a myth interpreted through funerary symbolism as an exaltation of conjugal devotion). The scenes alluding to the life of the deceased like the depiction of marriage, military life and sacrificial offerings were taken as a form of preparation for the afterlife.

How were the sarcophagi sculpted? Craftsmen worked from cartoons which were often inspired by paintings and then they used special tools such as drills to recreate the design on the marble obtaining remarkable naturalistic and chiaroscuro effects with the relief technique. The portrait of the deceased would be left roughly hewn as these coffins were mass produced and only finished off when they were commissioned.

The cult of the dead

There were various festivals associated with the cult of the dead which, through the ardent attention devoted to their mortal remains, had the specific aim of guaranteeing eternal renewal of life to the souls. The commemorative period officially dedicated to the dead was known as *Parentalia* (13th–21st February), the last day of which was intended for public ceremonies while the other days were reserved for private celebrations. There were also private occasions when the family would honour the dead at their own tomb, for example on the deceased's birthday (*dies natalis*). It is interesting to note here that Christian inscriptions indicated the date of death but not the birthday of the deceased as it was considered to be the day of rebirth to new life. As worshippers drew near to the tomb of the deceased, they would offer light with small burning oil-lamps, incense to burn, and flowers would be entwined to make garlands, immortalised in the scenes on the reliefs of the altars and the urns containing the ashes. Funeral banquets were held near the tomb and libations of wine and milk were poured directly inside in order to reach the deceased's remains and include them in the feast. The news of the death would be communicated through literary sources and funerary inscriptions, the words of these inscriptions would also indicate the bequest of money set aside to accrue interest, which would be spent on oil-lamps, incense and flowers for the tomb as well as funeral banquets.

■ *Sarcophagus of Lucius Cornelius Scipio Barbatus* **(1)**

In the Square Vestibule there is a sarcophagus from the tomb of the Scipiones, the monumental rock-cut tomb on the Appian way. These burial places, along with those of Etruscan origin, are the oldest known vestiges of the Italian funerary world. This sarcophagus was found along with other coffins and more especially with a great number of incredibly

Sarcophagus of Lucius Cornelius Scipio Barbatus,
3rd century BC, Square Vestibule

precious funerary inscriptions, on display both in this Vestibule and in the nearby *Apoxyomenos* Cabinet (3), which hand down important information about the Roman ruling-class Scipiones family. The coffin is made of peperino, a type of rock similar to tuff which has a dark-grey colour and small black inclusions (*Lapis albanus*); peperino was widely used before Rome was "decorated" in marble after the conquests in the East. The coffin looks like a large altar and its decorations evoke the Greek models with two volutes on the sides. A Doric frieze can be seen under the altar table (the Doric frieze is an architectural element typically seen on Greek temples and often decorated in relief with metopes, that is to say a quadrangular background sculpted in various styles of relief and triglyphs adorned with three vertical grooves). The cover holds an inscription with the name of the coffin's proprietor, 'Lucio Cornelio, figlio di Cneo, Scipione' ('Lucius Cornelius, son of Gnaeus, Scipio'); the coffin is inscribed with the *cursus honorum* (course of honours) of Scipio, who is described as being 'a strong, wise and brave man, consul, censor, aedile, conqueror of Taurasia and Cisauna in Samnium, and of all Lucania, also taking hostages'. This sarcophagus dates back to the 3rd century BC.

- *Front of a sarcophagus with a scene of Porto* (6)

In the east portico of the Octagonal Courtyard (Cortile Ottagono), only the front of a sarcophagus built into the wall is visible. The deceased is portrayed in the foreground in a state of heroic nudity with his wife next to him; the faces of both figures are only roughly-hewn. The subjects represented on marble coffins, which became widespread in the 2nd century AD, were very varied and the Romans, masters of the relief technique, were able to create real masterpieces. These coffins must be imagined, for example, inside house tombs, positioned against the walls. In this case there is a vibrant scene behind the married couple set in Porto, Rome's sea wharf, where buildings, small chapels dedicated to gods and boats with men on board are depicted amongst frenzied activity. This sarcophagus dates back to the 3rd century AD.

- *Sarcophagus with Dionysian thiasos* (6)

This sarcophagus was found in the area of the ancient necropolis near Via Cornelia during excavations to build the foundations for the new building of St. Peter's Sacristy. A *thiasos* is depicted in relief on the coffin, that is to say a portrayal of the procession which accompanied Dionysus in his festivities. Satyrs, the demons of nature, swing around in

Front of a sarcophagus with a scene of Porto, 3ʳᵈ century BC,
Octagonal Courtyard

a constant dance, their feral nature emphasised by the flowing tail of a
horse. In their frenzied movements the Maenads, personifications of or-
giastic spirits of nature, brandish the thyrsus (a staff covered with ivy or
vine branches, an attribute of the Dionysian procession), and hit timbrels
(tambourines). There are also some small-winged eroti or amorini (putti represented as infant cupids) on panthers, the animals which trium
phantly conveyed Dionysus. The sarcophagi with Dionysian scenes were
often not rectangular but took the form of a basin (*lenòs*), alluding to the
wooden vat used to crush grapes to obtain the must. This basin shape
was therefore easily associated with the god of wine and well-suited to
funerary symbolism as grapes made into wine were a symbol of new life,
just like the one on which the deceased was about to embark. This sarcophagus is also decorated with protomes and escutcheons (heads, in
this case in the form of lions, which were frequently used as decorative
elements) and it dates back to the 2ⁿᵈ century AD.

■ *Funerary altar of Quintus Gaius Mucius with a dedication by his wife
Volumnia Ianuaria* (8)

Funerary altars are vertical, marble parallelepipedon constructions
and usually have a cavity in the higher part to hold the ashes container.
The funerary inscription on the front indicates the dedicator and obviously the name of the dedicatee. These altars were placed in front of

Sarcophagus with a Dionysian scene, 2ⁿᵈ century AD,
Octagonal Courtyard

or inside house tombs, constituting a suitable alternative to the ashes containers which were set in niches around the walls. This altar has been dedicated by Volumnia Ianuaria to her husband Quintus Gavius Musicus, (*Quintus Gavius Musicus* on the inscription), and holds an invocation to the Manes-gods (*Dis Manibus*), the gods who oversaw the world of the dead and defended the inviolability and the sacredness of the deceased's burial place. This altar is also decorated with two lifelike sculpted portraits of the married couple on the front above the stone plaque. On the left-hand side Volumnia's late husband is in a seated position and seems to be entrusting his sons to a young man, probably a relative; on the right-hand side this same relative opens the funerary procession holding a sign which usually held the name of the deceased. The customary small jug and plate (*pàtera*) alluding to the items used to make libations in honour of the dead which usually ornament the short sides of altars are not depicted here, instead there are scenes which evoke parts of the deceased's life. This altar can be dated, partly thanks to the presence of the portraits, to the beginning of the 2nd century AD.

- *Front of a sarcophagus with a dead couple at the gates of Hades* (10)

The front of this sarcophagus has been built into the wall and is divided into architectural sections by small, elegant columns. The gates of Hades are in the centre, decorated with reliefs with the two doors half-open waiting for the dead people to go in. The dead married couple are depicted in a farewell stance. The man is wearing a *contabulata* toga which denotes his Roman citizenship and high social class (depending on their colour and style togas could reveal the person's age and social class) and he is holding a *volumen*, a papyrus scroll, as a sign of distinction. The woman's head is covered by a cloak (*capite velato*) and her stance conveys a sense of melancholy. Two genii crowned by winged victories are present at the couple's last farewell; these spirits not only dwelled within each individual but also in places, symbolising spiritual essence and consequently fulfilling the essential role of safeguarding the deceased's memory. Either side of the couple we can see Hades, the god of the dead, and Persephone, Queen of the underworld and Hades' consort. This sarcophagus dates back to the 3rd century AD.

Funerary altar of Quintus Gaius Mucius with a dedication by his wife Volumnia Ianuaria 2nd century AD, Octagonal Courtyard

Front of a sarcophagus with a dead couple at the gates of Hades,
3rd century AD, Octagonal Courtyard

■ *Sarcophagus with a scene of clemency* (12)

This sarcophagus holds a relief of a defeated and imprisoned barbarian
people in the act of submitting to the victorious commander who is depicted seated and crowned by a personification of victory. It was probably
destined for a high ranking Roman official of General Emperor Marcus
Aurelius (161–180 AD), who inflicted a decisive defeat on the Sarmatians.
On the left side of the coffin, two soldiers are transporting a prisoner
with his young son on a cart. On the right, prisoners are being carried on
a sort of stretcher in military triumph. The theme of the submission of
the barbarians was frequently used in Roman reliefs, mainly on official
monuments such as arches of triumph, or on the famous spiral columns
of the emperors Trajan and Marcus Aurelius, which record their victories
over the barbarian peoples. This theme was also used by ordinary individuals so it was not uncommon to find it depicted on the sarcophagi of
officers. It reflected a subject the Roman world felt very strongly about,
with the strong emotions of the winners set against the plight of the defeated. This sarcophagus was placed in an important position when it
first came to the Vatican, being initially used as the basin of the fountain
in the original niche of the *Ariadne* in Julius II's famous statue courtyard. It was placed in such a significant position because, at first, it was
thought the military feats on the sarcophagus could be attributed to the
Emperor Trajan, the noble figure with whom Julius II wanted to be associated. Another noteworthy aspect of this sarcophagus is the preference
for compositions full of figures. This stylistic arrangement was highly
valued in the relief genre as it concentrated a considerable number of

Sarcophagus with a scene of clemency, 2nd century AD,
Octagonal Courtyard

forms in a limited space. This style was studied by the Renaissance sculptors and artists, who drew on the work of the Ancients. This sarcophagus dates back to the 2nd century AD.

- ◼ *Sarcophagus of Constantia* **(21)**

On the two main sides of this great monumental coffin there are some eroti-amorini traditionally linked to Dionysus, the god of vines and wine, busy harvesting grapes in a decoration entwined with foliate designs and vine-shoots. In contrast, on the other two sides the eroti-amorini are pressing the grapes in a vat while the cover is decorated with floral festoons hung from masks. The themes represented derive from Dionysian iconography which was often represented on sarcophagi as the transformation of the grapes from must into wine and was considered to be an effective metaphor for the deceased's journey to a new life. The presence of the peacock on the coffin also has an important meaning in a funerary setting as in ancient times its flesh was thought to be imperishable. Consequently, it is depicted as a bearer of the message of hope of life after death, a meaning also found in pagan symbolism. Furthermore, the material used to sculpt the sarcophagus has its own meaning. Red porphyry, given its hardness and great value, was the type of marble used to depict emperors or the imperial family. This coffin could therefore only belong to a member of the imperial family. It was probably made in one of the highly specialised workshops in Alexandria in Egypt, the only ones able to achieve such incredible results bearing in mind how difficult it was to sculpt porphyry. This sarcophagus was sculpted in the 4th century AD for Constantia, the daughter of Constantine

Sarcophagus of Constantia, 4th century AD, Greek Cross Room

and Fausta and it came from the great Mausoleum of Constantia (Mausoleo di Costanza) which then became the Church of Santa Costanza (St Constantia) on the Via Nomentana next to the Basilica of Sant'Agnese (St. Agnes). During the Renaissance the presence of the grape harvesting eroti, which were also present in the mosaic decorating the vault of the small portico running around the inside of the mausoleum, caused people to think that the sarcophagus and the mausoleum were dedicated to Dionysus-Bacchus.

■ *Sarcophagus of St. Helena* **(21)**

On this coffin, galloping knights loom over barbarian prisoners sculpted in relief. The theme of military victory over an army of barbarians indicates that this sarcophagus was destined for an emperor, perhaps Constantine himself, his father Constantius Chlorus or one of the men of the imperial family. For unknown reasons, however, it was used for the body of St. Helena, Constantine's mother. The sarcophagus was found in Helena's Mausoleum between Via Prenestina and Via Labicana, two important consular roads leading away from Rome. In the case of dead members of the imperial family large buildings were constructed to make richly decorated mausoleums in brickwork to hold magnificent coffins, like in this case, often made from porphyry, the imperial stone par excellence. This sarcophagus was probably also sculpted in one of the highly specialised workshops in Alexandria in Egypt and dates back to the 4th century AD. The decorations are completed by two busts of the imperial family on the higher ledge, while the edge of the cover holds sculpted garlands with putti.

Sarcophagus of St. Helena, 4th century AD, Greek Cross Room

THE GALLERY OF MAPS

As we leave the Belvedere Palace and move down the long gallery on the second floor which connects the Papal Palace and the Sistine Chapel, we can admire, in one part of the corridor, the cycle of mural paintings dedicated to the Maps.

The main figures behind its design and creation at the end of the sixteenth century were Pope Gregory XIII (Boncompagni, 1572–1585), who wanted to dedicate a cartographic picture to the whole of Italy, and the cosmographer and mathematician Ignazio Danti, who painted the cartoons of the all the geographical panels and managed the whole project. Girolamo Muziano and Cesare Nebbia coordinated a small army of painters and stucco decorators. The "signatures" of the two protagonists are clearly recognisable: the Pope's coat of arms, a golden dragon on a red background placed over the entrance and exit to the Gallery, and the cartouche in which Ignazio Danti signs the project, discernible on the first map when entering from the right, north of the *Sallentina Hydrunti Terra* (Southern Puglia).

The innovative nature of the Gallery

The custom of decorating the walls of monumental buildings with depictions of maps can be traced back to ancient Rome. This trend continued throughout the Middle Ages but when compared with similar rooms from the time, the Vatican Gallery laid claim to undisputed originality both in terms of its considerable size (120 metres long) and more especially its display concept. The maps of Italy were set out along the walls in such a way as to form a three-dimensional model of the whole peninsula. The two long walls hold the regions touching the Adriatic coast on the right and those touching the Tyrrhenian Sea on the left. The cartographer

South entrance to the Gallery of Maps

Gallery of Maps

Danti prepared the cartoons of the 40 panels he and Pope Gregory had envisaged, starting off the route through the Gallery with two representations of Italy, one from the imperial Roman era (*Italia antiqua*, on the Adriatic side) and the other from the sixteenth century (*Italia nova*, on the Tyrrhenian side). The maps were done mainly by specialised painters including the Flemish artist Paul Bril, who worked on the landscapes and Cesare Nebbia, who worked on the painting and stucco decorations, which were not strictly cartographic. The subdivision of the various panels designed by Danti follows more of a political approach than a geographical one, especially as regards the territories of the Papal State even though the cartographer drew on a variety of sources including cartographic manuscripts, literary descriptions and printed material like *Italia illustrata* (*Italy illustrated*) by Flavio Biondo.

The Maps

Each panel is surrounded by a white and gold frame with geometric friezes in false stucco. These frames have inner borders which hold the scale of the latitudes and longitudes and, higher up above the frame, we can see the title of the panel written in Latin. Inside the frame each region bears a plate holding a written, schematic caption with the physical, economical or political characteristics of the area as well as a metric scale based on the Roman mile (one mile = 1480 metres), which allowed distances to be calculated. More often than not the maps also hold a compass rose.

Each map holds depictions of the populated areas; the places with a significant political, military, economic or religious role are often marked out by a cross symbol indicating a bishop's see. Towards the lower margin on a great number of panels there are small zenithal or perspectival

Gallery of Maps:

▲Ignazio Danti, *Latium et Sabina* (*Southern Lazio*)

▼Ignazio Danti, *Roma*, detail of *Latium et Sabina*

ROMA
PER SACRAM B.PETRI SEDEM CAPVT ORBIS EFFECTA. S.LEO.1

▲Ignazio Danti, *Anconitanus ager*
(*Cartouche with a view of Loreto*)

▼Ignazio Danti, *Picenum*, detail.

depictions of the most important cities in the region. Some also include small fortresses and ports. Last but not least, we can also admire the added detail of lovely landscapes.

In addition to the inhabited areas and the urban hubs there are also depictions of battles and political events from the classical and medieval eras as

▲Ignazio Danti, *The Battle of Cannae between the Romans and the Carthaginians (216 BC)*, part. di *Apulia* (northern Puglia), Gallery of Maps

▼Ignazio Danti, *The return of papal court from Avignon to Rome (1377)*, detail of *Avegnonen[sis] ditio et Venaisinus comitatus*, Gallery of Maps

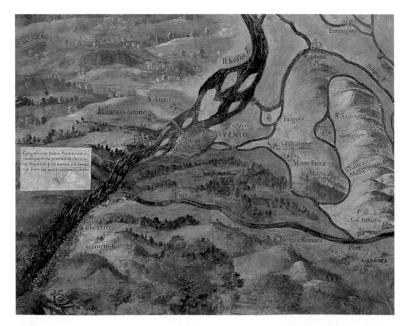

Ignazio Danti, *Civitas Vetus* (Civitavecchia), Gallery of Maps

well as more recent incidents, with the subjects indicated on small plaques. There are paintings of boats and ships in the areas covered by sea, as well as monsters and victories taken from classical mythology.

At the far ends of the Gallery there are some smaller panels. The ones by the south entrance hold the maps of four of the main Italian seaports (Civitavecchia, Ancona, Genoa and Venice) and the ones at the opposite end contain representations of the four smaller islands (the Tremiti islands, Elba, Corfu and Malta). Notably, in the map of the port of Civitavecchia, which was rebuilt by the Popes on the ancient ruins of the port of Emperor Trajan (98–117 AD), there is a depiction of an obelisk being transported from Egypt to Rome on a barge, the gnomon of Augustus' famous sundial in Campus Martius. In the painting of Corfu we can see the renowned naval battle of Lepanto, where the coalition forces of the Holy League prevailed over the fleet of the Ottoman Empire (1571).

Ignazio Danti, *Classis turcarum ad Crocyleium profligata* (Corfu Island), Gallery of Maps

101

The iconographic concept of the ceiling

The intertwined nature of geography and history on the walls is perfectly represented on the Gallery's barrel vault. In the central panels various painters, including Cesare Nebbia, frescoed scenes depicting exemplary episodes or miraculous deeds featuring apostles, saints, martyrs and other champions of faith. These scenes can then be linked in the geographical panels below to the cities and locations where each episode took place. These panels constitute a sort of figurative atlas of Christian history, a spiritual projection of the geographic history spread around the walls. This reflects the aim of the whole Gallery, showing how every episode and its corresponding region below consecrates Italy as the New Holy Land, the centre of Catholic teaching. The two illustrations on the following page show the *Transportation of the Holy House of Loreto* and *Domine quo vadis?*. The first depicts the miraculous voyage of the stones and bricks of the Virgin Mary's house in Nazareth to Loreto (in all likelihood transported by boat after the first Crusade). The second, *Domine quo vadis?*, shows St. Peter's meeting with Christ at the gates of Rome. Peter is about to flee the city, yet through the simple question he asks his master, he understands that his destiny is to return to Rome and be crucified.

At the head of the Gallery above the two maps of *Italia antiqua* and *Italia nova*, there are panels on the vault depicting two extremely important episodes in the history of all Italy: the *Apparition of the Cross to Constantine before the Battle of Milvian Bridge* above *Italia antiqua* and *St. Sylvester Pope baptises Constantine* above *Italia nova*. Consequently, the vault begins with a scene which represents the cornerstone of the Italian history of the Church. Constantine's baptism is the purifying rite of passage which forms the origins of *Italia nova*, heir to the glory of pagan Rome, defeated at the Battle of Milvian Bridge.

In the final panel of the vault at the opposite end of the Gallery (near the north door), we can see the baptism celebrated by St. Paul after the miraculous recovery of Publius' father, symbolising the conversion to Christianity of the pagan inhabitants of the island of Malta. The position of this rite of purification mirrors the initial panel with the *Baptism of Constantine*. The symmetry also continues with the *Apparition of the Cross to Constantine before the Battle of Milvian Bridge* corresponding to the *Apparition of St. Michel Archangel on Mount Gargano*.

Absolute pre-eminence is given to the centre of the Gallery where the vault holds the episode of *Christ telling St. Peter to look after the crowd of believers (Pasce oves meas)*, which does not correspond to any of the lower panels. This subject's important position highlights the significant message it bears, exalting both Peter's leadership and the divine institution of the Church of Rome. It also identifies the celebration of Mass and the administration of Holy Communion as the "nourishment" that the Church has the task of distributing, by the will of Christ, to the crowd of believers to lead them to salvation. This message was sent by Pope Gregory XIII to the schismatics and heretics, with particular reference to Protestants. It not only presented the Church as an invisible and transcendent concept, but also as an earthly institution which could lead the crowds of believers to salvation through the sacraments. Consequently, the Gallery recapitulated the beginning of a new phase in the Counter-Reformation coinciding with the Council of Trent. After the most dramatic period triggered by the protestant schism and after the sense of

▲ *Transportation of the Holy House of Loreto*, Gallery of Maps, Ceiling

▼ *St Peter meets Christ at the gates of Rome (Domine quo vadis)*, Gallery of Maps, Ceiling

103

▲*Apparition of the cross to Constantine before the Battle of Milvian Bridge*, Gallery of Maps, Ceiling

▼*St. Sylvester Pope baptises Emperor Constantine*, Gallery of Maps, Ceiling

PAVLVS·PVBLI·PARENTEM·MELITAE·SANAT·

▲ *St. Paul cures Publius' father on Malta,* Gallery of Maps, Ceiling

▼ *Christ tells St. Peter to look after the crowd of believers (Pasce oves meas),* Gallery of Maps, Ceiling

disorientation had passed, the Church used the Council to redefine its own doctrinal system.

The iconographic concept of the vault is completed by a series of monochrome scenes in a brownish-yellow colour. The *Cycle of the Sacrifices* illustrates the sacrificial rite of the Old Testament with the intention of consolidating the bond of continuity between Judaism and Christianity. The *Cycle of Christian Virtues* uses allegorical female figures and biblical characters to allude to specific godly virtues, spread around the central panel of the *Miracle* like diadems.

THE TOWER OF THE WINDS

When Gregory XIII created the Gallery of Maps he sought to use the space to represent a series of ideas. This project coincided with the construction of the nearby Tower of the Winds, the ultimate point and final destination of the long corridor where researchers could study the weather using an anemometer (an instrument used to measure and identify the direction of the wind) and Danti's sundial (a solar clock which uses the shadow of the gnomon on a dial, a wall or a paved area to calculate the time of day). The construction of this tower was largely entrusted to the same craftsmen who worked on the Gallery of Maps. Although the Tower of the Winds is not open to visitors, it must be regarded as an inseparable part of the representation of the whole of Italy in the Gallery.

The Tower of the Winds from the Pinecone Courtyard

The Gregorian calendar

This calendar came about as a result of the astronomical observation of the sun and the moon by the ancients who noted the existence of a cyclical temporal continuity. It became an essential instrument in the subdivision of time.

Our calendar is founded on the revolutionary changes promoted by Julius Caesar when he approved a new system which came into effect in 46 BC. This system divided each year (composed of 365 days in total) and identified an innovative method of drawing as near as possible to the astronomical year (*Julian calendar*). It created a four-year cycle with three years composed of 365 days and one with 366, known as a leap year. This was because the solar cycle lasted 365 days plus an excess of around 6 hours; every four years the surplus of 24 hours was compensated for by the addition of an extra day in February. During the Council of Nicaea in 325 AD, the first ecumenical council of Christianity organised by Emperor Constantine, various extremely important subjects were discussed such as the definition of the nature of Christ and the wording of the prayer of the Creed. They also produced a disquisition on the date of Easter, which was linked to the spring equinox (when the duration of the day and the night are the same all around the world). Based on astronomical observations they established that during that year the equinox would fall on the 21st March and, after a series of discussions, they decided Easter would be celebrated on the first Sunday after the full moon following the spring equinox. In 1582 Pope Gregory XIII ordered an astronomical assessment which revealed that the equinox would fall three days early every 400 years, so at that time the equinox was around the 11th March. In order to bring it back to the 21st March they decided to remove 10 days from the calendar, passing from the 4th to the 15th October to reinstate the beginning of spring on the 21st March. In the west, therefore, the days between the 5th and the 14th October 1582 have never existed. This calendar is known as the *Gregorian calendar*.

THE PAPAL PALACE

When was the first part of the Papal Palace built? In view of the ancient origins of the very first building and all the extensions which have been added over time, it is extremely difficult to isolate the original structure. In actual fact the Popes only lived solely in the Vatican after the Avignon Exile (1305–1377) and consequently Nicholas V's reign (1447–1455) and the construction work he carried out on the Palace coincided with the beginning of a new chapter as far as the Papal residence was concerned.

Even when the popes lived in the Lateran, they considered the Vatican area to be of the utmost importance and soon acquired a residence next to St. Peter's Basilica which would allow them to be near the Prince of the Apostles' tomb. The earliest available information dates back to the 5th century AD to the time of Pope Symmachus (498-514 AD), who built the first buildings *dextra levaque* of St. Peter's, that is to say along the north and south sides of the Basilica, although it seems as if these buildings fell into disrepair soon afterwards.

When Pope Leo IV (847-855) had a series of great walls built, the Vatican area started to become a safer place than the Lateran, but it was only after the year 1000 that a *palatium novum* was constructed on Symmachus' old worksite, extended years later by Pope Innocent III (Lotario di Segni, 1198-1216). This construction stood on the slopes of the *mons saccorum*, a hill to the north of St. Peter's which is now the Courtyard of St. Damasus (Cortile di San Damaso) (3). It looked like a small fortress and had a tower which corresponds to the current Chapel of Nicholas V (Cappella Niccolina) (5).

The building grew considerably under Pope Nicholas III (Orsini, 1277–1280), who began the construction work near the Parrot Courtyard (Cortile del Pappagallo) (1). It was at around this time that the Vatican began to be thought of as a possible permanent papal residence, especially considering how important it was for a Pope to live next to St. Peter's tomb. Consequently, the Popes began to live permanently at the Vatican and in an intentional move, none of the official acts issued by Nicholas III are dated from the Lateran. The only part of Nicholas III's building open to visitors today corresponds to the Chiaroscuro Room (Sala dei Chiaroscuri) (4) in the Chapel of Nicholas V and the Hall of Constantine (Sala di Costantino). The Palace of Nicholas III remained unfinished.

Finally, there was a *pomerium* next to Palace, a walled orchard-garden which stretched from the *mons saccorum* to the top of a hill to the north which is now roughly equivalent to Bramante's great Belvedere Courtyard (2).

Frescoed frieze with a parrot and festoons, detail. Roman school, 13th century, hollow space above the current wooden ceiling, Chiaroscuro Room, formerly the Parrot Room

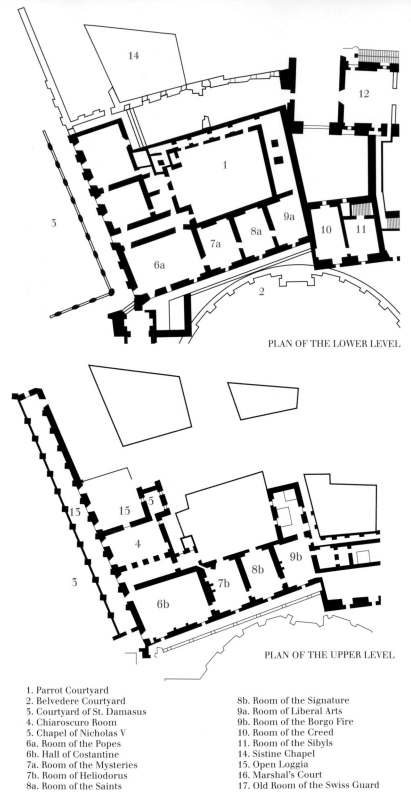

PLAN OF THE LOWER LEVEL

PLAN OF THE UPPER LEVEL

1. Parrot Courtyard
2. Belvedere Courtyard
3. Courtyard of St. Damasus
4. Chiaroscuro Room
5. Chapel of Nicholas V
6a. Room of the Popes
6b. Hall of Costantine
7a. Room of the Mysteries
7b. Room of Heliodorus
8a. Room of the Saints

8b. Room of the Signature
9a. Room of Liberal Arts
9b. Room of the Borgo Fire
10. Room of the Creed
11. Room of the Sibyls
14. Sistine Chapel
15. Open Loggia
16. Marshal's Court
17. Old Room of the Swiss Guard

Fra Angelico, View of the entrance wall and east wall,
Chapel of Nicholas V

Historical documents mention a certain *Jacobus Pictor* who 'pinxit in
Palatio S[ancti] Petri' (*Vat. Lat.* 9114, pp. 286–287) and can be identified as the famous artist Jacopo Torriti. At that time Torriti had one
of the most important workshops in the city. This information can be
verified on every floor of the Vatican Palace by the presence of traces of fresco decorations. These are fragments of decorative friezes
which would have ornamented the upper sections of the public and
private rooms in the Palace.

An important addition made in an unknown era, though certainly before
Nicholas V's papacy, was the construction of the *aulae pontificum*, now
the Room of the Popes (Sala dei Pontefici – in the current Borgia Apartment) on the first floor and the Hall of Constantine on the second floor
(Sala di Costantino) **(6b)**.

The great era of Nicholas V:
The Renaissance is welcomed into the Pope's residence

During Nicholas V's papacy (Parentucelli, 1447–1455) the Palace began to
take on the form it would have had under Julius II and Leo X. Pope Nicholas V was a highly cultured humanist and surrounded himself with artists and men of letters such as Marsilio Ficino, Leon Battista Alberti and
Fra Angelico. First of all he endorsed a magnificent urban design project
in Rome aimed at giving the city a new look. He renovated the ancient Au-
relian walls, built new Vatican defence towers, renovated the Sant'Angelo
bridge and adorned the city with new squares and fountains. Secondly, he

courageously tackled the problem of the deterioration of St. Peter's Basilica, calling in the architect Leon Battista Alberti and, as mentioned above, he was an active contributor to the enlargement of the Papal Palace with the construction of a wing which closed off its perimeter creating the Parrot Courtyard **(1)**. The new north wing built by Nicholas V included grana-ries and wine cellars on the ground floor, the rooms now occupied by the Borgia Apartment on the second floor, and Julius II's apartment frescoed by Raphael above **(7b, 8b, 9b)**.

THE CHAPEL OF NICHOLAS V

The Chapel of Nicholas V **(3)**, decorated by Fra Angelico, is a splendid commemoration of the Papal Palace's ornamentation during Nicholas V's era. It is cited in historical documents as "parva et secreta" (small and secret) and it was destined for the private or semi-private use of the Pope. It was accessible from the Studiolo-Cubicolo (small study/private bed chamber), situated in the room next to the small chapel, and constituted the Palace's most secluded wing. This little chapel is very different from the medieval Great Chapel (Cappella Magna), un-doubtedly constructed before Nicholas V's time, which, from the sec-ond half of the sixteenth century onwards, took on the name of the Sistine Chapel **(12)**, destined for hosting events on the liturgical and ceremonial calendar of the Papal court. The chapel occupied the third and fourth floors of the military tower constructed for Innocent III, and was then incorporated into the new Vatican residence built by Nicholas V. It is a rectangular-plan chapel with a cross vault and takes its name from the Pope who ordered the area to be frescoed by Friar Giovanni da Fiesole known as Fra Angelico (Beato Angelico), one of the greatest painters of the fifteenth century. This artist's real name was Guidolino di Pietro but when he took the habit of St. Domenic in the convent of Fiesole he also took the name Giovanni (John). He became known as Angelico and then Beato (Blessed) due to the sanctity of his conduct and the celestial beauty of the figures in his paintings.

How is the pictorial composition of the chapel organised? In line with mediaeval customs, a painted base runs around the lower section of the room with false drapes hanging from nails. Rows of compositions, one set above the other, narrate the main events in the life of the dea-con St. Stephen, the first martyr of the Eastern Church, and the deacon St. Lawrence, the first martyr of the Western Church. Who were the dea-cons of the early Church? The deacons were instituted both to carry out general charitable and benevolent activities and give assistance during Baptisms and Eucharistic celebrations. The *Doctors of the Church* such as St. Augustine and St. Thomas are frescoed in the upper corners in niches. The vault is divided into four sections by the ribs of the cross vaulting, holding the *Four Evangelists* with their symbols: Luke and the Bull, Mat-thew and the Angel, Mark and the Lion and John and the Eagle.

The *Stories of St. Stephen and St. Lawrence* are divided onto two levels on the side walls and the entrance wall by a string-course cornice between the last two floors of Innocent III's tower. A recent restoration returned this cycle to its original splendour, conveying the strength of the faith in which Fra Angelico deeply believed; he saw spiritual meaning and the divine order of the universe shining in everything and he was able to communicate it through his paintings. These are the only paintings to have survived from among those by this great master in the Vatican.

▲ Fra Angelico and studio, *Diaconal ordination of St. Stephen and distribution of alms*, Chapel of Nicholas V

▼ Fra Angelico and studio, *Capture and stoning of St. Stephen*, Chapel of Nicholas V

The cycle of the *Stories of St. Stephen* begins as we come into the Chapel on the right-hand wall. The lunette holds two episodes of the protomartyr's life. On the left we can see the moment in which St. Peter gives the deaconship to Saint Stephen in the presence of some Apostles inside a church, whose architecture evokes the ancient style in the shafts of the columns, the capitals and the friezes. On the right St. Stephen gives out alms, expressing the essence of Christianity – charity – in the slow rhythm of his solemn movements.

In the second lunette on the left we can see St. Stephen giving a sermon outdoors to a group of women sitting on the ground with pious simplicity while the men, in fourteenth-century clothing (some recognisable as Fra Angelico's contemporaries), are standing at the back. On the right we can see the *Disputation of St. Stephen*, when he is summoned by the Jews before the Council of Elders and the scribes. This scene is true to Luke's words in the *Acts of the Apostles* where he describes the opponents 'grinding their teeth' against the heroic confessor of the faith who points to the open skies to the 'Son of Man at the right hand of God' (*Acts of the Apostles*, VII, 54–55).

The architectural structures surrounding these two scenes, which take place both outdoors (the first) and indoors (the second), are half real and half imaginary, creating the impression of being in a sort of Jerusalem with buildings which evoke small Tuscan fifteenth-century towns. Furthermore, the intentional disproportion between the figures and the architectural setting accentuates the scene's almost dream-like quality.

In the third lunette St. Stephen is being led to his death: one of the executioners drags him by the arm while the other pushes him aggressively towards one of the gates of the city. The facial expressions of his persecutors do not reveal the ferocity we might have expected. This is because the Dominican painter believed in evil as a transitory element of earthly life and never depicted it in its most violent forms. The last fresco shows the stoning of St. Stephen. The kneeling deacon prays for his torturers, heedless of his injuries, with a serene air, deep in thought. When faced with this sight, some of the crowd are moved to compassion but not Saul, the future Paul, the Apostle of the People, as he has not yet been touched by Grace, standing on the left with a cloak over his arm, watching with contempt. The scene is divided in centre by a long turreted wall, which is reminiscent of those in Rome in the part rebuilt for Nicholas V. It is set in a landscape brought to life by rolling Tuscan hills, topped by villages and dotted with cypress trees.

The stories from the *Life of St. Lawrence* in the lower cycle repeat the episodes already illustrated in the *Life of St. Stephen* with clear parallels between the two.

Fra Angelico, *Diaconal ordination of St. Lawrence*, Chapel of Nicholas V

▲Fra Angelico, *St. Lawrence receives the treasures of the Church from Sixtus II and distributes alms*, Chapel of Nicholas V

▼Fra Angelico, *Trial and martyrdom of St. Lawrence*, Chapel of Nicholas V

In the first panel Pope Sixtus II (257–258 AD) confers a deaconship on St. Lawrence in a basilica characterised by a beautiful line of columns: the Pontiff, on an Episcopal chair, offers the kneeling saint the chalice and the paten. It is interesting to note that both the Pope and his assistants are dressed in blue, a colour which does not exist in liturgy (the liturgical colours are purple for Advent and Lent, white for festivals and solemnities, red in memory of martyrs and Good Friday, and green for ordinary occasions), but here Fra Angelico granted himself this digression in virtue of the celestial beauty of the colour; all the figures seem to be portraits of people from the time, like Pope Sixtus II, depicted with the features of Nicholas V.

In the second panel Sixtus II consigns the treasures of the Church to St. Lawrence. In times of persecution it was plausible for a Pope worried about confiscations of treasures belonging to the Church by the Roman authorities, to try to keep them safe by entrusting them to a deacon so he could then distribute them among the poor people in the city. The handover takes place in a porticoed courtyard, while two armed and armoured men try to break down the gate to take Lawrence prisoner. The building's elegant façade is characterised by a gate with a tympanum decorated with a bust of Christ benedictory in a shell and it reveals the refined architectural taste of the painter. Besides the porticoed courtyard we can see a little cloister in full sunlight which diffuses a monastic sense of peace, in contrast with the dramatic episode depicted in the foreground.

The most important of all virtues, charity, is represented in a wonderful scene in the second part of the fresco in which Lawrence distributes the Church's treasures to the poor. The saint is depicted standing on the threshold of a church, inside of which we can make out the central nave with a magnificent line of columns in a stern fifteenth-century style. Lawrence is surrounded by the poor as he distributes alms, a young mother with her baby in her arms, an old man who comes forward limping on a crutch with his hand held out, a beggar with amputated legs, and a blind man who tests the ground with the end of his stick and puts out his hand as if he senses an obstacle.

In the last panel we can see the final episodes from the deacon's life. St. Lawrence is depicted before the tribunal of Emperor Decius (249–251 AD), who points at the instruments of torture whilst seated on a throne, surrounded by elements reminiscent of Roman architecture. A Roman eagle in relief seems to loom over the whole scene above the niche with the throne, encircled by a bay wreath. As we look at the group, St. Lawrence naturally stands out with his transfigured face, already detached from earthly life. The young boy who looks away from the scene with his hands put together in prayer represents St. Roman, who was baptised in prison by Lawrence.

On the other half of the panel we can see St. Lawrence's martyrdom, unfortunately seriously damaged by the opening of a window which allowed the Swiss guards to attend mass in the next room. The façade of the imperial palace decorated with niches holding the *Cardinal Virtues* still survives. On the balcony we can see the Emperor with some of the members of his court. At the side of the façade we can see the tower where St. Lawrence was imprisoned and then converted his jailer, the future St. Hippolytus.

Domenico and Davide Ghirlandaio, *Lunette with St. James*, Apostolic Library, Latin Room

THE APOSTOLIC LIBRARY

Nicholas V gathered together the beginnings of the Vatican Library, which Pope Sixtus IV (della Rovere, 1471–1484) would then officially inaugurate. The number of codices grew so much that it became necessary to provide them with a suitable location. They decided to give the Library a series of rooms on the ground floor of Nicholas V's Palace with an entrance from the Parrot Courtyard (1) and a view over the Belvedere Courtyard (2), which were then being used as storerooms for grain and wine. Obviously, these rooms were completely remodelled to provide a worthy setting for the Library requested by Sixtus IV. The renovation project created a main hall to hold the Latin manuscripts called the *Bibliotheca latina*, a smaller hall for the *Bibliotheca graeca* and another area for the most valuable manuscripts called the *Bibliotheca secreta*. There was also a series of rooms following on from these areas up to the current Courtyard of St. Damasus (3) with a large hall called the *Bibliotheca pontificia* which held the papal archives.

The pictorial decorations included frescoes, one of which (now in the Pinacotaca) is a famous work by Melozzo da Forlì which the artist painted in the *Biblitheca latina* and which depicts the official foundation of the Vatican Library. Of course, Melozzo was not the only artist commissioned to decorate the rooms of Sixtus IV's Library, other renowned artists lent their services too.

In the lunettes on the higher part of the walls in the hall of the *Biblitheca latina*, Domenico Ghirlandaio painted half-length figures looking out from behind banisters. These philosophers and thinkers from antiquity, positioned next to Doctors and Fathers of the Church, highlighted the humanistic traits Sixtus IV wanted the library to reflect. The decorations are completed by classical-style ornamentation around the ribs of the vaults with large ceiling roses in the centre carrying Sixtus IV's coat of arms.

The hall of the *Bibliotheca graeca* is decorated by a false portico of columns. Their Corinthian capitals are characterised by elegant trabeations holding up a balustrade with vases of flowers. In the centre of the vault we can see Nicholas V's coat of arms, as he set up the library's first collections here.

Finally, in the hall known as the *Bibliotheca pontificia*, designed for archival documents, the vault decorated by Melozzo is composed of thick foliage on a white background in silvery grey and in the centre we can see Paul V's coat of arms (Borghese, 1605–1621) instead of the original one of Sixtus IV, as revealed by the remnants of some red bands around the edges.

THE BORGIA APARTMENT

The Borgia Apartment takes its name from the Italianised pronunciation of the Spanish surname of Alexander VI (Rodrigo de Borja y Doms, 1492–1503), who lived there during his papacy. The apartment occupies the first floor of Nicholas V's Palace and is made up of a suite of rooms called the Room of Mysteries (Sala dei Misteri) (7a), the Room of Saints (Sala dei Santi) and the Room of Liberal Arts (Sala delle Arti Liberali) (9a), known as the "secret rooms" or rather private rooms under Raphael's *Stanze* (7b, 8b and 9b). They also incorporate two rooms in the Borgia Tower, constructed for Alexander VI, known as the Room of the Creed (Sala del Credo) (10) and the Room of the Sibyls (Sala delle Sibile) (11). Finally we come to the Room of the Popes (Sala dei Pontefici) (6a), a vast audience apartment built in the medieval wing constructed after Nicholas III's papacy, along with the Hall of Constantine above. This suite also contains some small rooms which can be accessed from the Room of Liberal Arts including the Bedchamber of the Pope (Cubicolo del Pontefice). The Borgia Apartment was abandoned after Alexander VI's death when Julius II took up residence on the second floor to avoid sharing anything with his hated predecessor.

Amidst the decline of the Middle Ages and the dawn of the Modern Era, Pope Alexander VI maintained a prominent position, albeit among factionalism and intrigues at court. First of all he guaranteed the independence of the temporal State of the Church and its spiritual authority. Furthermore, in 1492 the discovery of America opened up opportunities for the Church to enlarge its community of believers through intense missionary activity. Alexander VI was also a man of the Renaissance and he surrounded himself with great artists to create highly ambitious public works of art. The work which most reflects his style and the refinement of his papacy was the Borgia Apartment. The Pope's presence is constantly called to mind by the depictions of his coat of arms, a bull on a gold background, which is practically everywhere in the rooms, even in new and unique ways in the portrayal of the Egyptian myth of Isis, Osiris and the bull Apis.

A letter dated the 29th March 1493 written by the Pope to the people of Orvieto gives us precious documentary evidence of the works commissioned for the Apartment, as Alexander VI explains that work had been suspended on Orvieto Cathedral because the painter Bernardino di Betto, known as Pinturicchio, was also working on the papal apartment in the Vatican. Besides Pinturicchio, who was entrusted with the iconographic design of the rooms and the general management of the project, other artists and craftsmen also worked there. The mark of the master, however, can be seen everywhere and this complex of rooms constitutes one of the most important manifestations in existence of his great ability as a decorator. Pinturicchio had great expressive skill and worked in Rome in the footsteps of Pietro Vannucci, known as Perugino, Raphael's master. He became famous for the ornamental nature of his style, characterised by his use of bright colours and gold embellishments, the minute detail on his luxurious depictions of clothing and the enchanting execution of the landscapes he used to enliven the narrative contents of his scenes. In short, he was able to make the customary sacred scenes more immediate and accessible.

The aim of the cycle as a whole is to outline the story of the salvation of humanity which occurs through the contents of faith. Faith attained through grace, however, is not the only form depicted here. We can also see faith acquired on the journey taken by science and through the good practice of the Liberal Arts (according to medieval traditions these were the sciences of the *Trivium*, grammar, rhetoric and dialectics, and of the *Quadrivium*, music, astronomy, geometry and mathematics) including the good use of astrology in the Room of Liberal Arts.

Obviously this theological programme was guided by a man of God, to be precise the Dominican friar Annio da Viterbo. It is based on writings by Boccaccio and Ovid and intertwined with the exaltation of the figure of the Pope, allegorically personified in the figure of the bull alluding to his family's coat of arms.

Room of the Sibyls (Sala delle Sibille)

This room is situated in the Borgia Tower **(11)**. Its upper section holds a series of lunettes each featuring a prophet from the Old Testament and a sibyl, according to the medieval tradition of setting the pagan world side by side with that of Israel, waiting for the Messiah promised to all

►Pinturicchio and his workshop, *Apollo and Alexander VI*, Borgia Apartment, Room of the Sibyls

▼Pinturicchio and his workshop, *Lunette with Peter and Jeremiah*, Borgia Apartment, Room of the Creed

men. Each figure is identified by their name inscribed in a cartouche with the text of the prophecy. This theme was very popular in Christian iconography and it was taken up again and brought to completion by Michelangelo in the frescoes in the Sistine Chapel. Octagonal panels on the ceiling complete the room's decorative ornamentation in which, in line with the artistic and literary traditions of the Middle Ages, we can see the personifications of the seven main planets depicted with their symbols. Chariots drawn by allegorical animals fly through the sky while the men and women on the ground act in accordance with the influence these celestial bodies were thought to have over them. The rest of the ceiling is decorated with painted or stuccoed motifs with the Pope's achievements and coat of arms and the customary doves in front of Venus' chariot have been substituted by bulls, a iconographic variation introduced to please Pope Borgia. The artist who carried out the pictorial decoration of this room, the last to be frescoed, was a pupil from Pinturicchio's studio. The aim was to show how the contents of faith could be acquired through listening to prophetic messages.

▲ Pinturicchio and his workshop, *Geometry*, Borgia Apartment, Room of the Liberal Arts

▼ Pinturicchio and his workshop, *Astronomy*, Borgia Apartment, Room of the Liberal Arts

Room of the Creed (Sala del Credo)

Situated in the Borgia Tower, the Room of the Creed **(10)** unites with the Room of the Sibyls to form a coherent pictorial programme aimed at portraying the main contents of the faith through listening to prophetic messages. In the previous room the Sibyls and the Prophets linked the pagan world to Israel; in this room Prophets and Apostles link the Old and the New Testament according to a traditional layout. In the lunettes there is a series of half-length figures of apostles and prophets, one after the other. They each hold unfurled cartouches with inscriptions of the articles of the Creed (which, according to tradition, each apostle would compose upon divine inspiration before leaving Jerusalem) and the verses of the Old Testament which heralded them. In the 4th century AD Rufino d'Aquileia recounts how the Apostles, before separating to evangelise the world, each wrote a verse of the compendium of Christian doctrine known in its early form as the Apostolic Symbol. The pictorial decoration in this room can also be attributed to one of Pinturicchio's pupils.

Room of Liberal Arts (Sala delle Arti Liberali)

This room was probably Alexander VI's study **(9a)** and takes its name from the ancient division of medieval advanced teaching into "arts" or subjects known as the *Trivium* and the *Quadrivium*. These subjects are personified by female figures seated on magnificent thrones, surrounded by the most prominent representatives of their respective subjects. The names of the various allegorical figures can be read on the steps leading up to the thrones. The room fits into the iconographic programme of the Apartment's rooms as it shows that faith can be acquired on the route followed by science and though the study of the Liberal Arts. Pinturicchio has inserted his own name "Penturichio" on the throne of *Rhetoric*, although we cannot rule out that his pupils worked on the scenes too.

Room of the Saints (Sala dei Santi)

The aim of this room **(8a)** is to show how the great gift of faith can be obtained through the practice of the virtues using emblematic examples from the lives of saints. The episodes are taken from the stories of saints, some more famous than others, and from classic and oriental mythology. These frescoes were also mostly done by Pinturicchio.

In the main lunette we can see the well-known *Disputation of St. Catherine of Alexandria* portraying the episode in which Emperor Maximinus (235–238 AD) forced the saint to debate the vanity of polytheism with the wise men of his court. The young girl succeeded in convincing the wise men thus arousing the Emperor's anger and after having her imprisoned, he condemned her to death. The episode is set in a pleasant landscape: on the left Emperor Maximinus is seated on a small baldachin throne surrounded by his court; straight in front of him the young girl defends the Christian faith, naming her various reasons one by one; on the right there is a group of spectators listening to the debate, some standing and some on horseback, including some learned men called upon to present the opposing arguments. The Arch of Constantine rises up in the middle of the scene, partly decorated in relief in gilded stucco with a Lat-

Pinturicchio, *Disputation of St. Catherine of Alexandria*, Borgia Apartment, Room of the Saints

in epigraph clearly visible on the attic which reads "Pacis cultori". This was the motto of Pope Alexander Borgia, who fostered belief in a kind of peace which could be obtained only through a perfect knowledge of faith. The portraits of some of the figures from the court and family of Alexander Borgia can also be seen in the fresco.

The *Martyrdom of St. Sebastian*. The saint is bound to a column and looks up towards an angel who appears in the sky to comfort him. There are darters on each side, some wearing "ancient" clothing and others dressed according to fashions of the time. The Coliseum looms on the horizon along with the Palatine Hill, thought to be the location of the saint's execution. The fragments of roman columns and capitals lying around represent the end of the pagan world, defeated by faith in Christ which is persecuted in vain.

Susannah and the Elders. This young girl is spied upon whilst bathing naked and protests. She is unjustly accused but in the end she is freed from blame. The scene is set in a small garden with various animals drawn from life while a monumental fountain sculpted in relief dominates the composition in the centre. In the foreground we can see the biblical heroine molested by two elders, and in the background on the right we can see the two slanderers being punished.

Finally, a complex iconographic concept is depicted on the ceiling alluding to the Egyptian myth of Isis, Osiris and the ox Apis, which is none

Pinturicchio, *Annunciation*, Borgia
Apartment, Room of the Mysteries

other than an exaltation of the Pope with this theme being chosen as a pretext to allude yet again to the heraldic animal of the Borgia family.

Room of the Mysteries (Sala dei Misteri)

In the Room of the Mysteries **(7a)** we can see the foremost mysteries of the life of Christ and the Blessed Virgin in the lunettes. The salvation of Humanity, therefore, can also be reached through the contemplation of the unfathomable Mysteries of Faith. On the vault, among the gilded emblems of heraldic bulls, there are medallions with figures of prophets who are holding up a cartouche with a biblical verse heralding the subject of the fresco below. With the prophecy 'Ecce ego mittam angelum meum', the prophet Malachi introduces the theme of the Annunciation.

The words of Isaiah's verse ('Cognovit bos possessorem suum') introduce the lunette below with the *Nativity*. They are reflected by the presence of the ox in the stable and metaphorically by the open subjection of the Pope (represented by the bull/ox) to Christ the Word of God incarnate. David's verse 'Adorabunt eum omnes reges terrae' heralds the *Adoration of the Magi*.

The highest quality fresco in the whole cycle is the *Resurrection*, introduced by the words of Sophonias' verse 'Expectate in die Resurrectionis meae', where Alexander VI has been put into the scene as a witness of the event. The glorious figure of Christ is surrounded by the heads of angels and appears in a mandorla of light. His right hand is raised in a blessing, revealing

Pinturicchio, *Resurrection of Christ*, Borgia
Apartment, Room of the Mysteries

the wound on his chest, while his other hand holds the banner with the cross. Lower down, amidst the rocky background, we can see the open tomb with three young men to one side nearby. They are richly dressed and armed and one of them is still in a deep sleep. On the other side we can see a magnificent portrait of Pope Alexander VI in a luxuriant jewel-encrusted golden cope (a sacred vestment in the form of a cloak held together over the chest by a clasp), as he kneels to adore Christ resurrected.

The figure of Christ appears once more in the Ascension in a mandorla as he rises into the sky, while the Virgin Mary and the apostles look on in prayer. In the corresponding web Micah heralds the event with the prophecy 'Ascendet pandens iter ante eos'. In the next two lunettes the Mysteries more directly linked to Marian spirituality can be seen, the *Descent of the Holy Spirit*, heralded by Joel's words 'Effundam de spiritu meo super omnem carnem', and the *Assumption of the Virgin* introduced by Solomon's words 'Quasi cedrus exaltata sum in Libano' with the Virgin Mary's tomb open and filled with flowers. Above, the Mother of God, dressed in white, is seated on clouds in a mandorla of light.

Room of the Popes (Sala dei Pontefici)

The Room of the Popes **(6a)**, the largest room in the Borgia Apartment, is situated in the medieval wing of the Papal Palace under the Hall of Constantine on the second floor and was used for official functions such as audiences, banquets and consistories. Originally the ceiling was covered by a heavy beamed structure which collapsed and could have killed Alexander VI. The lunettes each contain a painted shell and a plaque inscribed with a Latin epigraph with the name of a Pope. According to Giorgio Vasari (1511–1574) these *Tituli* corresponded to an equal number of portraits of the Popes done by Giotto which gave the room its name, although they are presumed to have been lost after the ceiling collapsed. The current ceiling is made up of a typical "grotesque" design and panels holding personifications of the then-known planets and constellations accompanied by their respective animals. The decorations were carried out for Leo X

Giovanni da Udine and Perin del Vaga, *Ceiling of the Room of the Popes*

View of St. Peter's Basilica with the dome under construction,
Julius III's Apartment (formerly Noble Guard)

by the Perin del Vaga with stuccoes by Giovanni da Udine, as both artists had come to Rome to work with Raphael on decorating the loggias **(13)**.

RAPHAEL'S ROOMS:
JULIUS II AND LEO X'S APARTMENT

The Apartment used by Julius II (della Rovere, 1503–1513) and Leo X (Medici, 1513–1521) is on the second floor of the Papal Palace and consists of the rooms in Nicholas III's medieval wing. The areas open to visitors include: the Chiaroscuro Room **(4)**; the Chapel of Nicholas V **(5)** situated in the ancient tower of Innocent III; the area built after Nicholas III's papacy which is now known as the Hall of Constantine **(6b)**; the wing Nicholas V had built to close off the Parrot Courtyard which now holds the Room of Heliodorus (Stanza di Eliodoro); the Room of the Signature (Stanza della Segnatura); and the Room of the Borgo Fire (Stanza dell'Incendio) **(7b, 8b, 9b)**.

Julius II moved onto the second floor of the Papal Palace as he felt very strongly about not wanting to live in the Apartment occupied by his reviled predecessor Alexander VI, and in the context of the general renovation work in the Vatican Palace he decided to completely refurbish the rooms. The oldest rooms had already been frescoed in the thirteenth century although some remains of medieval friezes are conserved above the current wooden ceilings. In the fifteenth century Nicholas V commissioned the decoration of the second floor from the most famous painters of the time such as Fra Angelico and Piero della Francesca. Seeing as Julius II had these paintings torn down during the refurbishment work and asked Raphael to do the new frescoes we can still admire today, we do not have any information about the previous designs, apart from a few medieval fragments and the Chapel of Nicholas V.

Julius II first commissioned the frescoes for the new rooms from two of the foremost artists of the time, Perugino and Luca Signorelli, who had been

View of St. Peter's Basilica and St. Peter's Square,
Julius III's Apartment (formerly Noble Guard)

two of the main contributors to the wall decorations of the Sistine Chapel. According to Giorgio Vasari, Bramante, the architect of the Sacred Palaces at the time, also called upon his fellow countryman and distant relative Raphael to collaborate on the work already underway on the frescoes. When Julius II first saw Raphael's work he was said to be so enthusiastic about the young painter that he ordered the frescoes the other painters had begun to be destroyed and entrusted the decoration of all the rooms to him. In homage to his master Perugino, Raphael saved the vault painted by the great Umbrian artist in the current Room of the Fire. The refurbishments and decorative work went on long after Julius II's papacy and continued under his successor Leo X, only coming to an end under Clement VII (Giulio de' Medici, 1523–1534). The description of each room follows a chronological order starting with Raphael's first work under Julius II up to his last compositions which were completed by pupils from the master's designs under Leo X and his successor Clement VII. The route which visitors must follow starts in the Hall of Constantine, the last room to be frescoed.

Raphael worked actively in these rooms but he also availed himself of helpers to complete the decorations. He frescoed the main scenes on the walls, with help from others in decorating the bases, the vaults and sometimes even the most important scenes if he was overloaded with too much work. The illustration shows the entrance to the Papal Palace with its characteristic clock to the right of the ancient façade of St. Peter's.

Room of the Signature (Stanza della Segnatura)

The first room to be frescoed was the Room of the Signature (**8b**), thus called by the Ecclesiastical Tribunal of the same name which was based there for some time. Originally, however, the room was intended to be a study and a library for Julius II, who wanted the decorations to be closely linked to the room's purpose. The decorative design concept was undoubtedly guided by a theologian or man of letters of the Roman Curia, although Raphael's training at the refined court of Urbino cannot be called into question. Urbino was a hub of Renaissance Platonism reexperienced from a Christian standpoint based on the work of the philosopher Marsilio Ficino. In the four tondos on the vault Raphael painted

▶Raphael, *Theology*,
Ceiling of the Room of
the Signature

▼Raphael, *Disputation
of the Holy Sacrament*,
Room of the Signature

female allegories or rather personifications of the subjects chosen for
Julius II's study. *Theology*, *Philosophy*, *Poetry* and *Justice* in the frescoes
are linked to each of the walls below in line with the decorative design
concepts of humanistic and renaissance libraries.

The aim of this cycle is to illustrate and exalt the highest forms of the human spirit through the depiction of these subjects, that is to say Truth,
Goodness and Beauty. Truth is exalted through theology and philosophy
both in its supernatural and rational forms. Goodness, entwined with
personifications of the virtues of Fortitude, Prudence and Temperance, is
exalted through law and depicted both in its objective standards and subjective principles. Beauty is shown in the guise of music and poetry.

The allegory of *Theology*, marked out with a cartouche holding the inscription 'Divinarum rerum notitia', is linked to the depiction of theology represented in the double guise of the Church Triumphant and the
Church Militant. The genius of the master Raphael is expressed here

in his capacity to translate abstract and universal concepts into images by giving flesh, movement, colour, light and life, to the invisible all'invisibile. The Eucharistic bread is at the perspectival centre and heart of the composition with the Church Triumphant and Church Militant around it. The Church Triumphant, or rather the glorious Church contemplates the mystery of the Trinity from above while the Church Militant, or rather the earthly Church, contemplates the Trinitarian mystery from below through faith in the daily miracle of the presence of Christ in the consecrated Host.

The higher part of the composition shows Jesus in majesty between the Virgin Mary and St. John the Baptist, who is surmounted by God the Father in an aureole of angels while the dove of the Holy Spirit flies down towards the earth. At the sides of the Trinitarian mystery we can see alternate saints and patriarchs from the Old Testament, seated in a semicircle in the clouds. In the area below, on an altar adorned with an elegant frontal, we can see a golden ostensory forming the converging point of all the composition's main elements, the point where the symbolic dove connects the sky and the earth. The Doctors of the Church are positioned around the altar, Jerome, Ambrose, Augustine, Thomas Aquinas, St. Bonaventure and other sacred authors. In the crowd to the right we can make out Dante, above all a *Theologus* and also an outstanding poet and, almost hidden under a black hood, the Dominican Savonarola, who was inspired to radical asceticism and conducted a fervent predication against the Church of the time. After being excommunicated by Alexander VI Borgia, Savonarola was burned at the stake.

This fresco is also mentioned in historical sources by the title the *Disputation of the Holy Sacrament*, alluding to the impassioned debate which flared up in the sixteenth century about the real presence of the Saviour's body in the Host. This assertion was cast into doubt by Luther, causing a schism which inflicted significant damage to the Church's unity.

The aim of this scene was to exalt supernatural and revealed truth through theology.

The personification of *Philosophy* in the tondo on the vault, clearly marked by a cartouche with the inscription 'Causarum cognition', is wearing a cloak divided into sections representing the four elements of nature (yellow decorated with oak leaves for earth, green scattered with fish for water, red for fire and blue dotted with golden stars for sky). On the wall below a crowd of thinkers from antiquity gather together under an imposing architectural structure inspired by Bramante's design for the new St. Peter's Basilica. They are grouped according to their various subjects with some deep in silent thought and others engaged in lively conversation. In the centre of the scene, Plato and Aristotle preside over the erudite gathering as representatives of the two most important schools of classical thought. Plato stands for the world of ideas as the only reality, the essence of his way of thinking. Aristotle, on the other hand, holds out his open hand between the sky and the earth to show that universals do not actually exist but are incarnate and subsist in a particular form. With their other hands the two thinkers hold two works: Plato holds the *Timaeus* treatise which studies the genesis of the universe and Aristotle holds *Ethics*.

Theology and philosophy are represented as two sides of the same coin, as they form the two ways of exploring the truth. Theology explores a supernatural truth, as revealed in the Sacred Scriptures where faith and reason move forward as one. Philosophy explores the truth according to the principles of reason alone.

► Raphael, *Philosophy*, Ceiling of the Room of the Signature

▼ Raphael, *School of Athens*, Room of the Signature

Some figures' identities are unclear while others can be easily identified. At the bottom of the building, either side of the flight of steps, two philosophers are in a prominent position surrounded by students intently observing a slate. The figure on the left is Pythagoras, the discoverer of the science of numbers who is thought to have been the first person to teach his students to write numbers on a table called an *abacus*. The figure on the right is Euclid, the greatest representative of the science of forms or rather geometry, who bends over the slate measuring a star-shaped geometric figure with a compass. The great flight of steps is not only an architectural component of the scene; it also represents the materialisation of "steps" made up of the various subjects required as part of a philosopher's education. According to Plato, philosophers, deemed to be the sentinels of an ideal state, had to receive an education worthy of guiding

them in the right direction beyond the world of appearances towards the world of ideas, and the mathematical subjects were considered to be at the core of this education. Hence the intentional presence, in a prominent position at the sides of this flight of steps, of the two foremost representatives of arithmetic and geometry, Pythagoras and Euclid.

Other identifiable philosophers include Ptolemy, the ancient upholder of the geocentric system, on the right holding a globe. In front we can see Zoroaster, the legendary discoverer of Astronomy defined as the science and study of the movement of celestial bodies, who is significantly holding a globe dotted with stars. Further to Plato's right on the steps we can make out Socrates in an olive-coloured cloak in profile as he converses with his companions. The figure half lying on the steps is Diogenes, known as the Cynic, his stance revealing the essence of his way of thinking, namely his rejection of social conventions and a return to nature. In the foreground on the left we can see Epicurus wearing a wreath of vine leaves as he lectures on the subject of hedonism, the founding principle of his way of thinking with feeling being considered as the only rule of truth. The figure with the turban behind Pythagoras can be identified as Averroes, Aristotle's Arab glossator lauded by Dante as he 'who made commentary vast' (*Inferno*, IV: 144). Finally, seated in the foreground with his head leaning on his arm we can make out Heraclitus as he seems to meditate with sadness on the principle of his way thinking which was based on the knowledge of the eternal flow of everything ('*Panta rei*'). The artist's initials can be seen on the neckline of Euclid's tunic in

Raphael, *School of Athens* (detail), Room of the Signature

gold letters: 'R.V.S.M.', *Raphael urbinas sua manu*. Furthermore, the artist not only painted himself in the far right corner looking towards the viewer, he also depicted some philosophers with the features of some of his contemporaries. Euclid is depicted as Donato Bramante, Plato looks a little like Leonardo da Vinci, and Michelangelo appears as Heraclitus. We must also note that these years came to form a unique period in the history of art as Raphael was working on his rooms at the same time as Michelangelo was working on the ceiling of the Sistine Chapel, and Bramante was the architect of the Sacred Palaces. A story related by Vasari about this period recounts that Bramante, in possession of the keys to the Chapel in his role as the Palace's architect, is said to have let Raphael in secretly when Michelangelo had not finished the ceiling 'and showed him Michelangelo's methods so that he might understand them', deftly summarising this wonderful and absolutely unique period in the history of art.

The tondo on the ceiling with the personification of *Poetry* is marked by a cartouche with the words 'Numine afflatur' to show that poetry originated in divine inspiration. It is also conceptually linked to the depiction of poetry on the wall below. How did Raphael sensitively and effectively portray poetry? The artist painted a small hill with a copse to represent Parnassus, the famous Greek mountain thought to be the ancient seat of the Muses. Apollo, the god of music and poetry, is in the centre of the composition

◄ Raphael, *Poetry*, Ceiling of the Room of the Signature

▼ Raphael, *The Parnassus*, Room of the Signature

presiding over the meeting of the Muses. The god is depicted playing a lyre under the shade of laurel trees, demonstrating that the connection between music and poetry was almost inseparable, keeping to a tradition which was then lost over the centuries. The Muses are depicted around him and in the foreground at either side of the god we can make out Calliope, the inspirer of epic poetry, with a tuba and Terpsichore, the inspirer of lyric poetry, with a cithara, both seated at the god's feet.

The meeting of the Muses is attended by poets from antiquity and the following centuries in an idealised timeless group. Homer is blind and sings his verses annotated by the poet Ennius, who is seated on his right. Virgil is behind him as he converses with Dante, crowned with a bay-wreath and swathed in a red cloak. Sappho is in the foreground below on the left, with her name inscribed on a scroll, along with Petrarch in a yellow robe. In the foreground on the other side we can see Aristotle and

Boccaccio in a blue robe. It almost seems as if we can hear Apollo playing his lyre, the rustling of the laurel leaves and the water gushing from
the Castalia spring on Mount Parnassus, which was thought to have provided inspiration for poetry. These elements were then re-evoked in Julius II's courtyard-garden of orange trees and his *antiquarium* of statues
adorned with fountains, as this was where the famous statue of Apollo
came to be positioned, subsequently named the "Belvedere Apollo", at
exactly the same time as Raphael was working on the papal apartment.
The concept of beauty lauded in this scene is represented in the guise of
poetry and music.

Finally, the tondo of *Justice* on the ceiling is represented according to
tradition with scales and a sword. This personification is linked to the
scenes on either side of the window depicting key events in the history
of law. On the left we can see the institution of Civil Law with Trebonian
presenting the *Digest* (a compilation of decisions and opinions of Roman
jurists put together in the 6th century AD) to Justinian (527-565 AD). On
the right we can see the institution of Canon Law, with Pope Gregory IX
(dei Conti di Segni, 1227–1241) depicted with the features of Julius II receiving the decretals (*Corpus iuris canonici*) from St. Raymond. In the
large lunette above the window we can see personifications of the *Cardinal Virtues*: Fortitude with an oak branch, Prudence looking at herself
in a mirror, and Temperance with her reins entwined in the *Theological
Virtues* represented in the guise of angels: Faith pointing to the sky, Hope

Raphael, *Expulsion of Heliodorus from the Temple*, Room of Heliodorus

holding a lit torch, and Charity catching hold of the oak branch.

The aim of this scene is to exalt goodness, depicted in a dual guise of objective goodness (law) and subjective goodness (the virtues).

Room of Heliodorus (Stanza di Eliodoro)

This room **(7b)** was set up by Julius II for the private audiences the Pope would grant to the foremost political, religious and diplomatic representatives. The pictorial decoration he commissioned therefore reflects the importance of the room's purpose and the meetings which took place there. The pictorial design concept is political and is aimed at illustrating the protection bestowed by God on the Church from the Old Testament and the stories of the Apostles to the origins of Christianity in the Middle Ages. In contrast with the Room of the Signature where the scenes are timeless and abstract with the aim of exalting Man's intellectual capacity, this room holds representations of historical episodes which actually took place.

Raphael, *Liberation of St. Peter*, Room of Heliodorus

Raphael completed the four main scenes on the large wall arches, while the caryatids on the base, like the framework of the ceiling decorated in grotesques, were done by other artists. The decorations on the ceiling are related to those on the walls with scenes designed by Raphael based on episodes from the Old Testament. These scenes fit into the general decorative concept by illustrating the recurring theme of the divine assistance bestowed on the Church.

The scene illustrating the Old Testament story of the *Expulsion of Heliodorus from the Temple* symbolically represents the protection accorded by God whenever the Church is threatened on its own territory. Here we can see the climactic moment of the angels sent by God to punish and expel Heliodorus, who had come to steal from the Temple of Jerusalem. In commissioning this subject from Raphael, Julius II undoubtedly sought to allude to a policy he resolutely followed of expelling all usurpers from the Church's lands. In order to make this message even clearer, the Pope had himself depicted in the left-hand corner in a gestatorial chair, surrounded by his attendants who are closely watching the scene of God's judgement in defence of sacred property. This judgement is shown with particular vehemence in the right-hand corner of the scene where the celestial knight comes crashing down with his horse upon the overpowered Heliodorus. In the middle of the fresco there is an architectural structure which is reminiscent once again of Bramante's design, where the High Priest Onias prays by candlelight forming the perspectival centre of the scene.

Whenever the Church was threatened, God would provide his own miraculous protection. One of the stories in the Acts of the Apostles recounts how Peter, imprisoned in Jerusalem, dreamed that an angel was leading him out of the prison while the guards were asleep. Raphael has translated the dream into images here with St. Peter chained up in the centre in a deep sleep behind bars; in a supernatural glow the angel bends over him to show him the door of the prison cell; on the right of the scene the apostle is being led by the angel as they are about to go down the stairs where two soldiers are sleeping. On the opposite side a soldier with a lit torch

Raphael, *Mass at Bolsena,* Room of Heliodorus

Raphael and helpers, *Meeting between St. Leo I the Great and Attila*, Room of Heliodorus

wakes his companions to raise the alarm. The most significant aspect of this fresco is the light, which appears in various glowing forms: the supernatural light of the angel, whose radiant aura glows in bright contrast with the prison's dark iron grating, the light of the moon, the light of the dawn and the light of the torch reflected off the armour.

All cardinals are appointed a titular church when they are nominated and it is worth noting that Julius II commissioned this fresco because he received the titulus of San Pietro in Vincoli (St. Peter in Chains – the Church where St. Peter's chains are kept).

The fresco with the *Mass at Bolsena* portrays God's miraculous intervention to protect the Church, threatened in its faith. The episode occurred in the 13th century when a Bohemian priest, who harboured doubts about real presence of Christ in the Eucharist, saw blood exuding from the Host while he was celebrating Mass in the Church of St. Christine in Bolsena. After this, the Cathedral of Orvieto was built as an immense reliquary to hold the corporal, which was stained when the miracle occurred. The event also gave rise to the festival of *Corpus Christi* which Julius II revered, so much so that he had himself depicted as a spectator on the right-hand side of the scene. Raphael used the available space skilfully, restricted as it was by a large, decentralised window. The episode is depicted at the climatic point when the priest near the altar, significantly positioned in the centre of the scene under an open archway, witnesses the miraculous occurrence with amazement. Behind him a small crowd is roused by the sight of the miracle and on the opposite side a Pope depicted with the features of Julius II kneels before the altar. On the right we can also make out some cardinals and members of the Swiss Guard (instituted by Julius II himself in 1506) with their characteristic uniforms as well as some gestatorial chair carriers (those who were charged with carrying the gestatorial chair used to transport the Pope short distances).

In contrast with the first three frescos portraying the divine protection accorded to the Church's patrimony, the sacred figure of the Vicar of Christ and the integrity of faith, the fresco with the *Meeting between St. Leo I the Great and Attila* aims to show God safeguarding Peter's resting place in

Rome, watched over by Providence. The papal procession comes in from the left with Pope Leo I the Great (440-461 AD) who, as tradition has it, stopped Attila, the King of the Huns. The episode actually happened in northern Italy (near Mantua) but the artist transferred the scene to the gates of Rome as the city was considered to be the heart of Christianity. In the background we can make out some of the fated city's most identifiable monuments such as the coliseum, an aqueduct, a basilica and an obelisk. In the centre of the scene Attila, on his black horse, throws up his head in terror at the vision which appears in the sky of the apostles Peter and Paul, armed with swords, and he turns his body instinctively to flee. As the fresco was being done, Julius II died and Leo I the Great was depicted with the features of the new Pope Leo X.

Room of the Fire (Stanza dell'Incendio)

During Julius II's papacy this room (9b) was used as the seat of the highest tribunal of the Papal Curia, whose gatherings were presided over by the Pope. Leo X, who remodelled the apartment, set up his own "triclinium poenitior", or rather "a smaller dining room". This name differentiated its purpose as a private dining room from a room for public festivities like the Hall of Constantine, with the Pope using this smaller room to have lunch with cardinals or visiting ambassadors. Besides changing this room's function, the new Pope also hastened the completion of its decoration, continuing to avail himself of Raphael's services. Raphael found the ceiling already frescoed by his old master Perugino, who had been commissioned by Julius II to paint the medallions in the four sections of

Perugino, *Christ between Justice and Mercy,*
Ceiling of the Room of the Fire

Raphael, *Fire in the Borgo*, Room of the Fire

the vault. The aim was to show the glory of the Lord: the *Supreme Creator enthroned*, *Christ tempted by the devil*, the *Holy Trinity with the twelve apostles*, and *Christ between Justice and Mercy*, and it is thought that Julius II sat under this fresco as he signed acts of pardon.

Raphael kept both the medallions and the architectural structure and worked only on the four large wall arches in this room, the last one to be decorated by the artist himself. When writing on this subject Vasari emphasised that 'he nevertheless continued his work in the Pope's chambers and halls, where he kept men constantly employed in carrying on the work from his designs, while he supervised the whole, giving assistance as well as he knew how'.

The aim of the decorative design concept was to exalt the reigning Pope Leo X and illustrate the course of his papacy through stories taken from the lives of two great Popes who bore the same name, Leo III (795-816) and Leo IV(847-855), depicted with the features of Leo X.

The fresco of the *Fire in the Borgo* is a very well-known work and gives the room its name. It shows a dramatic episode with Leo IV; according to the *Liber Pontificalis*, the primary historical source of Pope's biographies, in the year 847 AD Leo IV managed to put out a serious fire which had broken out in the *borgo* (area) between St. Peter's Basilica and the Tiber by making a simple gesture of the sign of the cross. The fresco portrays the event and shows Pope Leo IV in the background facing the Loggia of the Blessings (Loggia delle Benedizioni) of the ancient Constantinian St. Peter's Basilica while making the miraculous gesture.

The episode is represented at a culminating and dramatic moment and takes place in a scene which appears to be divided into two parts. In the foreground the lavish buildings in the classical style in flames do not belong to Rome but almost seem to be reminiscent of ancient Troy, evidently portrayed through the eyes of a Renaissance man. In the background we can see precious documentary evidence of the façade decorated with mosaics of the ancient St. Peter's Basilica constructed for Constantine, and the Loggia of the Blessings behind it. To the left of the scene, from the top of the crumbling wall of a building,

Raphael (studio), *Coronation of Charlemagne*, Room of the Fire

a mother ignores the danger and leans out in a desperate attempt to save her baby. In the left-hand corner three figures evoke the famous Virgilian group of Aeneas with old Anchises on his shoulders and his young son Ascanius. In the centre of the scene a group of frightened women and children beg for the Pope's help and on the bottom right there is a well under a portico where men and women are drawing water to put out the flames.

This fresco reveals a transformation in Raphael's style: his works in the other rooms show his attention to the harmonious composition, whereas here he concentrates on the expressivity of each figurative element.

The *Battle of Ostia* depicts Leo IV's naval battle against the Saracens. In the background on the right we can see the battle still underway while the barbarian prisoners are dragged ashore in the foreground and presented on their knees to the Pope (depicted with the features of Leo X) who is seated on a sculpted marble platform looking up to the sky as he gives thanks for his victory. By choosing this episode the Pope sought to express his specific intention of fighting the Turks. As often happened, aside from the features of Leo X on the Carolingian Pope, we can also make out some of his contemporaries in the figures around him. Furthermore, the building in the background is the Fortress of Ostia, built for Cardinal Giuliano della Rovere, the future Julius II, to defend the mouth of the Tiber. The *Battle of Ostia* was prepared by Raphael with designs on cartoons but it was actually frescoed by his pupil Giulio Romano.

On the wall opposite the *Battle* we can see the *Coronation of Charlemagne* which took place in the year 800 in the ancient St. Peter's Basilica officiated by Pope Leo III. The Pope is once again depicted with the features of Leo X while the Emperor has been given the features of Francis I to allude to the concordat reached between France and the Church. Just as Leo II sealed an accord and a wish of friendship with the highly significant act of the coronation of a sovereign in St. Peter's, the agreement reached with France under Leo X signified, once again, a desire for peace and harmony with the then dominant governing powers. The attribution of the work on this fresco is unclear as it was carried out by Raphael's school.

Finally, the fresco in the lunette above the window holds the *Justification of Leo III*. Raphael arranged the composition of each of the frescoes in the Room of the Fire, preparing them with his designs but he received help for the cartoons from his students, overseeing their work as much as he could in view of the immense amount of work he took on during the last years of his life. As a result there are very few sections which bear evidence of his personal intervention.

The base around the room was painted by Raphael's pupil Giulio Romano with Egyptian telamons, based on the ancient originals excavated at the beginning of the sixteenth century at Hadrian's Villa. According to Vasari, Perugino had frescoed the vault which Raphael 'from respect to his memory and from the affection that he bore him would not destroy, given that it was by his instruction Raphael himself was first conducted to the path which had led him to so high a position in art'.

The poet Baraballo

In addition to the pictorial decorations, the rooms of this Apartment used by Julius II and Leo X were enriched with furnishings which were just as magnificent, splendid flooring (as seen in the Room of the Signature) with a beautiful marble carpet of geometric motifs made up of little polychrome tesserae), chimneys and elegantly carved doors.

Many of these furnishings have been lost but echoes of the past still remain in the form of the original doors, and in particularly the door-knockers between the Room of the Signature and the Room of Heliodorus. Looking closely at the inside door-knocker we can see a little inlay of a man with an oak branch in his hand on the back of an elephant, with the saddle cloth holding the inscription *Poeta Barabul*. The presumed poet enjoyed a certain level of fame during Leo X's time owing to a practical joke immortalised in this little inlaid scene. The figure was the abbot Cosimo Baraballo da Gaeta, a humanist, courtier and improviser of classic hexameters who was full of himself. One day, people convinced him that he was going to be crowned on Capitol Hill like the great poet Petrarch, only with more pomp and splendour as he would be conveyed there in triumph in the ancient style of Roman generals on an elephant called Hanno (named after the Carthaginian general), which the Pope had received as a gift. The poor poet, unaware of the joke, left the Vatican on the pachyderm's back but the unlikely procession did not manage to go any further than the Sant'Angelo bridge, where the elephant threw the graduand to the ground, terrified by the crowds gathered to make fun of the new Petrarch.

Wooden door with a carving of the poet Barballo, Raphael's Rooms, between the Room of the Signature and the Room of Heliodorus

Chiaroscuro Room (Sala dei Chiaroscuri)

Leo X spared no efforts to bring the Apartment he had inherited from Julius II to completion, hence the inauguration, at the same time as the one in the Room of the Fire, of a second project at the other end of the Apartment in what is now known as the Chiaroscuro Room **(4)**. As mentioned above, this room was part of the medieval structure of the Vatican and along with Innocent III's tower it is the oldest wing in the Palace.

Where was the entrance to the new Palace? It is difficult to say where the entrance was under Nicholas III and Nicholas V, but during and after Julius II's papacy people came directly into the Chiaroscuro Room. Julius II asked Bramante to build a monumental staircase from the Marshal's Court (Cortile del Maresciallo) **(14)** with a ramp the Pope could be carried along to attend public ceremonies in St. Peter's or in the Sistine Chapel. Guests such as heads of state or ambassadors could also come up the ramp on horseback until the second floor to come right to the threshold of the Papal Apartment.

Here, the sequence of rooms starts with the Old Room of the Swiss Guard (Sala Vecchia degli Svizzeri), which is next to the Chiaroscuro Room but not open to visitors **(15)** – this was an antechamber which the entrance guards, the *ostiaries*, used to monitor access to the other rooms. Here, for example, ambassadors would wait until they were allowed to enter. The next room was the Parrot Room which took its name from the real parrot who lived there, a gift from the King of Denmark to Leo IX (1049–1054), who is said to have been able to repeat the Pope's name or rather "Papa Leo". This room also became marked

View of the wall decorations, Chiaroscuro Room

139

out visually with the image of a parrot, conserved in the hollow space above the current wooden ceiling among the medieval pictorial fragments. The parrot was therefore evoked with a certain continuity, almost as a living emblem of temporal power. This room was used by the Pope for the solemn dressing ritual before taking part in ceremonies. It was furnished with an altar and a bed the Pope would use, not to sleep in, but to sit on during the clothing ceremony, following European royal protocol.

The Pope would then sit in the gestatorial chair before being carried to public ceremonies by the *Palafrenieri* or rather grooms (this name derives from the word *Palafreno*, the horse used by the Pope when he travelled). Consequently this room was also known as the Room of the Grooms (Sala dei Palafrenieri or *Cubiculari*, from *cubiculum* – the Pope's bedchamber – used to refer to the Pope's manservants).

Essentially this room can be counted among the Pope's most private apartments. The clothing ceremony took place here as it was next to the Chapel of Nicholas V, the Pope's private chapel, while a second adjacent door led to his *cubiculum*. The Parrot Room was also used for the last clothing ceremony of a deceased Pope before the body was laid in the coffin. Finally, secret consistories happened here, that is to say deliberative and executive meetings between the Pope and his college of cardinals.

The pictorial decoration was coordinated under Pope Leo X, who commissioned the magnificent coffered ceiling in carved wood. The Pope set up a second worksite at the same time as the decorative work went ahead on the Room of the Fire and charged Raphael with its management. This time the painter did not work on the decorations himself but called upon Giovanni da Udine, an artist he had already employed previously as a decorator. The walls are covered by a false portico of columns crowned with Corinthian capitals with niches holding depictions of the *Twelve Apostles and Saints*. The use of false niches with illustrious figures can also be seen in the villas of noble families, where apostles and champions of faith were substituted with secular figures who had distinguished themselves as famous condottieres or able men of government.

Hall of Constantine (Sala di Costantino)

The Hall of Costantine is the largest room in the whole apartment **(6b)** and was mainly used for formal occasions such as banquets, weddings of the Pope's relatives or large semi-public audiences. The Hall of Costantine and the Room of the Pope in the Borgia Apartment below both belong to the *aulae pontificum* (papal rooms) which were built at an unspecified time, like the Room of the Grooms (or the *Cubiculari*) and the adjoining Room of the Swiss Guards. The Hall of Costantine is now named after the subject of its frescoes but in ancient times it was known for obvious reasons as the Superior Hall of the Popes (Sala Superiore dei Pontefici).

This room was decorated by artists working in Raphael's former studio as the painter himself had died, leaving only his designs for his pupils to copy. The work was finally completed under Clement VII. The iconographic concept follows the same criteria as the other cycles, namely the celebration of the Church's apotheosis. There are historical scenes depicted on false tapestries on the walls which mark the definitive

Raphael's school, *Apparition of the Cross*, Hall of Constantine

defeat of paganism and the establishment of the Church of Rome. The work is thought to have been carried out by Giulio Romano, assisted by Gian Francesco Penni, guided by the master's designs. On the base we can see monochrome depictions of less important episodes from Constantine's life divided by pairs of caryatids. The magnificent false tapestries of the middle section are separated by Popes who had contributed to strengthening the temporal and spiritual power of the Church, enthroned under baldachins in false niches next to allegorical figures alluding to their virtues.

In the *Apparition of the Cross*, Emperor Constantine addresses the troops gathered on the field before the battle against the pagan Emperor Maxentius and raises his eyes to the sky where a cross shines with a warning written in Greek which says "with this sign you will win". In compliance with this vision, as tradition has it, he had the monogram of Christ affixed to the Roman *labara* (square military banners which were raised only when the emperor was with the army). The iconography faithfully portrays a subject frequently depicted in Roman reliefs, namely the *adlucutio* (the commander's rousing speech to the soldiers before a battle). In this scene we can make out intentional references and elements in homage to ancient Rome in the background: Hadrian's Mausoleum (Castel Sant' Angelo), the Ponte Elio (Elio Bridge) which crosses the Tiber at that point and, on the far right, the famous Mausoleum of Augustus in Campus Martius (the current Piazza Augusto Imperatore) in which the urn with the Emperor's ashes was kept along with those of his relatives and friends.

The *Battle of Milvian Bridge* depicts Constantine's famous victory over the pagan Emperor Maxentius at Milvian Bridge to the north of Rome. At the centre of the fray the Emperor rises up on his white horse in a composition inspired by Roman reliefs with condottieres and emperors, protected by three angels in the sky while his defeated rival drowns in the waters of the River Tiber. The battle is captured at the climactic moment when Constantine claims victory. This predilection for compositions full of figures derives from Roman reliefs with sculptors preferring to depict battles at their most active point when the two sides are locked in conflict and irremediably intertwined.

In the *Baptism* we can Constantine receiving the sacrament from Pope Sylvester (314–335 AD), depicted as Clement VII, in a baptistery

Raphael's school, *Battle of Milvian Bridge*, Hall of Constantine

which still stands near the Basilica of San Giovanni in Laterano (St. John Lateran). The interior of the octagonal building is skilfully reproduced and is reminiscent of the classical and monumental structures of ancient Rome with polychrome marble and columns with elegant capitals. Many figures from the papal court at the time can be seen depicted as participants of the ceremony.

In the *Donation of Rome*, based on a legend, Constantine is portrayed in the Vatican Basilica offering Pope Sylvester temporal sovereignty (symbolised by a small golden statue of the goddess Roma) before he transferred the capital of the Empire to Constantinople. This symbolic gesture emphasises the legitimacy of the temporal power of the Church which was strongly supported in the sixteenth century. According to this concept the possession of territory was a basis and a guarantee of a much higher and important spiritual power. This fresco has great documentary value as it shows the inside of Constantine's Basilica: Emperor Constantine had a Basilica built in the 4th century AD above St. Peter's tomb which fell into irremediable disrepair and was progressively demolished over the centuries to make room for the new construction site of St. Peter's Basilica. Consequently, in order to form an idea of what the ancient building looked like, we must study descriptive literary sources, iconographic sources and fragments of remains. This fresco of the *Donation* has turned out to be a remarkable historical source as it shows the interior of the ancient St. Peter's Basilica before it was completely destroyed. In particular, at the back of the central nave, we can see a presbytery area raised up from the paving, a common practice in the twelfth century. The altar here stands directly above St. Peter's tomb, decorated with a baldachin held up by small, porphyry columns. Behind the grate under the altar we must imagine the sight of the first altar built by Constantine on the apostle's tomb. Consequently, when remodelling work was carried out to build another altar in this area over the course of the centuries, the new structures were built on a higher level but never strayed from the area directly above the tomb itself. The presbytery area is set apart from the rest of the Church by a sort of barrier made up of a series of small, white, spiral columns, imported, as tradition has it, from the Temple of Jerusalem. These small columns are some of the few fragments still conserved today from the ancient structure and they have been reused in the four large pillars holding up the current Basilica's dome.

▲Raphael's school, *Baptism of Constantine*, Hall of Constantine

▼Raphael's school, *Donation of Rome*, Hall of Constantine

The original raftered ceiling of this room was substituted under Pius IV (Medici, 1559–1565) with the current false vault done by the painter Tommaso Laureti. Laureti frescoed the central panel with *The Triumph of Christianity*, creating a rather extreme synthesis of the message portrayed in the false tapestries below. This scene shows a remarkable perspectival view of a temple decorated in polychrome marble with Christ's cross set on a small altar and a statue of a broken pagan divinity at his feet, symbolising the death of pagan idols.

Tommaso Laureti, *Triumph of Christianity*, Ceiling of the Hall of Constantine

THE SISTINE CHAPEL

The construction of the chapel

The new chapel was built for Sixtus IV and also bears his name. It stands in the place of an earlier mediaeval building which fulfilled the same role of Papal Chapel. Based on architectural inspections carried out on the new building it has been revealed that the previous one would have been an imposing structure with the same rectangular lay-out and dimensions (40 metres long and 13 metres wide). We do not have any information about its height and type of roofing but we know it was situated among the very first buildings of the Papal Palace built by Pope Nicholas III (Orsini, 1277–1280). Besides the topographical similarity of the Sistine Chapel to the previous building, the mediaeval walls were incorporated at least up to a certain point while the Sistine brickwork starts above the windows, reaching a total height of about 20 metres. The crenellated exterior of the Sistine Chapel, reveals its double purpose as a chapel and a fortress. Due to repeated structural problems over the following centuries, the exterior walls were progressively covered with buttresses and a new brick wall.

This section shows the various stages of the Sistine Chapel's construction. The barrel vaults of three rooms with Sixtus IV's coat of arms can be seen below the paving, the elevation of the actual Chapel is set out on three floors and the rooms under the roof, which would become the guard-house, looked over the open projecting gangway.

Who was the architect of the Sistine Chapel? In historical sources two names are mentioned - Baccio Pontelli and Giovannino de' Dolci. Pontelli is named by the well-known artists' biographer, Giorgio Vasari, as the designer of the Chapel. Giovannino de' Dolci, according to archive documents, received payments for the Chapel's construction although he is thought to have been a sort of building contractor with the capacity to set up a large construction site rather than

▼External view of the Sistine Chapel

▼Section of the Sistine Chapel

Pietro Perugino,
*Consignment of the Keys
to St. Peter*, detail, Sistine
Chapel

an architect. In the famous fresco of the *Consignment of the Keys to St. Peter* we can make out two portraits of figures from the time on the right holding architectural instruments. Could these two figures be portraits of the architect and the master mason? Their identification as such remains hypothetical.

The architectural structure of the Chapel, whose proportions are the same as those of the temple of Jerusalem described in the Old Testament, was first decided upon as a result of practical considerations based on functionality.

The Pope had a Daily Chapel or rather Secret Chapel at his disposal in his private apartments where Mass was celebrated every day. Sixtus IV used the renowned Chapel of Nicholas V (Parentucelli, 1447–1455) on the third floor of the Papal Palace, which was decorated by Fra Angelico. The liturgical calendar, however, envisaged a series of occasions during the year, in addition to daily Mass, which were not all celebrated in St. Peter's Basilica. Most of these took place in the Palace's great Chapel.

The term Papal Chapel was used to indicate both the building, known as the Sistine Chapel, and the religious and secular representatives admitted to the celebrations. These people were accommodated in a special area separated by a railing from the laymen who were non-accredited yet still allowed to be admitted to the Chapel.

The Chapel is also universally known because the election of the Pope takes place here. At first, cells were set up along the walls for the cardinals for the entire duration of the voting process, although this practice was abandoned partly because the number of people taking part in the conclave increased. During the conclave, the cardinals stay completely isolated and use an oven fitted with a long duct to communicate the result of each round of voting to the faithful in St. Peter's Square with white or black smoke. Finally, another solemn ceremony still celebrated in the Chapel is the Sacrament of Baptism carried out by the Pope during the festival of the baptism of Jesus (the first Sunday after the Epiphany).

View of the entire Sistine Chapel

Stone furnishings in the Chapel: The screen and the choir

As well as overseeing the building work on the Chapel, Sixtus IV also arranged the internal decorating work on the walls, the paving, the elegant marble screen and the choir.

The screen divides the presbytery, the sacred and restricted part of the Chapel, from the area designated for the congregation. It derives from the *iconostasis*, the part of early Christian churches separating the presbytery from the *quadratum populi*. The ancient *iconostasis* was a sort of low wall decorated around the edges with marble slabs. It supported a series of balusters leading up to an architrave where sacred images (icons) would be hung. The elegant Sistine screen is made up of panels decorated in relief supporting a fine grate between balusters under an architrave with eight candelabras. There were originally seven can-

Mino da Fiesole, *Presbyterial screen*,
details, Sistine Chapel

Mino da Fiesole, *Choir*, Sistine Chapel

delabras, in an obvious reference to the seven wings of the Temple of Jerusalem. At first the screen divided the room at approximately a half-way point and sat on a step which still elevates the presbytery area today forming an inseparable unit with the choir both in terms of its layout and decorations. Later the screen was moved back towards the doorway to the position in which it currently stands.

Notably, the lower part of the screen is made up of marble recessed panels decorated in relief, alternately bearing festoons of fruit (in a clear reference to the ancient style) and putti holding Sixtus IV's coat of arms – a shield with an oak tree.

The choir area in the Chapel is literally the seat of the *schola cantorum*, the choir which attended the ceremonies. Singing played an extremely important role in accompanying prayers. This choir area is situated in the right-hand wall and has a coffered ceiling with an elegantly decorated and gilded balustrade looking over the Chapel.
A stone bench runs around the perimeter walls of the Sistine Chapel, except in the area holding the altar where the ground is raised.

The floor

The decoration of the floor began either when the Chapel was still being built or just after the construction work had been completed and it follows in the wake of the great tradition of the Roman masters of marble, the Cosmati family. This family of highly skilled craftsmen used ancient marble to create magnificent inlaid flooring made up of countless pieces in various colours and shapes, examples of which can be seen in ancient churches in Rome. The design for the Chapel's floor, however, was not based purely on geometrical forms, it also reflected the functional layout of the liturgical areas ensuring the orderly positioning and movements of the participants.
This diagram shows the original layout when the screen divided the room into two almost equal parts (before it was moved to its current position, standing on the first of the decorative circles). Notably, in the first part of the Chapel coming in from the main entrance, the spiral pattern

Reconstruction of the Sistine Chapel in Sixtus IV's time

continues and encloses six circles defining the processional route the celebrants would follow with their attendants as they moved towards the altar. After the railing the geometric design is made up of *quadratura*, seats for cardinals placed symmetrically on three sides of a square with the fourth side left open towards the altar. The long space along the side between the *quadratura* and the three steps made up of a series of rectangles was reserved for the lower ranking members of the Papal family who sat in rows perpendicular to the steps in front of the Pope enthroned on the left. The design in the largest square indicates the four positions of the censing, one for each of the cardinals' seats and one facing the altar.

Of the six circles indicating the processional route, the one nearest the entrance in porphyry is the *rota porphyretica* (porphyry disc), which can be seen in the same place in many of the more important Roman churches including the old and new Basilica of St. Peter. This circle marks the point where the Pope, the celebrant or simply pilgrims would stop to bend or touch one knee to the floor in worship as they came into the Chapel. Porphyry had become a symbol of imperial power during classical antiquity as the stone was associated with the figure of the Emperor, so much so that at one point (4th century AD) it was used exclusively for

Diagram of the floor of the Sistine Chapel

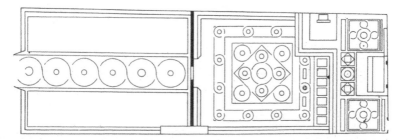

the decoration and ornamentation of his palaces and for his portraits. The sacred and celebratory value of the stone was further confirmed by palace protocol when it became customary to kneel down and worship the Emperor on porphyry *rotae* (discs). In early churches, these *rotae* indicated the place where you had to kneel (if positioned at the entrance), and the place where the sovereign kneeled to be crowned by the Pope (if positioned near the main altar).

SIXTUS IV'S FRESCOES

Architecture and pictorial decoration inseparably connected

When the Chapel was designed and built, the architecture and pictorial decoration were conceived as being inseparably connected. The Pope was able to count on the best painters of the fifteenth century from Umbria and Tuscany as he recruited artists and their workshops including Pietro Perugino (Raphael's master), Sandro Botticello, Domenico Ghirlandaio, Cosimo Rosselli (who sometimes divided his work with Biagio d'Antonio) and Luca Signorelli, the last artist to join the group. Various other artists, for example Bartolomeo della Gatta, collaborated on lesser assignments. This venture must therefore be considered as the result of a collaboration on which the painters committed to work following a common ideology imposed by the Pope and one of his theological advisors, who would have designed the general layout of the decorations together. It was agreed upon that the paintings would commence "a capite altaris" or rather above the altar, taking advantage of the winter months as this was the most suitable season for working in the fresco technique.

The four walls are divided by painted architectural elements into three horizontal tiers holding, from the lower level upwards, painted drapes, the biblical cycles of the *Life of Moses* and the *Life of Christ*, and the *Gallery of Popes*. The false drapes in the lower tier are either yellow or blue, the heraldic colours of Sixtus IV's family, and they are divided vertically by elegant, painted pilasters (half pillars set in the walls).

The second tier holds depictions of two parallel cycles of stories from

Wall with false drapes, Sistine Chapel

Sandro Botticelli, *St. Sixtus II*, Sistine Chapel

the Old and New Testaments, which start at the altar and unfold in perfect synchrony towards the entrance. The episodes are paired off, one intended as a forecast of events, the other as their fulfilment; they show the law delivered to Moses and the teaching of Christ in a design concept which was often portrayed in the decorations of the basilicas in Rome. This series of paintings was then curtailed, however, by the work which took place to make space for Michelangelo's *Last Judgement*, leading to the loss of two of the original frescoes: the *Finding of Moses in the Nile* and the *Birth of Jesus*.

The aim of these two biblical cycles was to reassert the extensiveness of the powers conferred on the Pope. Moses, the elected guide of the people prefigures Christ, the new teacher, just as the Law was fulfilled in the Evangelical teachings of Christ (whose power passed on to Peter and his successors).

The third tier holds depictions of the first Popes in painted niches, the first part of Chapel to be worked on by Michelangelo. The series begins at the altar wall with the figures of Christ and Peter in the centre in a ring of union between the foundation of the Church itself and the transfer of authority to the Popes. This gallery therefore completes the other two cycles below of the *Stories of the Life of Moses and Christ*, when interpreted in light of the Sistine concept aimed at illustrating the Stories of Salvation. It represents the beginning of the history of the Church and the supremacy of Peter. It is also natural that the Sistine iconographic concept should conclude, before Michelangelo's project began, with the exaltation of the Bishop of Rome. The Chapel was essentially meant for the supremacy of Peter, constructed for ceremonies, as well as for the election process in the conclave. The bases of the niches holding the figures carry Latin inscriptions of each Pope's name done by Platina, the renowned prefect of the Vatican Library.

Finally, according to the original decorative design, the vault was conceived as a starry sky. Spheres of gilded wax were applied to a blue background and in the flickering candle light they seemed exactly like the sparkling stars in the heavens. The depiction of starry skies stemmed from an ancient trend which can be traced back to the first mosaics in Early Christian churches and it suited the profound, fifteenth-century decorative harmony of the Chapel.

As the Chapel was dedicated to Our Lady of the Assumption, the decorations were completed by an altarpiece by Pietro Perugino with the *Assumption of the Virgin*. A drawing of this work is still conserved where we can see the Virgin Mary rising into the sky in the presence of apostles and Pope Sixtus IV, kneeling and presented by Peter.

The biblical cycles in the Sistine Chapel

The Sistine painters agreed upon a common course of action regarding the general layout of the decorations so a series of general rules were established which each master and their respective assistants had to respect. This was done to ensure that the cycles would be consistent and viewers would not be disorientated: the height of the horizon line and consequently the observer's viewpoint had to be the same, as well as the dimensions and the proportions of the figures.

We can identify the artist behind the separate frescoes without too much difficulty as the great masters left their unmistakable, sometimes bizarre signatures on the works. For example, in a nice little play on his name, Cosimo Rosselli painted a bowl with a paintbrush resting on it filled in with the colour red (in Italian *rosso*) in the lower corner of the *Adoration of the Golden Calf*.

Sometimes the artists, according to tradition at the time, depicted themselves in the paintings as spectators of the scene, using their portrait as their signature. Pietro Perugino painted himself looking out at the viewer on the right-hand side of the *Circumcision of the Son of Moses*, while the young man crowned with a garland of flowers (*ghirlanda*) on the left-hand side of the *Vocation of the first Apostles* alludes to the nickname of the painter Domenico Bigordi known as Ghirlandaio. He was given the nickname because of the profession of his father, who weaved crowns and garlands as hair adornments for the young girls of Florence.

Now we come to the descriptions of each panel from the biblical cycles starting with the *Stories of Life of Moses*. As the *Finding of Moses* has been lost, the sequence begins on the right-hand wall of the Chapel with *Moses' journey into Egypt* by Pietro Perugino. This event is depicted towards the right-hand side of the panel, while a more prominent position is given to the extremely beautiful, white figure of the angel, who stops the group with an authoritative gesture. Moses' journey can only continue after his youngest son has been circumcised. In the background, deep in the landscape, we can make out Moses bidding farewell to his father-in-law.

The common connection between the two cycles is to show the divine investiture of these two figures from the Old and the New Testament through emblematic episodes, substantiated through the course of prodigious events. As the first scene of the *Nativity* has been lost, the cycle starts on

► Cosimo Rosselli, *Adoration of the Golden Calf*, detail, Sistine Chapel

▼ Pietro Perugino, *Moses' journey into Egypt*, detail, Sistine Chapel

▼ ► Domenico Ghirlandaio, *Vocation of the first Apostles*, detail, Sistine Chapel

the left-hand wall with an emblematic episode from the New Testament, the *Baptism of Jesus* by Pietro Perugino. Jesus stands in the centre being baptised by John the Baptist as the dove of the Holy Spirit descends over his head. Above, the tondo with God the Father blesses the scene, surrounded by a circle of cherubs. A crowd of men watch the scene from the banks of the river Jordan. The Sistine painters depicted numerous portraits of their contemporaries in the biblical cycles in order to create a bond of understanding between the stories narrated and the visitors.

Next we come to the *Stories of Life of Moses* by Sandro Botticelli and his workshop. As the fifteenth-century painters had to represent numerous episodes of the *Lives*, they put several events in each fresco. In this case we can see as many as seven events with the narration beginning in the

Pietro Perugino, *Moses' journey into Egypt*, Sistine Chapel

153

lower right-hand corner: Moses kills an Egyptian who has mistreated a fellow Israelite and he is forced to flee; in the centre of the scene Moses helps to water Jethro's daughters' flock after defending the girls from the pestering shepherds in an area of the desert called Madian; on a small hill representing Mount Horeb, Moses kneels before the burning bush and is appointed by God to go into Egypt and free the Israelites from the slavery they had been forced into by the Pharaoh, who was intolerant of their prolificacy and economic prosperity; and finally Moses leads the Israelites out of Egypt, obeying an order from God. In the centre of the panel there is a large oak tree which was originally full of acorns supplely shaped in golden wax. This panel lies above the place where Pope Sixtus IV sat on his throne during ceremonies, in an obvious reference to the oak tree on his coat of arms.

The *Temptations of Christ* by Sandro Botticelli and his workshop is set in contrast with the *Stories of Life of Moses*. In the *Temptations of Christ* the painter has used an unusual composition, as the main theme is set in the background while more importance is given to a sacrificial scene typical of the Old Testament in the foreground. The narration of Jesus' ordeals begins on the upper left-hand side. The devil is in a thicket wrapped in a monk's habit with the wings of a bat and the claws of a hen. He invites Jesus to change the stones into loaves of bread with a rosary in his hand and then, as he cannot persuade him, he incites Jesus to throw himself off the top of the Temple of Jerusalem, (represented by a fifteenth-century building) so the angels of God can save him. Finally, while three angels behind the figures prepare the table on the right, Jesus unmasks the devil who reveals his true form and flees after being invited by Jesus to kneel and worship him. In the foreground a young acolyte stands in front of the altar where the fire of sacrifice is burning and presents the High Priest with a basin with the blood of the sacrificed animal. This scene can be interpreted as foreshadowing the sacrifice of Christ, the Lamb without blame.

'Moses stretched out his hand over the sea, and at daybreak the sea went back to its place. The Egyptians were fleeing toward it, and the Lord swept them into the sea. The water flowed back and covered the

Pietro Perugino, *Baptism of Christ*, Sistine Chapel

Sandro Botticelli, *Stories of Life of Moses*, Sistine Chapel

chariots and horsemen – the entire army of Pharaoh that had followed the Israelites into the sea' (Exodus, 14:27–28). The *Crossing of the Red Sea*, by Biagio d'Antonio and his assistants, is a representation of this passage from the bible. Under a leaden and stormy sky the Egyptian army is engulfed by waves with a warrior in the foreground traditionally identified as the Pharaoh (although the Bible does not actually indicate his personal presence). The Israelites with Moses at the forefront look over the scene from the shore, safe and protected by a column of fire in the centre. They are all bathed in the light of a rainbow, a sign of the alliance between God and his people.

The *Vocation of the first Apostles* by Domenico Ghirlandaio and his workshop is framed by the serene lacustrine landscape around the lake of Gennesaret. In the background on the left, Jesus summons Peter and his brother Andrew who are on their boat with fishing nets still in their hands. On the right of the composition he summons John and

Sandro Botticelli, *Temptations of Christ*, Sistine Chapel

▲Biagio d'Antonio, *Crossing of the Red Sea*, Sistine Chapel   ▼Domenico Ghirlandaio, *Vocation of the first Apostles*, Sistine Chapel

James, the other two brothers, positioned symmetrically at the same height. Jesus is in the centre and forms the climactic point of the scene in the foreground as he reveals his teachings to the first two apostles Peter and Andrew, who are kneeling before him deep in prayer. In accordance with traditions, numerous figures from Sixtus IV's time watch over the scene forming a magnificent gallery of portraits.

In the fresco *Moses receiving the Tablets of the Law* by Cosimo Rosselli and his workshop the most important element of the composition is Mount Sinai, where the prophet Moses kneels to receive the Tablets of the Law from the Eternal Father, surrounded by a cloud of angels. When Moses comes down the mountain with his son Joshua, his face transfigured, he breaks the Tablets he has received in anger at the sight of the golden calf, a pagan idol the Israelites had begun to worship guided by Aaron as they were incapable of waiting patiently for Moses to return.

▲Cosimo Rosselli, *Moses receiving the Tablets of the Law*, Sistine Chapel

▼Cosimo Rosselli, *Sermon on the Mount*, Sistine Chapel

In the *Sermon on the Mount*, by Cosimo Rosselli and his workshop, Jesus is depicted in the background with his disciples as he walks along the path leading to the place where the Beatitudes will be announced. Jesus makes this speech in front of a large crowd of people, for which the painter has reserved a privileged position, spreading them out in the foreground. Lower down in the centre of the composition, the young boy playing with the lamb is a clear symbolic reference to Christ's sacrifice. On the right, in a scene obviously set at a later time, we can see the healing of a leper, a recurrent theme in Christian iconography metaphorically interpreted as physical illness being equal to moral evil, or rather paganism and heresy.

In the *Punishment of Korah, Dathan and Abiram* and the *Consignment of the Keys to St. Peter* on the opposite wall, we can see a theme which constitutes the focal point of the whole iconographic concept of the Sistine Chapel – the affirmation of the divine origin of Papal authority legitimised

▲ Sandro Botticelli, *Punishment of Korah, Dathan and Abiram*, Sistine Chapel

▼ Pietro Perugino, *Consignment of the Keys to St. Peter*, Sistine Chapel

by the transmission of power from Christ to Peter (Christ's vicar on earth and the first Pope). Just as Moses defeats the rebels as a result of God's protection, the Church of all time carries out its mission according to its divine mandate, ably defeating the forces of evil.

This fresco by Sandro Botticelli shows one of the rebellions which disrupted the Israelites' journey through the desert and the subsequent punishment inflicted by Moses. In the centre of the fresco, Moses and his brother Aaron intervene in a riot taking place around a sacrificial altar, where the rebels are being hit with censers. The dramatic and tumultuous state of this scene is in contrast with the stately gravity of the *Consignment of the Keys to St. Peter*, although there are similarities in the scenographic backdrop dominated by the triumphal Arch of Constantine, a symbol of the triumph of Christianity over pagan Rome. A noteworthy aspect of this scene is the quote from the *Letter to the Israelites* (5:4) written by the apostle Paul, which substitutes the Roman inscription on the attic of the Arch and aims to highlight the fact that the priesthood stems from a divine calling.

Luca Signorelli and Bartolomeo della Gatta,
Testament of Moses, Sistine Chapel

In the *Consignment of the Keys to St. Peter*, by Pietro Perugino, Luca Signorelli and his workshop, we can see the metaphoric institution of the vicariate of Christ. A large number of Sixtus IV's contemporaries have been depicted in this fresco, witnessing the establishment of the papacy and the first Pope taking office and contemplating the moment in which Jesus consigns the two keys to Peter, one in gold and the other in iron, symbols of spiritual and temporal power respectively.

The event takes place in a square with a central plan temple standing out in the centre, the point where the vanishing lines converge. Two triumphal arches stand on either side of the composition, based on Constantine's famous Arch. These buildings are symbolic monuments: the temple represents Judaism and the Temple of Jerusalem while the arches represent paganism in an explicit reference to Roman antiquity. The aim is therefore to lay emphasis on the great cultures of the past which prepared and raised Christianity.

In the fresco of the *Testament of Moses*, by Luca Signorelli and Bartolomeo della Gatta, God in the guise of an angel shows Moses the Promised Land he will never be able to reach on a rocky spur representing Mount Nebo. In the foreground we can see depictions of two events which take place immediately before Moses climbs the mountain. In the first, Moses gives his staff of command to his kneeling son Joshua and in the second, he gives his last speech to the crowd, held before the urn with the Tablets of the Law and the manna, precious gifts from God. Finally we can make out the dead prophet, far in the background on the left of the painting, lying on the ground surrounded by sorrowful figures.

The *Last Supper* by Cosimo Rosselli, Biagio d'Antonio and his workshop, is the only scene in an interior location, set in an octagonal room with a magnificent coffered ceiling. Here, on both sides, two pairs of figures from the time witness the Last Supper which Jesus celebrates in Jerusalem with his disciples. The disciples, along with their master, are seated behind a table and the only one with his back to the viewer is Judas, who has a small devil sitting on his shoulders (a popular addition in mediaeval iconography). A noteworthy aspect of this composition is the depiction of three episodes from the life of Christ which

Cosimo Rosselli and Biagio d'Antonio, *Last Supper*, Sistine Chapel

will take place after the Last Supper, set in the three windows behind the figures in the dining room. From the left, the episodes portray the *Prayer in the olive grove*, the *Capture of Jesus* and the *Crucifixion*.

The two original frescos on the entrance wall of the Chapel, the *Dispute over the body of Moses* by Domenico Ghirlandaio and the *Resurrection* by Luca Signorelli, were destroyed when the marble architrave over the door collapsed and killed a Swiss guard just as Pope Adrian VI (Florensz, 1522–1523) was coming in to celebrate Christmas Mass. After this they were substituted by frescoes of the same subject by Mateo Pérez de Alesio known as Matteo da Leccia and Hendrick van den Broeck, during the papacy of Pius IV (Medici di Marignano, 1559–1565).

▲ Hendrick van den Broeck, *Resurrection*, Sistine Chapel

◄ Matteo da Leccia, *Dispute over the body of Moses*, Sistine Chapel

MICHELANGELO'S FRESCOES

Sixtus IV created a complete decorative concept in the Chapel from the vault to the floor which effectively conditioned any subsequent projects, including Michelangelo's frescoes. Before long, the structural problems from which the Chapel had always suffered resurfaced. In particular, because of the uneven foundations caused by the unusual nature of ground on the site, cracks formed on the vault. Hence, under the papacy of Julius II (della Rovere, 1503–1513), the necessary renovations took place to stabilise the building including the insertion of tie rods over the main vault. While this was taking place the Pope commissioned a new decoration to substitute Piermatteo d'Amelia's starry sky which had been damaged by the structural instability. The decision to entrust the vault project to Michelangelo was greeted with great surprise by the artist as he considered himself a sculptor, not a painter. Aside from this, he was also very annoyed by the suspension of the construction work Julius had imposed on the monumental *Tomb* the Pope had commissioned for St. Peter's.

The contract to which the artist eventually agreed was therefore the result of long negotiations. A considerable period of time was also needed to search for collaborators and assistants, set up the scaffolding, prepare the vault's surfaces and design the cartoons.

The first problem Michelangelo had to resolve in order to start the decorative work on the vault was that of the scaffolding. As the Chapel had become an essential part of the liturgical and ceremonial life of the Papal Palace, he had to use a structure which would not impede the use of the room for the whole duration of the work. A tiered stand topped with a platform was designed for the two sides so Michelangelo could paint the stories, prophets, sibyls, webs and lunettes from the same scaffold. He proceeded from the entrance of the Chapel towards the altar in two separate phases with a break between the *Creation of Eve* and the *Creation of Adam* to allow the Pope to see the work "from the door up to midway along the vault".

This scaffolding, however, led to a problem with the light. Michelangelo could not work in ideal conditions as natural light only came into the Chapel from the upper part of the windows. This was because of the presence of the scaffolding structure below, built for safety and

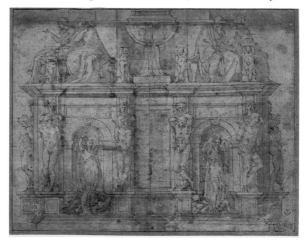

Michelangelo,
*Second design
for Julius II's
tomb*, Florence,
Gabinetto Disegni
e Stampe degli
Uffizi

aesthetical reasons. As the Pope had insisted on a structure which would not block the worshipping area, it is difficult to believe he would have accepted the sight of a multitude of girders without insisting they be concealed.

An analysis of the scaffolding's structure allows us to understand the position Michelangelo must have been in when he painted. The tiers were designed in such a way as to allow the artist to stand at the best possible distance from the surface to be frescoed. This ideal distance was equal to the artist's height with his arm stretched out upwards plus the length of the paintbrush. The hypothesis that the artist worked on his back stems from the interpretation of a statement from the time which reads 'resupinus, uti necesse erat' (P. Giovio, *Michaelis Angelis vita*), where the term 'respinus' (supine) may just refer to the artist's head and not his whole body, thus translatable as 'with his head bent backwards'. More evidence of this can be seen in a sketch Michelangelo drew next to a sonnet addressed to Giovanni di Benedetto da Pistoia, where he depicts himself standing on the scaffolding with his arm streched upwards painting on the vault.

The presence, or rather absence, of collaborators is a difficult subject which historical sources can only partially clarify. Bearing in mind that the involvement of assistants was limited and strictly controlled, the presence of other hands has partly been revealed thanks to recent restorations. An extremely important monitoring tool for the frescoes was the drawing up of precise cartoons which left absolutely no room for initiative from assistants as they were obliged to follow the plans carefully laid down by the master.

Michelangelo, *'I' ho già fatto un gozzo in questo stento'* (*'I've grown a goitre by dwelling in this den'*), signed manuscript addressed to Giovanni di Benedetto da Pistoia, Florence, Casa Buonarroti Museum

The lunettes and the webs

The lunettes and the webs are architectural elements which connect the vault to the walls over the windows. We cannot ascertain if they were already decorated when Michelangelo began his project as there is no evidence of their designs in the project showing the earlier decoration of the vault with the starry sky.

The lunettes hold figures of the *Ancestors of Christ* from Abraham to Joseph, that is to say all those who bore witness to the coming of the Messiah. They are positioned according to the sequence of the forty generations listed at the beginning of the Gospel of Matthew forming a gallery of figures with their names inscribed in a plaque in the centre of each lunette.

The series is completed by the figures in the webs below. The chronological order begins at the altar and proceeds in a criss-cross manner on the two side walls until it reaches the entrance wall. It follows the same

▲Michelangelo, *Achim-Eliud*, Sistine Chapel, lunette

▼Michelangelo, *Salmon-Booz-Obeth*, Sistine Chapel, lunette

163

pattern as the series of Popes frescoed in Sixtus IV's time, taking into account that the two lunettes on the altar wall were destroyed to make room for the *Last Judgement*. This concept led to an extraordinary representation of human archetypes diversely portrayed with great depth both in terms of their positioning (in classical and real poses) and their psychological characteristics. These psychological characteristics are portrayed with predominant variations on some specific themes, like, for example, the maternity and filial tenderness of the female figures, and the meditation and anxious solitude of the male figures.

When Michelangelo came down from the vault to the lunettes he found himself working on vertical surfaces instead of curved ones, which allowed him to work in a less tiring position and also to move freely to see his work as he painted. This explains why the lunettes were often painted without relying on preparatory cartoons and completed very quickly in an almost unfinished state like a draft. In this way the artist established a more direct rapport with the surface he was painting, similar to the approach he used, as a sculptor, when he handled stone. This becomes more evident especially in the second half of the Chapel when the artist, under pressure from Julius II who was impatient to see the work finished, painted with such zeal that he left brush bristles in the plaster of one of the lunettes. The first area he worked on was always the plaque, as this was the part that gave the whole composition its balanced structure. It was for this reason that Michelangelo did not fresco this part freehand, but incised vertical and horizontal lines in the fresh plaster with the help of nails, string and a straight edge, which would have given him the certainty of respecting the plumb lines. This process therefore created a central element on which the rest of the composition could be based.

The example illustrated (*Achim-Eliud* lunette) shows the meditative stance of the male figure, full of energy. This is set in contrast with the naturalness and spontaneity of the actions of the female figure opposite who reaches out to take some food from a plate as she turns towards her son. The positioning of these two figures opposite each other can be interpreted as a comparison between active life and contemplative life.

Michelangelo's frescoes suffered from general and progressive darkening and the lunettes were particularly affected because of their position. Besides the smoke from the candles, layers of animal glue were applied to the surface over the course of the centuries with the aim of concealing the saltpetre deposits which built up due to water infiltration through the cracks. As a result, travellers from the late eighteenth century like Johann Wolfgang Goethe (1749–1832) were left with impression that the frescoes in the lunettes were colourless and they ended up being almost overlooked by visitors as they came to be interpreted as gloomy and nocturnal scenes. The recent restorations have returned all the decorative works, including the lunettes, to their ancient chromatic magnificence. Michelangelo transferred his talent for sculpture to painting, making more use of colours than lines to give substance to the images depicted. Colour, therefore, played a fundamental structural role, becoming a tool of primary importance in creating volume and giving depth to the figures. The artist also shaped the images thanks to the use of brushes of different widths and hardness as well as the differences in body of the pigments. Furthermore, instead of the traditional fifteenth-century chiaroscuro technique used to portray light and shadows, Michelangelo used the colour technique of *cangiantismo* (changing hues) to give substance to light. This is why we can see colours placed next to each other which are often astonishing, where the darker colour is used to define the shadowy areas and the lighter colours for those in the light.

The vault: A summary of architecture, sculpture and painting in light of theological renaissance thinking

The initial phase of work was dedicated to the creation of compositional sketches followed by the first cartoons, the construction of the scaffolding and the preparation of the surfaces to be frescoed with mortar (a mix of lime and sand or, in Michelangelo's case, lime and pozzolana).

In order to define the theme which would take the place of the starry sky, the artist probably turned to the theologians of the papal court for guidance, and then submitted the outline of the project to the Pope for his approval. The project required the space of the vault to be divided by a painted architectural structure made up of frames which encased the *Stories of Genesis* in the centre, from the *Separation of Light and Darkness* to the *Drunkenness of Noah*, depicted as visions over the main area of the Chapel. *Prophets* and *Sibyls* lie opposite each other at either side of these scenes. The figures sit on painted marble thrones and are flanked by balusters decorated with pairs of putti. *Ignudi* sit above the *Prophets* and *Sibyls* on plinths holding bronze medallions on festoons of oak leaves. These medallions illustrate episodes from the Old Testament with *exempla* of obedience and disobedience of divine law. Finally, in the corner pendentives we can see depictions of biblical scenes which show God as he works, through his servants, to bring about the salvation of his people.

The *Sibyls*, who had the gift of foresight in the pagan world, and the *Prophets*, through whom God spoke in the Old Testament, are the most prominent "moving forces" of the whole vault in terms of meaning as they represent the two fundamental components on which Christian culture is founded – Greco-Roman culture and Hebraism. The *Sibyls* and the *Prophets* are therefore significantly positioned on the same plane as they

▶Michelangelo,
Zechariah, Sistine Chapel,
vault

following pages:
Vault of the Sistine Chapel
and iconographic design

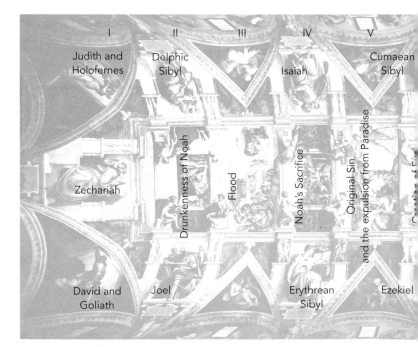

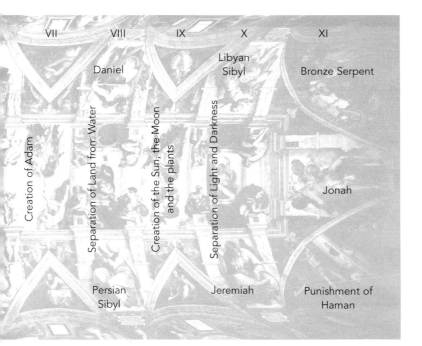

VII	VIII	IX	X	XI
	Daniel		Libyan Sibyl	Bronze Serpent
Creation of Adam	Separation of Land from Water	Creation of the Sun, the Moon and the plants	Separation of Light and Darkness	Jonah
	Persian Sibyl		Jeremiah	Punishment of Haman

were the first to reveal, when times were not yet ripe, the light of the Revelation upon which the Kingdom of Christ would be established. Among the *Prophets*, *Zechariah* and *Jonah* are especially noteworthy, significantly positioned next to the entrance wall and the altar wall respectively. *Zechariah*, in particular, was the prophet who foretold Jesus' arrival in Jerusalem with the words 'Rejoice greatly, O daughter of Zion! Shout in triumph, O daughter of Jerusalem! Behold, your king is coming to you; He is just and endowed with salvation, humble, and mounted on a donkey...' (Zechariah, 9:9). This episode was evoked on Palm Sunday, when the Pope crossed the threshold of the Chapel in full ceremony.

Jonah, prefiguring Christ resurrected, is in a dominating position above the altar where the Eucharistic sacrifice was celebrated: 'A wicked and adulterous generation asks for a miraculous sign! But none will be given it except the sign of the prophet Jonah. For as Jonah was three days and three nights in the belly of a huge fish, so the Son of Man will be three days and three nights in the heart of the earth' (Matthew, 12:38–40). From a stylistic point of view we cannot fail to mention the magnificent foreshortened perspective of the prophet's body as it seems to lean almost too far backwards.

The first three sections Michelangelo worked on from the main entrance side feature Noah, the new man saved from the flood and singled out after sin. The first section holds the *Drunkenness of Noah*, characterised by the figure of Noah lying on the ground before his sons as one of them, Japheth, moves to cover his father's naked body.

The scene of the *Flood* was probably the first to be painted and it got off to a difficult start. According to historical sources 'this technique caused considerable problems. When he had started work and completed the

Michelangelo, *Jonah*, Sistine Chapel, vault

Michelangelo, *Drunkenness of Noah; Flood; Noah's sacrifice*, Sistine Chapel, vault

panel with the Flood, mould began to grow on the fresco, so much that the figures could not be seen clearly. A considerable number of figures, mostly ignudi in a variety of different positions, are depicted in distinct groups as they try to flee from the perilous water. Some crowd onto rocks while others climb aboard boats and even the external platform of the Ark in the background. The *Flood* can be interpreted through the *New Testament* as a prefiguration of Baptism, with the Ark embodying the Church which, although rocked with storms, remains steadfast for the salvation of Man.

The last scene in this group is *Noah's Sacrifice*, where the patriarch celebrates the sacrifice of an animal on the altar, giving thanks for being saved from the waters.

The next three scenes hold depictions of events linked to the forefathers: in the first section Michelangelo portrayed *Original Sin and the expulsion from Paradise*. As we move towards the altar we can see that the figures are becoming larger in less cluttered compositions and the main figures are making powerful movements. This section is divided into two parts by the tree of knowledge: on the left Michelangelo has depicted a scene of dia-

Michelangelo, *Original Sin and the expulsion from Paradise; Creation of Eve*, Sistine Chapel, vault

logue between the serpent tempter, who is depicted in the guise of a woman, and the forefathers; to the right the Angel holding the sword shows the sinners towards exile from the garden of Eden. The tree is a prefiguration of the wood of life, the *lignum vitae*, or rather the Cross of Christ, which can be interpreted as a new tree and a means of redemption.

Michelangelo frescoed the *Creation of Eve* in a significant position in the centre of the vault, directly above the railing which, at that time, divided the Chapel into two almost equal parts. Following the reading order of the scenes of *Genesis* (the reverse order of the painted sequence), the *Creation of Eve*'s central position above the entrance to the altar area can be interpreted as Eve as a prefiguration of Mary, who would, in her turn, come to represent the Mother of the Church in Christian theology.

This interpretation is confirmed by the presence of the prophet *Ezekiel* and the *Cumaean Sibyl* on either side of the scene. Ezekiel's prophesies included the birth of the Virgin and the construction of a new temple, in which the Eternal would return. The presence of the *Cumaean Sibyl* is just as meaningful, as she owed her fame in the Latin Christian world to the *Eclogue IV* by Virgil, in which she recounts a prophecy. According to this prophecy a baby boy born of a virgin under the reign of Augustus would be destined to substantially change the course of history and inaugurate a new golden age: 'Ultima Cumaei venit iam carminis aetas; / magnus ab integro saeclorum nascitur ordo; / iam redit et Virgo, redeunt Saturnia regna / iam nova progenies caelo demittitur alto' [The last era of Cumaean song is now arrived: / the great series of ages begins anew. / Now, too, the Virgin Astraea returns, the reign of Saturn returns; / now a new progeny is sent down from high heaven]. These words resulted in the idea that the whole of antiquity had to be seen as a preparative period leading up to the good news, along with the conviction that, although God had showed himself in a more direct way through the prophets of the Old Testament, at least some fragments of the Revelation were also transmitted to the pagan world through the Sibyls. This concept was widespread during the Renaissance and linked to an attempt to tie classic culture to Christian doctrine.

The *Creation of Adam* excited great admiration, in part from Michelangelo's contemporaries as they could see the incarnation of one of the most important ideals of Renaissance culture – man made in the image and

Michelangelo, *Cumean Sibyl*, Sistine Chapel, vault

Michelangelo, *Ezekiel*, Sistine Chapel, vault

likeness of God. In the homilies the preachers held in the Chapel, the exaltation of the intellectual and spiritual faculties of man was never detached from that of corporal beauty, a mirror of the divine and the culmination of creation. Nevertheless, man without God is nothing and this concept is well expressed by the artist, who depicts the figure of Adam against an indistinct background as if it were the dawn of time. The young man reaches his arm out to the Eternal, who flies down towards him swathed in a drape. The conception of the stretched out fingers is extraordinary, captured at the moment they are about to touch in a metaphor of the vital energy which passes from the Creator to the created.

The last three scenes portray the creation of the world. The common aspect is the figure of the Eternal in flight above undefined spaces as he creates the magnificence of the physical universe from nothing. The first section holds the *Separation of Land from Water*, where God soars through the air with his angelic retinue, flying above the water stretched out below.

In the *Creation of the Sun, the Moon and the plants* the Eternal appears two times: 'God made the two great lights: the greater light to rule the day, and the lesser light to rule the night.' (Genesis, 1:16); and on the opposite side: 'Then God said, "Let the land produce vegetation: seed-bearing plants and trees on the land that bear fruit with seed in it, according to their various kinds." And it was so' (Genesis, 1:11). God's creative acts are expressed here once again through the metaphor of flight.

The *Separation of Light and Darkness* marks the beginning of the Creation cycle and is represented with the figure of God who forms swirls of light with his arms in the impending shadows.

pages 172–173:

Michelangelo, *Creation of Adam*, Sistine Chapel, vault

◀ Michelangelo, *Separation of Land from Water*; *Creation of the Sun, the Moon and the plants*; *Separation of Light and Darkness*, Sistine Chapel, vault

▶ Michelangelo, *Libyan Sibyl*, Sistine Chapel, vault

The *Last Judgment*

When Michelangelo completed the decorative work on the Sistine Chapel he forever altered the concept laid out by Sixtus IV both in terms of iconography and the spatial organisation of the room.

The Pope who commissioned the *Last Judgement* was Clement VII (Giulio de' Medici, 1523–1534) and Michelangelo's appointment was confirmed by his successor Paul III (Farnese, 1534–1549). After studies for the composition and for the cartoons had been made, and after the wall had been prepared, the artist climbed up the scaffolding and worked on the fresco for over five years.

Michelangelo conceived the work as a vision which spread beyond the

Michelangelo, *Last Judgement*, Sistine Chapel

physical space of the Chapel: visitors behold an "alternative reality" of extraordinary vastness, in which the second coming of Christ is depicted at the end of time. Firstly, in order to create spatial depth the artist decided not to use the trompe l'oeil architectural elements which are present in the other frescoed surfaces. Secondly, he used lapis lazuli blue for the background as it was the ideal colour to make the figures stand out. In this regard the start date of the work was delayed because of the time needed to find and buy the colours which would fully satisfy the artist, particularly the deep blue.

Although the exact literary sources Michelangelo used to create the *Judgement*, including Dante's *Divine Comedy*, are disputed, it is certain that he studied previous representations of the scene so he could

Michelangelo, *Christ the Judge and the Virgin Mary*, detail of the *Last Judgement*, Sistine Chapel

then revolutionise the traditional iconographic concept. This traditional composition had a rigorous structural form divided into two areas, one above the other, with a clear distinction between the sky and the earth. Michelangelo undoubtedly began composing his scene with this iconography in mind, although he went on to revolutionise it through a remarkably strong, dynamic layout. The lynchpin and perspectival heart of the scene is still the figure of Christ the Judge. The new element, however, was the circular movement he makes with his hands. His right hand moves downwards to expel the damned towards the abyss of hell, while he raises his left hand upwards to lift the blessed into the sky.

In this portrayal of the *Judgement*, although the artist has modified the traditional structure, we can still make out three main areas. The first is the area above in the lunettes where the angels are holding the instruments of the Passion of Christ – the cross, the crown of thorns and the column – symbols of his sacrifice and the redemption of humanity.

In the centre Christ the Judge with the Virgin Mary is surrounded by apostles and a crowd of the blessed. Aside from taking away the traditional apostles' thrones, Michelangelo substituted the motifs of the Virgin and John the Baptist in the act of interceding, with only the figure of the mother present next to her son with her arms folded. The extremely wide range of gestures and movements of the bodies is extraordinary, as too is the intense expressiveness of the faces and their gazes. The artist shows both his unsurpassable talent in the depiction of the human body, which seems to want to compete with classical models, and his extraordinary capacity to portray the variety and intensity of the passions of the soul.

Christ is surrounded by the following figures: on the right, St. Peter returns the keys, the symbols of the power to set free and detain conferred on the popes; opposite Peter on the left, we can see the dominant figure of John the Baptist; we can make out other saints underneath with

Michelangelo, *Angels with the Column of Flagellation,*
detail of the *Last Judgement*, Sistine Chapel

Michelangelo, *St. Peter and St. John the Evangelist*,
detail of the *Last Judgement*, Sistine Chapel

the attributes from their martyrdom such as St. Lawrence with the gridiron and Bartholomew with the skin (flayed from his own body). Their important position in the choir of the elect is explained by the fact that their Saint's days were celebrated with particular solemnity in the Sistine Chapel, as they were linked respectively to the anniversary of the Chapel's foundation and Sixtus IV's coronation.

At the edge of the group of the blessed, there is a crowd of female saints, martyrs and heroines from the Old Testament on the left, in contrast with the male saints, martyrs and prophets on the right. Among the male figures we can make out Simon of Cyrene as he helps Christ on his way to Calvary by carrying the cross, which almost looks as though it is leaning against the frame. We can also make out St. Sebastian as he grasps the arrows, the symbols of his martyrdom, St. Catherine of Alexandria with the spiked wheel, and St. Blaise with the iron carding combs.

Finally, lower down, some angels with trumpets announce the end of time to two groups of figures. The first is the group of the resurrected,

▲ Michelangelo, *Trumpet-playing angels*, detail of the *Last Judgement*, Sistine Chapel

▼ Michelangelo, *St. Bartholomew* (self-portrait of Michelangelo), detail of the *Last Judgement*, Sistine Chapel

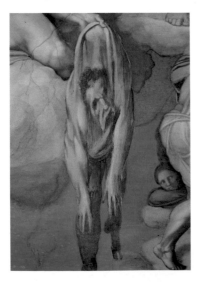

who come out from their graves, take possession of their bodies once again and ascend into the sky. The second is the group of the damned, who are expelled again towards the infernal abyss with brutal violence. In particular, the artist has admirably represented the resurrected figures' repossession of their flesh as they express a sense of slow awakening and a return to consciousness after a long slumber in their movements and their faces. On the opposite side, the tragedy of the damned reaches an intense climax heightened by the brutality of the demons. The scene is set between the boat of Charon (the ferry of the souls) and the figure of Minos (the infernal judge), both elements inspired by the words of Dante in the *Divine Comedy*.

A dramatic self-portrait of the artist has been identified in the skin St. Bartholomew is holding in his hand. Here, Michelangelo expresses his dread of the "second death" and worry when faced with sin.

The restoration of the frescoes

The Chapel was built on a pre-existing mediaeval construction and soon began to develop cracks because of the movement of the land, perhaps due to the massive excavation work taking place for the foundations of the new St. Peter's Basilica nearby. The ceiling, however, did not collapse, partly thanks to the well tested construction technique which was based on Roman traditions (vaults made of blocks of tuff stuck together with a mixture of lime and pozzolana on wooden centring). Unfortunately, they were unable to prevent the damage caused by the rain water leaking in and consequently saltpetre deposits built up on the frescoes.

As early as the mid-sixteenth century the evidence of this damage led the doctor and historian Paolo Giovio to write worriedly to Giorgio Vasari (letter dated 7 May 1547) saying 'the whole of the vault is being destroyed by saltpetre and cracks'. The smoke deposits from the candles used during ceremonies and braziers used to heat the room added to the structural damage. Lastly, we must also take into account the restorations which took place over the course of the eighteenth and nineteenth centuries when animal glues were applied to the frescoes with the aim of brightening the colours and hiding the white patches caused by the salt deposits.

The most recent restorations aimed to return the pictorial film to its original state. The first phase began in the 1960s with the cleaning of the fifteenth-century frescoes of the *Stories of Moses and Christ*, finishing in the 1980s with the restoration of Michelangelo's frescoes. All the restoration work was carried out by the Paintings Restoration Laboratories of the Vatican Museums.

Before the restoration of the surfaces frescoed by Michelangelo began, preliminary tests were done to analyse the pictorial techniques. These tests resulted in the discovery of the widespread presence of the "buon fresco" technique. This technique involved the use of good plaster to cover the pictorial surface and although Michelangelo was aware of the existence of mortar made up of lime (obtained through the pulverisation of calcareous rock) and river sand, he decided to use a type of mortar made up of lime and pozzolana (a soil of volcanic origin) which gave excellent results. Mortar made with pozzolana dried more slowly, thus guaranteeing a higher compactness and hold of the frescoes making them resistant to water infiltration, even though the use of a slower drying mortar increased the risk of mould growing on the pictorial surface. The fresco technique has been around since antiquity and takes its name from its use of fresh plaster. Pigments diluted in water are worked directly into the wall and become permanently fixed there through a naturally occurring chemical reaction. The artist has a certain amount of time available to complete the pigmentation of the fresh plaster before it dries, usually about six hours, although this can vary depending on the time of year and the quality of the plaster. The artist can therefore only work on sections of the whole composition at one time, with the help of preparatory drawings; these sections are called "giornate" ("day's work"). Michelangelo's working technique was extremely rigorous, so much so that he refused to use both the "a secco" method (when the pigments diluted in water are painted onto the dry plaster and covered with artificial fixatives) and the intermediate technique known as "affresco aiutato" (when the scene, though painted using the buon fresco method, is finished off with strokes of colours mixed with animal based binders or vegetable oils such as linseed or walnut.

The actual restoration took place between 1980 and 1989 on the ceiling and in 1994 on the *Last Judgement*. The work centred mainly on cleaning the frescoes with solvents or deionised water to remove the layers of foreign substances (smoke from the candles and braziers, and animal glues) which had built up on the colours and darkened them. Animal glues in particular constituted a serious threat to the frescoes as they suffocated the delicate pictorial film and prevented the plaster from breathing. Over time, the continual strain caused by humidity trying to pass from through from the inside out and viceversa, would lead to the pictorial film becoming detached and eventually falling away from the surface.

The work carried out on the *Last Judgement* over the centuries did not always arise from restoration efforts. Some parts were famously censored after the judgement passed at the Council of Trent. This overpainting work took place straight after Michelangelo died (1564) and included the addition of drapery covering the nudity of the figures known as the "braghe" ("breeches"). The initial retouching work was done by Daniele da Volterra, who consequently became known as "braghettone" ("the breeches painter"), but additions continued to be made the eighteenth and nineteenth centuries. During the most recent restoration the censorship from later centuries was removed but the retouching from the sixteenth century was conserved as a historical testament reflecting an important moment in which the Church found itself having to face the schism of Luther, responding with the Counter-Reformation and the Council of Trent.

Michelangelo, *Christ the Judge and the Virgin Mary*, detail of the *Last Judgement* under restoration

The solemn mass celebrated in the Sistine Chapel by John Paul II on the 8 April 1994 marked the end of the restorations. Aside from being valuable from a conservation point of view, the cleaning work played an extremely important historical role as it allowed the scene to be interpreted in a new and correct light. Michelangelo's colours re-emerged, creating shapes and variations of light on the pictorial surface known as *cangiantismo* (changing hues). His absolute perfection in the art of representing the human body could also be seen, praised for its beauty and considered as the height of divine creation. The artist revealed his anatomical knowledge by portraying the figures in countless positions making a wide variety of movements and gestures, all interrelated in a rhythmic rapport, a mirror of the motions of the soul.

Luca Beltrami, Pinacoteca, view from
the Square Garden

THE PINACOTECA

The word Pinacoteca comes from the Greek *pinakes*, a term which in-dicates painted wooden or terracotta panels. These were identified in ancient historical sources as types of easel paintings attributed to the great masters of Greek painting. The Romans picked up on the idea and used the panels as part of their wall decorations in houses with the aim of imitating real paintings – an unimaginable luxury for most people. The *pinakes* of the great masters were put on display in incredibly rich private collections as well as in public buildings, which would have had different rules and regulations governing public access and fruition than they do today. These buildings (*pinakothekai*) rarely opened their doors and only did so to show the prestige and wealth of the owners.

The Vatican, too, soon arranged to add a collection of paintings next to the Pius-Clementine Museum, as revealed in the weekly Roman ga-zette the *Diario Ordinario* on the 10 April 1790: 'Furthermore the Mu-seum (Pius-Clementine), thanks to the Holy Father's munificence, was enriched with a large and very fine collection of paintings, all originals by the most well-known artists both ancient and modern, too many in number to even make a brief description; all we can say is that the col-lection excited the general admiration not just of the superintendents but also of all the numerous guests, who were admitted to admire its merit'.

A detailed history of how the collection came together can be found in the chapter *The history*. Pius XI (Ratti, 1922-1932) inaugurated the magnificent new building for the paintings and, according to modern exhibiting crite-ria, they were put on display there in chronological order. We must not for-get, however, that the first, original group of paintings was made up almost entirely of 16th and 17th-century altarpieces from St. Peter's Basilica. Little by little, the altarpieces were replaced with mosaic copies which can still be seen on the Basilica's altars today. Consequently, these so-called "*Primitivi*" ("Primitives") only joined the main collection at a later date.

The precious sources which can help us piece together the history behind the works in this collection include *Il Libro dell'Arte* (*The Book of Art*) from the end of the 14th century by Cennino Cennini, and the *Lives of the most eminent Italian architects, painters and sculptors* by the 16th-century art historian Giorgio Vasari.

AN ANCIENT PICTURE GALLERY

As visitors leave the Sistine Chapel from one of the side entrances and walk along the long west wing lined with cabinets from the ancient Vatican Library, there is a small room near the Christian Museum which holds important evidence of an ancient picture gallery. Gregory XVI (Cappellari, 1831-1846) reserved one of the rooms belonging to the Library, later known as the Room of the Aldobrandini Nuptials (*Sala delle Nozze Aldobrandine*), for some ancient paintings which arrived in the Vatican at the beginning of the 19th century. These paintings were frescoes which had been removed from the walls of ancient villas. This small, early collection was then enhanced by other examples of classical painting including the renowned *Landscapes with scenes from the Odyssey*. This small, yet fine ancient picture gallery was conceived as an essential Greco-Roman counterpart to the modern picture gallery. In a significant move, ancient gilded frames were affixed to the fragments of ancient frescoes, transforming the mural paintings from the ancient villas into modern easel paintings.

The room takes its name from the famous Augustan-era fresco (1st century AD) on the far wall, which was found at the beginning of the 17th century on Esquiline Hill.

After it had been discovered the fresco was put on display in a specially constructed loggia in a villa belonging to Cardinal Pietro Aldobrandini. It was copied there by eminent artists and became the most admired ancient painting of the time, until the discovery of Pompeii and Herculaneum. The scene depicts the preparations for a wedding following a Greek iconographic concept. The two groups on either side are performing the ritual preparations for the nuptials. The scene in the centre shows the bride and groom with Aphrodite-Venus, which can be interpreted, according to some historians, as a reference to the nuptials of Alexander the Great to Roxanne.

In the mid-19th century, as work was being carried out near the Church of Santa Maria Maggiore (St. Mary Major) on Esquiline Hill, remains of ancient paintings were found on a wall and later became known as the *Landscapes with scenes from the Odyssey*. These scenes were originally panels hung on the upper section of the walls of a room in a Roman house. These frescoes were detached and transferred onto canvas. They can be dated to the 1st century AD and are based on Greek models. They constitute the oldest known examples of landscape painting in European art although we must keep in mind that these are fictional landscapes, not scenes painted from life. In Roman wall painting, scenes with figures were used as part of the decorative design concept partly with the aim of imitating real paintings, which were an unimaginable luxury for most people. The scenes often derived from the paintings on wood or *pinakes* attributed in historical sources to the great masters of Greek painting. These reproductions on the walls of people's houses can therefore be compared with our photographic replicas of great pictorial works. Generally, the paintings in the middle section of the wall

The Aldobrabdini Nuptials, 1st century AD, Room of the Aldobrandini Nuptials, formerly Vatican Apostolic Library

▲▲ *The Laestrygonians destroy Odysseus'*
fleet, 1st century BC, Room of the
Aldobrandini Nuptials, formerly Vatican
Apostolic Library

▲*Odysseus in the Underworld*, 1st century
BC, Room of the Aldobrandini Nuptials,
formerly Vatican Apostolic Library

would have a mythological subject, while the far ends of the wall would
hold the painted *pinakes* in false frames depicting small genre scenes,
idyllic rural landscapes or seascapes and views of villas. A noteworthy
example can be seen in the series of panels featuring the *errationes
Ulixis*, a sort of narrative cycle set beyond in a painted colonnade on the
far end of the walls. The Homeric events almost seem to be a pretext for
moving towards the representation of vast landscape compositions in a
succession of rocky peaks, creeks and copses.

When did landscape painting begin? Elements of landscapes can be
found depicted even in early artistic civilisations forming descriptive
representations of outdoor areas. Another thing altogether, however,
was the representation of a landscape as a main feature either with or
without the presence of human figures or animals, which remain secondary to the landscape even though they are used to characterise it.

This form of landscape representation, interpreted from a modern point
of view, must be attributed to the Greek world. Scenes like these on the
errationes Ulixis reveal how Greek painting, which Roman painting reflects, has really come full circle, having brought its original premise of
naturalistic, perspectival and colouristic research to its finishing con-
clusions.

In particular, the first panel holds two scenes set in the rocky land of the
Laestrygonians, the giants and cannibals Odysseus and his companions met with on their travels. In the first panel, three of Odysseus' companions meet the ruler's daughter. In the second panel, the Laestrygonians
gather together and prepare to attack the fleet. In the end, Odysseus
manages to escape their land with just one boat.

185

Myrrha, 3rd century AD, Room of the Aldobrandini Nuptials, formerly Vatican Apostolic Library

In the second panel Odysseus is depicted arriving in the underworld, where he will meet the soothsayer Tiresias (who predicts his return home), as well as numerous "shadows" of heroes and heroines. The second panel is smaller because the wall decorations were interrupted at this point by a door.

The decorations in this room are completed by a cycle of tragic heroines from Greek mythology who suffered for their guilty love. It can be dated to the 3rd century AD and is based on Greek models. This cycle formed the pictorial decoration of a Roman villa outside the St. Sebastian Gate (Porta San Sebastiano) and was found during excavations in the 19th century. The illustration shows one of the heroines, Myrrha, who was the protagonist of a Syrian legend. The young girl, the King of Syria's daughter, is punished by Aphrodite and compelled to lust after her father. In the end Myrrha turns into a tree – the myrrh tree – and her baby, Adonis, is born from the bark.

Ancient painting

Roman art is rarely seen in the form of a painting by itself, that is to say a framed picture or painting on wood hung on a wall (easel paintings), although in most cases paintings were conceived to be put on walls and, along with paving mosaics, made up an integral part of decorations in buildings. As commonly known, on the other hand, we have hardly any examples of large-scale Greek painting, although some information can be gleaned from literary sources, which provide the names of the craftsmen and artists, from vase painting and mosaics. Consequently, we know of the existence of a high level of Greek painting by which Roman painting was influenced, and which dealt with the problems European artists would go on to face once more in the 15th and 16th centuries. Essentially, Greece was the point of origin of all the pictorial problems which were later identified. The first problem was to overcome the introduction of colour in drawing in the search for volume and shape by means of mixing colours together. This was the stage at which developments in painting came to a halt in the ancient civilisations of the Eastern Mediterranean. Greek painters were also the first artists to pose the problem of setting the figures in a real – instead of an abstract – background, which would root the figures. They studied perspective, and although it was not equal to the Renaissance concept, which was the science of a depiction of what the eyes sees, it was still the first attempt at portraying figures as they moved into the background with a foreshortened view. They invented the chiaroscuro technique, or rather the first sketches of light and shadow. They studied portraiture and "still life" (which presupposes the presence of an advanced artistic culture as it indulged pictorial skill more than the subject). They studied genre painting and they also studied landscape painting. In short, Greek painting trod a path of conquests which culminated in painting with patches or rather impressionistic painting which did not define form, but hint at it with colour.

Naturally, when we talk about Roman painting we think of the Vesuvian cities which provided us with a considerable number of decorative layout concepts from houses and public buildings done between the 1st century BC and the year 79 AD, when Vesuvius erupted and buried the towns in the surrounding area. We must remember, however, that Rome itself is a much richer source than we are generally led to believe. For example, what was the decorative option of choice for the walls of the houses? There are many decorative schemes which are not mentioned in historical sources but they have been discovered thanks to material found during excavations. Walls were usually divided into three horizontal sections with a wainscot, a mid-section and an upper section which sometimes had two parts, creating a fourth level in the case of rooms with very high ceilings.

In general the following elements could be found:

- Imitations of marble slabs.

- The mid-section above the wainscot held architectural or landscape scenes with the aim of making the room seem larger. Sometimes this area was also used for both *megalographiae* (large-scale scenes) with almost life-size historical figures from mythological stories, and paintings of gardens which were ornamented with fountains, seats and gates as well as life-size plants and trees which stood out on blue backgrounds with birds.

- The shapes diverged from the actual architectural structure in the room to appear devoid of three-dimensionality and to accentuate the decorative aspects. This led to a loss of depth on the wall but gave great prominence to the "painting" in the centre of the wall itself which, as the only "way of escape", was open like a window allowing us to enter the world of fables and mythology.

- The constant use of architectural forms and decorative elements, as mentioned above, heightens the imaginary and unreal aspect.

The pictorial methods used in antiquity included the fresco, tempera and encaustic techniques. In tempera painting, pigments were diluted with egg yolk or egg white and water, while in encaustic painting, the pigments were dissolved in beeswax and applied hot. For walls, the most commonly used technique was fresco painting, which necessitated the preparation of the surface in advance with plaster made mainly of lime (pulverised calcareous rock) and sand. Pigments diluted in water were then worked into the fresh plaster. As regards the colours, most of the pigments were mineral-based, some were vegetable-based and others were obtained by mixing various pigments together.

ICONS IN THE VATICAN COLLECTIONS

The collection of Vatican icons (Room XVIII) provides evidence of the Church of Rome's awareness of objects of art and of worship in the orthodox religion. The collection includes icons which cover a historical period from the 15th to the 19th century (the post-Byzantine era). This period began on the 29th May 1473 with the fall of Constantinople (the administrative and religious capital of the Eastern Empire), when it buckled under the military might of the ottoman Turks. Istanbul continued to exert its influence over the Balkans just as Constantinople had done for a thousand years previously, and under the rule of the sultans this extraordinary point of exchange between east and west prospered for another five centuries. Consequently, for Christians, this meant that a considerable number of talented artists and craftsmen and spiritual resources were transferred abroad. It also led to the emergence of lesser artistic hubs which continued the Byzantine traditions, where those who found themselves in regions under Latin government assimilated the influence of western art. This long period of time confirms how icon painting became an integral part of European culture both in the East and the West, and how this artistic genre, using tempera on wood, kept its profound content the same. The time span of the collection is quite vast as it includes icons from Crete and Venice (Crete was under Venetian jurisdiction for a long period of time and a flourishing Cretan community became established in the lagoon town), Russia and the Balkans, Poland and outlying areas such as Asia Minor and Syria.

Icons were made in accordance with pre-established principles which had been maintained over time and they were not usually signed. Finding a signed icon is a relatively rare occurrence, although signatures are not uncommonly discovered on works from some schools in the Creto-Venetian area, which worked in a western cultural context. The date and the name of the buyer were often added to the name

Slavo-Macedonian Art, *Icon of the Twelve Festivals (Dodekàorton)*, 16th–17th century, Pinacoteca, Room XVIII

Emmanuele Tzanfournaris, *Death of St. Ephrem the Syrian*, 17th century, Pinacoteca, Room XVIII

of the painter. These were important elements which allowed some works without signatures to be attributed and dated.

How did this collection come together? The Venetian Popes undoubtedly had a particular reverence for icons as Venice had been a centre of their production for centuries. An emblematic figure in the 15th century was the Venetian merchant Pietro Barbo, the first patriarch of Venice. Barbo became a cardinal and lived in Rome in his residence in Piazza Venezia where, among other things, he collected icons. When he became Pope Paul II (Barbo, 1464-1471) he continued to show an interest in art and antiques. Before the icons were definitively grouped together in the Vatican Pinacoteca, they were part of the *Sacred Museum* (see the *History of the Museums* chapter, page 11) founded by Pope Benedict XIV (Lambertini, 1740-1758) in order to exhibit tokens from early Christianity.

■ The icon of the so-called Twelve Saint's Days or *Dodekàorton* originates from the Balkan region and can be traced back to the 16th and 17th centuries. It holds a series of images of evangelical episodes corresponding to the great festivals of the Byzantine liturgical year: the *Presentation of Mary at the Temple*, the *Annunciation*, the *Nativity of Christ*, the *Theophany* or the *Baptism of Christ*, the *Resurrection of Lazarus*, *Jesus entering Jerusalem*, the *Crucifixion*, the *Descent into the Underworld* or *Anastasis*, the *Ascension*, the *Pentecost*, the *Transfiguration of the Lord*, the *Dormition of the Mother of God*.

A noteworthy aspect of this cycle is that it does not make any distinction in the order of the festivals whether they were celebrations of the Lord or the Mother of God, as she was closely linked to the events in her son's life as an essential and special part of God's plan for the salvation of man.

■ The icon with the *Death of St. Ephrem the Syrian* can be dated to the 17th century and seeing as it is from the Creto-Venetian area, there is a visible signature. The artist, Emmanuele Tzanfournaris is of Greek origin and he worked in Venice in the 17th century. He is biographically referred to in historical sources as being part of the town's local Greek community. The work depicts the death of St. Ephrem, a theologian and saint of Syria who lived in the 4th century. He wrote various exegetic works of poetry and asceticism and he was later acknowledged as a Doctor of the Church. In this icon his appearance as a monk is emphasised. This aspect was exalted by the Eastern Church in recognition of the difficult ascesis he practised. Consequently this icon can be interpreted as a sort of manual of hermitic life in moments of prayer, work, meditation and charity. Various moments of the daily life of ascetics are depicted in a rocky landscape in a series of grottoes. The figures are absorbed in various moments of active and contemplative life and the centre of the composition is dominated by a column with a monk receiving food from one of his brothers at the top. Ephrem is depicted in a prominent position, stretched out on the ground and wrapped in a monastic habit, surrounded by his companions and disciples.

Icons

As early as the 6th century Gregory the Great realised how images could be interpreted as signs, as they possessed the capacity to guide people towards invisible concepts through visible shape and form. From the 8th century onwards, however, a violent condemnation of the worship of images erupted in the East (the iconoclastic controversy). This was both because images were considered to be deficient in their capacity to represent a supersensible reality, and because of the fear that they could attract the attention of those observing them for their "beauty", or rather the quality of the drawing and the magnificence of the colours. Essentially the dispute grew around the irreconcilable differences between the Greco-Roman tradition, which sought to create images to be as lifelike as possible, and the fear that the images would come to life before the worshippers, interposing in the relationship between the worshipper and God. The second Council of Nicaea was held at the end of the 8th century and established that the *structure* of the image (iconography does not refer so much to the style of the work as to the content) would fall back under the control of the Church and would not involve the artist's own imagination. The painter's role was comprised solely of *ars*, that is to say technique and execution, and they were obliged to follow series of rules or rather an iconographic format. The repetition of this format characterised mediaeval art in general but it became an obligation of primary importance for Byzantine artists. Icons became a revelation and not a description of the divine world. They were seen as theophanies, so the painters were required to dematerialise the forms through the complete removal or reduction of their size, the drastic cancellation of any space-time references, and the presence of a gold background, a symbol of divine light.

Eastern Christian churches had an *iconostasis*, that is to say an architectural structure which divided the presbytery from the naves (closed off by two wooden shutters), on which sacred images or icons would be exhibited. Given the presence of this screen, there was nothing behind the Eucharistic table which could be compared to the Latin altarpieces. Furthermore, icons could always be found in believers' houses, as they would pray in front of them, and some even possessed folding, portable icons. The icons which were particularly worshipped by their owners, who wished to offer them as a votive offerings, were often covered with embossed silver leaf which left only the faces and hands visible, or in some cases, a silver aureole was added around the heads of the sacred figures depicted.

How were icons positioned on an iconostasis? They were set out on various levels. The main icons were of Christ and, when space was available, of the saint or the festival to whom or to which the temple was dedicated. The higher level held a row of smaller icons which portrayed the most important festivals of the Christological cycle and the mother of God (the so-called Twelve Festivals or *Dodekàorton*). Above the Twelve Festivals there was often a row of icons featuring the half-length or enthroned figures of the twelve apostles, usually with an icon of the *Deesis* in the centre, or rather Christ implored by the Mother of God (known as *Theotokos*) and St. John. Finally, on top of the iconostasis, there was a large wooden cross sculpted with a painted depiction of the crucified Christ. Icons were also positioned either side of the nave and on the saint's day of the patron saint of the church, that saint's icon would be taken from the nave and positioned on a special lectern near the entrance so the faithful could come and worship and kiss it as they entered and left the church.

LEADING IN...

As we begin this journey through the history of painting based on mediaeval sources, and find ourselves in front of the works of art, after the indispensable introduction to ancient painting the following points are worth considering in order to clearly identify the developments artists made over the course of time:

- The subject or theme depicted
- The drawing and the colour which created shape and form
- The presence of gilded backgrounds, architectural structures, perspective and landscape
- Light and shadow
- Identifiable figures, portraits, clothing and furnishings
- Techniques and the type of support on which the artists painted
- The commission and origin of the work

■ The *Last Judgement*

The oldest work in the collection is the painting on wood of the *Last Judgement* (Room I), a round painting with a rectangular appendix on the base. Its shape may allude to the fact that the event takes place in the whole universe which, according to mediaeval notions, was round. This panel was probably used as an altarpiece and can be dated to the 12ᵗʰ century. The depiction of the last judgement unfolds on five levels, each one above the other, and each accompanied by an explanatory *titulus*. On the highest level Christ is depicted as the Pantocrater ("Ruler of All"), seated in a mandorla with a cross and orb among celestial hierarchies (two pairs of angels and seraphs). On the level below, on the other hand, Christ is depicted dressed as a priest with his arms raised in an ancient gesture of prayer in front of an altar with the symbols of the Passion, flanked by two archangels and the twelve apostles. On the third level three distinct scenes are portrayed: on the right we can see the *Works of Mercy* (*Dressing the Ignudi, Visiting the Prisoners and Quenching the Thirsty*). The *Virgin interceding on behalf of the Innocent Saints* is in the centre and *St. Paul guiding the resurrection of the elect* is on the left. The fourth level holds the *Resurrection of the bodies* with the depiction of a *Personification of the Sea* and a *Personification of the Earth*, where the bodies are awakened from their graves by the sound of the angels' trumpets. Finally, in the rectangular part, the damned

Nicolò and Giovanni, *Last Judgement*, Tempera on wood, 12ᵗʰ century, Room I

appear on the right, driven into the mouth of hell and identified by their sins which are written in Latin. *Heavenly Jerusalem* is on the left, with the Virgin Mary surrounded by the elect in front of the jewelled walls.

The iconography of the last judgement was a theme many painters chose to depict over the course of time. In this case, this mediaeval work suffers in comparison to the Byzantine tradition. Here, we can see all the elements which characterised works from this period before the great "revolution" of Giotto: the separation of the scene onto levels following a rigid and hierarchical composition, the prevalence of an outlined style favouring two-dimensional figures, emotionless faces and the absence of perspective and depth.

Painting on wood

Movable mediaeval paintings were done mainly on wood, they had sacred subjects and were mostly commissioned by religious institutions as ornaments for sacred places. Consequently, as paintings were seen as objects for contemplation and hence a channel of prayer to the entity depicted in the period in question, they were characterised by a certain fixedness. They displayed an outlined style with accentuated two dimensional figures, emotionless facial expressions, a composition divided onto levels in a rigid, hierarchical design concept and a predilection for gold backgrounds. These paintings can generally be identified as anconas (altarpieces), intended to adorn altars, and they were often made up of several panels (polyptychs) which had a base added to them (a predella) holding figures or events closely connected to the theme on the main part. Polyptychs were often painted on both sides and enhanced with arched frames. They were constructed according to the size of the altars in the mediaeval churches for which they were destined.

Firstly, the choice of wood for a painting was extremely important and the panel had to be prepared by a master carpenter. The most commonly used wood in the southern Europe was poplar while northern Europeans preferred oak. Given the extreme elasticity of wood in general and its sensitivity to humidity in the air, this first phase of preparation had to be carried out very carefully in order to avoid cracks in the painted surface in the future. The wood, seasoned and without knots, was then smoothed and the various parts were stuck together and reinforced with wooden pegs inserted into the join. The panel, thus formed of several pieces of wood, was then reinforced further with cross-beams along the lower section

Secondly, the surface of the wood had to be prepared for painting (priming). The front was covered in white canvas, then a layer of course gesso mixed with glue was added. This was followed by a second layer of finer gesso also mixed with glue. Finally, before any colour was laid down, the preparatory design would be drawn on the surface. On perfectly smooth gesso artists drew with charcoal, marking out the faces and shading in areas of depth which would then be finished off with ink.

And the colours? Tempera was the medium of colour used on mediaeval wood panels. The widespread use of tempera came before the development and popularisation of oil painting between the 15th and 16th centuries. The colours were obtained from semi-precious stones, "earths", plants and animals. They were carefully ground and diluted with water until they became powders; the base of the various pigments. A binder then had to be added for the colours to be able to stay on the surface of the panel. The colours used in the fresco technique were absorbed easily as they benefited from a naturally occurring chemical process which "fixed" the colour into the plaster on the wall, while painting on wood required the presence of substances which held the colour in place and made it adherent – this function was fulfilled by the binder which, in tempera, could be egg yolk, milk, animal based glues or wax. The term "tempera" originates from the verb "temperare" (to temper), in the sense of diluting the colours or mixing them in the correct quantity with binders. The colours obtained through this process provided a base; when darker or lighter shades were required a white colour was added (lead white). Originally, surfaces painted with tempera consisted simply of areas of homogenous colour laid next to each other. Over the course of time the need gradually arose for more shades of colour with more gradual changes of tone. The introduction of oil painting led to excellent results in this area as more shading and hence more naturalistic effects could be achieved.

We must bear in mind, however, that panel painting began, before any other colours were added, with the gold background. Artists used a thin layer of gold which was applied to the panel over a substance called bole, an argillaceous and oily earth diluted in water. Several layers of this substance were spread on the panel to allow a thin layer of gold leaf to adhere to the surface. Once all the gold had been applied, punches were used to create decorative patterns.

THE "PRIMITIVES"

The first two rooms of the Pinacoteca hold a series of mediaeval paintings on wood known as the "Primitives" (*"Primitivi"*). At first they were kept out of the papal Pinacoteca because it had been conceived as a gallery for Renaissance and early 17th century works of art. Originally, the paintings on wood belonged to the art collections of the Vatican Library and the Sacred Museum (now the Christian Museum), created by Benedict XIV (Lambertini, 1740-1758) with the aim of showing the beauty of Christian truth through art. The predominant interest behind the choice and acquisition of the panels was therefore thematic. As the Sacred Museum was created for didactic-apologetic purposes, the works were chosen mainly based on their iconographic content rather than for aesthetic reasons. It was perhaps for this reason that very few polyptychs were bought whole, while numerous acquisitions were made of separate panels. The most frequently occurring themes are Christological and they illustrate events from the Saviour's life. A considerable number of panels portray the Virgin Mary and there is also a sort of typological repertoire of Saints, mostly identifiable through their attributes.

■ The birth of Christ appears in several forms: on the following page there is an example of a small painting on wood from the 14th century (Room II). At first glance the scene seems to be just a *Nativity*, where we can make out typical narrative elements such as the cave surrounded by hosanna-singing and music-playing angels, the Virgin Mary and Saint Joseph praying before the child lying in the straw, the ox and the donkey at the back of the cave and the shepherds just awakened by the angel Gabriel in the background. The real subject, however, is the *Vision* St. Bridget of Sweden had in 1370 in Bethlehem when she travelled to the Holy Land. The Virgin Mary appeared before her and revealed that she had given birth on her knees to her child, without help or suffering any pain. The saint is depicted in the foreground on the right, kneeling like the Virgin with a rosary in her hand and a pilgrim's staff behind her.

■ Numerous panels are also dedicated to the theme of the *Crucifixion*: this small painting on wood (Room I) on the following page may have originally been the spire panel of a polyptych from the 14th century. The scene is enriched both by the usual group of the devout women supporting the Virgin, Mary Magdalene kneeling at the foot of the cross and the sorrowful image of St. John, as well as other narrative elements. In the background on the left we can see Longinus on horseback, armed with a lance and dressed in mediaeval clothing. On the right, on the other hand, we can make out the man who handed Jesus the sponge soaked in vinegar with the staff and the bucket. The cross also has some distinctive characteristics. It is made up of two, un-planed logs in a clear indication of the origin of its wood from the *Tree of Life*. A tondo is positioned above the cross with the mystical pelican which sacrificed itself for its young, just as Christ sacrificed himself for humanity.

■ Contrary to the panels with Christological subjects illustrating the events of the Saviour's life, those portraying the Virgin Mary are mostly iconic (depicting the figure alone or with her child). A frequently occurring theme is that of the *Madonna of Humility*, in which the Virgin is not seated on a throne but on a cushion on the ground, a rug or on grass in an act of humility before the divine nature of her son as she nurses him. The theme of the Madonna of Humility is therefore based on that of the Madonna of the Milk. In this regard, a noteworthy work is the small prayer altar by Francescuccio Ghissi from the 14th century (Room I). On a characteristic gold background the Madonna, in a richly ornate cloak, is seated on a rug as she nurses her child.

■ Among the various saints, St. Francis' iconography captured the Sacred Museum's curators' interest more than the others, as shown by the number of works in the collection featuring the most canonical images

Niccolò di Tommaso, *St. Bridget and the vision of the Nativity*, 14th century, Pinacoteca, Room II

▶ School of Pietro da Rimini, *Crucifixion*, 14th century, Pinacoteca, Room I

from his life and the miracles he performed of a popular devotional nature. One particularly interesting painting is the Pseudo Jacopino's *Exequies of St. Francis* from the 14th century (Room I), which depicts the saint's body lying in state in the Porziuncola (a small church), visited by a large number of religious and lay people. At the foot of the bier we can see a gentleman kneeling in prayer as he looks at St. Francis. This man can be identified as a person mentioned by the saint's biographers, a renowned doctor and man of letters who, having always been incredulous of the authenticity of the stigmata, verified the truth of the claim at that moment and became convinced and converted. The scene is completed by a priest with a censer assisted by some friars, standing behind the bier used to transport St. Francis to Assisi while a crowd of Franciscans and lay people follow them. Among the friars we can make out a Francis-

▼ Francescuccio Ghissi, *Madonna of Humility*, 14th century, Pinacoteca, Room I

Pseudo Jacopino, *Exequies of St. Francis*,
14th century, Pinacoteca, Room I

can with a scroll as he looks up to see St. Francis' soul rising into the sky.
The episode with the doctor actually took place some time beforehand
but it is re-evoked here to coincide with the recognition of the stigmata,
almost aiming to reunite two of the elements scrutinised during the be-
atification process.

■ Giotto and assistants, *Stefaneschi Triptych*

The *Stefaneschi Triptych* (Room II) was painted for the main altar of the
Constantinian Basilica of St. Peter. It was done for Cardinal Jacopo Ca-
etani degli Stefaneschi, who commissioned all the works by Giotto (1267-
1337) for St. Peter's and was one of the most important buyers in Italy
during the early 14th century. With this in mind we can think back to the
famous mosaic with the *Small boat* requested of Giotto by the Cardinal
himself. This work was originally in the four-sided portico of the old basilica but we can now admire a recreated version in the atrium of the
current basilica. The apostle's boat dashed by the waves is a symbol of
the Church, a small boat continually threatened by storms which never
sinks as it is sustained by its founder, Jesus Christ.
The altarpiece in question is painted both on the front and the back

because it would have been seen by both the Pope, seated on a throne in the apse along with his court (who assisted with the rites from behind the altar), and the faithful from the nave. The side facing the public holds *St. Peter Enthroned* in the middle section, with the buyer Cardinal Stefaneschi depicted kneeling at the saint's feet in ceremonial robes with a model of the triptych in his hand. The side section on the viewer's right holds *St. John the Evangelist* and *St. Andrew*, while the section on the left holds *St. James* and *St. Paul*. The only part which remains of the predella is a section with depictions of other saints. The side facing the apse holds *Christ Enthroned*, with the Cardinal who commissioned the work depicted once again, kneeling before Christ in more humble clothing. Instead of the usual depictions of saints in the side sections, we can see two narrative scenes: the *Crucifixion of St. Peter* with two famous pyramid-shaped funerary monuments in the background which, in traditional iconography, were depicted to indicate the Vatican, and the *Martyrdom of St. Paul* with a roughly sketched landscape in the background where, after the apostles martyrdom, angels give Plautilla the veil she lent to Paul to cover his eyes. The middle section of the predella holds the *Madonna enthroned* surrounded by angels and saints.

This work is dated to the early 14th century and Giotto used assistants to complete it, a common practice in mediaeval studios. Giotto was actually an artist-contractor and the manager of his own studio. As such, he designed the works and assigned them to his pupils, frequently intervening in various areas of the painting.

By the 14th century people began to talk about a revival of figurative arts and Boccaccio exalted Giotto's talent for imitating nature, declaring that 'he had revived that art of painting which had been buried for many centuries

Giotto and assistants, *St. Peter and Saints (Stefaneschi Triptych)* (back), *c.* 1320, Pinacoteca, Room II

under the errors of various artists who painted more to delight the eyes of the ignorant than to please the intellect of wise men' (*The Decameron*, Day 6 Story 5). Essentially, the Giottesque style was a reaction to the Greek or rather Byzantine tradition and it came to be seen as a rebirth of art. In real terms, what actually happened? First of all, Giotto, in breaking unequivocally away from the previous traditions, wanted to find a significant solution to the problem of creating the illusion of three dimensions on a two dimensional surface. Giotto's figures are solid masses placed in open landscapes or architectural backgrounds and they have humanised faces far removed from the impassiveness of those from the Byzantine tradition. Disengaging himself even further from the Byzantine conventions, which attributed symbolic value to each colour, Giotto used colour to create space and volume, thus laying down the founding principles of Renaissance art.

In short, although the *Stefaneschi Triptych* is still affected by the mediaeval decorative concepts from which it derives (such as the rigid and frontal position of the figures either side of the middle section and the gold background which creates a metaphysical atmosphere, just like in ancient mosaics), it reflects the developments lauded by Giotto's contemporaries. The rendering of the paving under the thrones belonging respectively to Jesus and Peter, or the steps on the thrones themselves, are all elements which give depth to the scene. The plasticity and monumentality of the figures of Christ and Peter also aim to create three-dimensionality. The humanised faces of the groups of figures watching the respective martyrdoms of Peter and Paul also reveal their full emotional involvement in the sorrowful events and atone for the impassiveness of the Byzantine tradition.

Giotto and helpers, *Crucifixion of St. Peter, Christ Enthroned, Martyrdom of St. Paul (Stefaneschi Triptych)* (front), *c.* 1320, Pinacoteca, Room II

THE FIFTEENTH CENTURY

■ Fra Angelico, *Stories of St. Nicholas of Bari: the Birth of the Saint, the Vocation, Giving dowry to the three poor girls*

Renaissance painters abandoned the gold background and set their scenes in natural environments or architectural structures inspired by the buildings from their time. Paintings became a window overlooking an artificially created space following the principles of imitation of reality where man, as a spectator of the world, acquired centrality because the painting, rendered in perspective, reproduced the perception of the eye. These ideas were defined by the architect Leon Battista Alberti in *De pictura*.

The *Stories of St. Nicholas of Bari* (Room III) are small rectangular panels and form the predella of the *Polyptych of Perugia*. This work was done by Giovanni da Fiesole (1400-1455) for the Order of the Dominicans and destined for a chapel dedicated to St. Nicholas in the Church of San Domenico (St. Dominic) in Perugia. This humble Dominican friar was also a great artist who found a balance between the Renaissance advances in art and the need for paintings to be firmly linked to elements of religious devotion. He was known as Beato Angelico (Blessed Angelico), usually referred to in English as Fra Angelico (Friar Angelico).

The *Birth of St. Nicholas*, the *Vocation* and the *Giving dowry to the three poor girls* constitute the first episodes from the saint's life and were positioned in the lower left section of the polyptych. Fra Angelico recreates the main miracles from Saint Nicholas' life, opening the narration with his birth and closing it with his death, which occurred around the middle of the 4th century. St. Nicholas was of noble origin and came from Asia Minor. He became a bishop and performed miracles and acts of charity, the most famous of which being the episode depicted in the last of these panels. It shows three girls ordered to become prostitutes by their father, he himself forced into making the decision due to their lack of money. St. Nicholas is said to have gone to the young girls' home during the night and thrown three bags full

Fra Angelico, *Stories of St. Nicholas of Bari: the Birth of the Saint, the Vocation, Giving dowry to the three poor girls*, c. 1437, Pinacoteca, Room III

of gold coins into the house so they could get married honourably. This panel is an emblematic example of a modern *historia figurata* (figured history), a style of representation which arose in the 15th century in which solidly formed figures were placed in harmony with each other and their background. The backgrounds in this style of painting were made up of Renaissance architectural structures depicted according to the rules of perspective. The figures are portrayed in a coherent narration in which the protagonist is represented at various different chronological moments of his life. Finally, the natural light which comes in from the left unifies the whole scene and contributes to giving the images an objectiveness which is typical of the high Renaissance.

■ Filippo Lippi, *Coronation of the Virgin, angels, saints and donors*

This triptych shows the *Coronation of the Virgin* (Room III) by the Carmelite friar Filippo Lippi (1406-1469). It was commissioned by a convent and depicts the kneeling donors among angel musicians on the sides. In the middle section, they are introduced by saint monks in contemplation of the divine event of the coronation. Another immediately recognisable historical figure, depicted among the donors, is St. Gregory the Great, a pope from the 6th century, depicted in the foreground on the left and characterised by the attribute of the dove of the Holy Spirit near his ear. Both a friar and a painter, like Fra Angelico, Fra Filippo Lippi embraces the advances in art which we can also see in the work of his contemporaries such as the plastic rendering of the figures, the attention given to their faces (which had the expressive strength of models painted from life), the solid rendering of the throne raised up on a dais (characterised by steps painted in perspective and preciously decorated with flecked marble also visible on the parapet), the blue sky in the background (instead of gold), and

Filippo Lippi, *Coronation of the Virgin, angels, saints and donors*, post 1444, Pinacoteca, Room III

the rendering of the light coming in from the left creating a area of shadow. The depiction of the light here conforms to Cennino Cennini's indications as he defined light as 'a helm and steersman', adding: 'arrange to have the light diffused when you are drawing; and have the sun fall on your left side'.

As we make our way through the rooms on this metaphorical journey through the history of painting, we can recognise various new advances. Some of these developments were made in the construction and appearance of altarpieces. As they moved towards a transformation in the modern sense of the word, they broke away from the rigid and predetermined mould of traditional polyptychs. Traditionally, the panels on either side of the middle section were dedicated to a single figure. As time went by, artists started to unite all the figures in a common setting enclosed in a single frame. The favoured theme became the so-called *Sacred Conversation*, in which the Madonna is enthroned with her child on a magnificent raised seat flanked by saints, set in a architectural or landscape background. In this case, although the three panels are separated by a wooden frame, the artist has still sought to create a unified architectural setting which would cancel out the fact the scene was divided into three sections. Consequently, the raised dais continues into the side sections by way of the steps in the middle section where the throne stands, contributing to the scene's sense of unity.

Portraiture from the Middle Ages to the Renaissance

The spread of portraiture is one of the most characteristic aspects of Renaissance civilisation: the culture of this era reconnected with classical art after a rupture which had lasted for centuries. After the fall of the Roman Empire portraiture no longer aimed to recreate a faithful portrayal of a person's features or individual psychology, but from the fourth to the twelfth centuries artists depicted archetypes and not individuals or high profile figures in society. Man became interesting to artists only as the possessor of a role: they exalted the attributes of man's power but not the individual features of his face or body. The first individual portraits reappeared amidst the cultural ambit we can define as the proto-humanistic period, that is to say with Giotto, although occurrences were rare and did not tend to be generalised until the trend gathered pace in the 15th century. In order for this budding inclination for individual portraits to spread, we must presuppose that artists began to perceive the value of portraying an individual; this concept became fully established in the 15th century. In the north of Italy for example, in the second half of the 15th century, marriages were arranged between young princes and princesses from different courts. The engaged couple could find out what their future husband or wife looked like by exchanging portraits, a custom which would have been inconceivable in mediaeval times. The transition, however, was long and in Florence, for example, figures in portraits were done in profile in the style of ancient coins with a celebratory purpose for the whole of the first half of the 15th century. This phase came to an end when the profile pose was replaced with the three-quarter pose, a style which was better suited to portraying the character of the subject. Naturally, this revolution was followed by the emergence of group portraits set in monumental contexts.

Melozzo and the Vatican Library

After the Vatican Library's first collection was set up on the first floor of the Papal Palace, mainly made up of what was left of the rich Library of Constantinople after the city fell into the hands of the Turks, Sixtus IV (della Rovere, 1471-1484) had the rooms enlarged. With a papal bull issued on the 15 June 1475, the Pope institutionalised the prestigious Library declaring the humanist Bartolomeo Sacchi (known as Platina) the *Gubernator et Custos* (Director and Custodian) of the codices. The rooms were divided into three sections dedicated respectively to the conservation of Greek, Latin and Papal codices. The bull also established rules for the consultation, conservation and census of the volumes, the duties of the librarians and it provided the Library with an autonomous location in the wing it had used previously. Furthermore, Sixtus IV called upon the foremost artists of the time to decorate the new rooms. Domenico Ghirlandaio, who was then working on the Sistine Chapel, was asked to paint the lunettes of the *bibliotheca latina* (latin library) with philosophers from antiquity next to the Doctors and Fathers of the Church. Melozzo da Forli (1438-1494) was asked to paint the central episode of the cycle frescoed in the *bibliotheca latina*, cel-

Melozzo da Forlì, *Sixtus IV and Platina*,
Pinacoteca, Room IV

ebrating the foundation of the new Library and the appointment of the first Prefect (Platina). Melozzo's fresco was detached in the 19th century and put on display in the Pinacoteca after being transferred onto canvas (Room IV). It can be linked to the opening to the public of the Latin and Greek Rooms.

In this work Sixtus IV is depicted in the foreground seated on a throne while Platina, kneeling before him, accepts his appointment to the position of Prefect. The Pope's Cardinal nephews can be seen next to their uncle, including Giuliano della Rovere, the future Pope Julius II (1503-1513). On the opposite side, we can see his other nephews – laymen – depicted in a separate position to underline the distinction between the secular and ecclesiastic spheres. Platina is indicating the inscription underneath which celebrates the work carried out in Rome by order of Sixtus IV, providing clear evidence of the commemorative nature of the painting. The scene takes place in front of a magnificent structure with pillars drawn in perspective under a commendably foreshortened coffered ceiling, enhanced by the light which glides over the precious marble, the gold and lapis lazuli blue, accentuating their brightness. This formal architectural structure aims to pay homage to the humanistic culture and to the greatness of the Pope and his court.

Fresco painting

When artists decorated walls the most widely used technique was fresco painting. This technique involved working colours into fresh plaster which then became permanently bound to the underlying layer through a naturally occurring chemical process. As a result the surface became compact, and took on the consistency of marble.

The layers of plaster were spread on the wall in two phases. During the first phase the surface to be frescoed was covered with a type of plaster called the "arriccio" ("floating coat"). This was made up of slaked lime (obtained through grinding calcareous rock) and coarse river sand, and it created a rough finish on the wall. Vertical and horizontal lines were then traced onto the surface with the help of string, nails and plumb lines. This was done to provide a guide to draw the preparatory design known as the sinopia, creating an idea of the outcome of the actual fresco. During next phase the plaster intended to receive the colour was laid down. This type of plaster was known as the "tonachino" ("stucco finish"), and it was made up of slaked lime, fine sand and marble dust. This layer was only applied to the wall in quantities which could be painted during one day as the plaster had to stay wet enough to take the colour (which is why the technique was known as "affresco" or rather "fresh" painting). On average about 6 hours made up one day's work, however, the plaster couldn't be touched for the first two hours because it was too wet and nor could it be touched for the last two hours because it would have dried out too much. In the end, only the middle two hours provided the optimal conditions for working. Artists used life-size cartoons to guide them as they worked. These preparatory drawings were especially useful when the sinopia had been covered by the "tonachino".

The preparatory drawing for the day's work was transferred onto the fresh plaster using one of two methods. The first method was known as "spolvero" ("pouncing"). The outlines of the life-size preparatory drawing were punched with very small holes and then the sheet was laid over the fresh plaster. A small bag made of canvas and filled with charcoal powder was then beaten against the surface so the drawing would be transposed onto the fresh plaster thanks to the black dust passing through the small holes in the paper. This technique required a considerable amount of preparation time because of the meticulous hole punching, but the resulting image was much more precise and well-defined. The second method was known as "indirect incision" and was much faster. The preparatory design would be drawn on a sheet of thick paper or cardboard. The cardboard was placed over the fresh plaster and the outline of the drawing was retraced with a pointed metal instrument, thus transferring the contours of the figures onto the soft surface and leaving a guideline for the painting. This method was of no use in the case of more minute and complex designs so the artist had to be capable of improvising more than he would have to when working from a drawing transferred using the "spolvero" technique.

When the time came to lay down the colours, the painter had to be sure in his work and could not afford to make any mistakes, otherwise the whole day's work would have to be destroyed and started from scratch. The outline of each the day's work can be identified by looking at the joining lines in the plaster. The colours were carefully diluted in water, but not all of them could be used in fresco painting (mineral-based pigments were better suited to the technique). As fresco painting had to be done quickly, various shades of colours were usually prepared in advance to create areas of shadow and light or the folds of drapery, always keeping the final result in mind as the colours would become darker on the plaster as it dried.

Perspectival ilusionism

■ Melozzo da Forlì, *Angel musicians*

Just after he had completed the fresco in the Vatican Library, Melozzo was asked to decorate the apse in the Church of the Santi Apostoli (Saint Apostles) in Rome with a portrayal of the *Ascension of Christ*. The fresco was commissioned after the Church had been renovated by order of its titular Cardinal Giuliano della Rovere (the future Pope Julius II). During the renovations the apse was redecorated using the mosaics in the apsidal vaults of early Christian churches as a reference. In the 18th century, when the church was modernised, the apse was destroyed and fragments of the fresco were detached and placed in different locations. The fragment with *Christ Benedictory* was put at the top of the main staircase in the Palazzo del Quirinale (the then Apostolic Palace and seat of the Pope). The fragments with the *Angel musicians* and the *Heads of the Apostles* were first housed in the Belvedere Palace, then they were moved to join the works in the Pinacoteca (Room IV). The revolutionary new advancement made by Melozzo in this composition was his use of foreshortening. He portrayed the figures from the point of view of the viewer standing under the fresco in the apse according to the principles of perspectival illusionism. When perspective was invented and developed in the 15th century, artists set about solving the problem, in the case of ceiling decorations, of how to put together a composition for a viewer standing directly underneath it. Melozzo tested the first solutions to the problem, which were then developed in full by Raphael. This composition envisaged Christ in an important position in the centre surrounded by angels, each with a characteristic musical instrument accompanying the celestial event of the return of the Redeemer to the heavens. Below, in the earthly sphere, the apostles are depicted as they contemplate the divine mystery. The wide variety of musical instruments shows once again how important music was in religious celebrations, being considered a formidable instrument of spiritual elevation.

Melozzo da Forlì, *Angel musicians*, c. 1480, Pinacoteca, Room IV

■ Perugino, *Altarpiece of the Decemviri*

Pietro Vannucci known as Perugino (1445-1523) came, like Melozzo, from the Court of Urbino. He was an extremely productive artist and his studio in Perugia was one of the most important of the 15ᵗʰ century. In particular, Perugino met with immense success in his religious painting of altarpieces thanks to the tenderness of his figures and the poetry of his landscapes. He demonstrated great ability in being able to bring people closer to religious mysteries and, especially during prayers, representations of figures and places which were immediate and evocative at first sight were in demand.

The Decemviri or Priors were members of one of the most important magistratures in Perugia, which was in charge of governing the city. These men commissioned the artist to do an altarpiece for the chapel of the Palazzo dei Priori. When he finished the work Perugino left his name in clear letters around the step of the Madonna's throne in the form of a false Latin inscription: 'Hoc Petrus De Chastro Plebis Pinxit' or rather 'Peter from Città della Pieve painted this work'. The scene's theme is the so-called Sacred Conversation. This term is used to indicate one of the most common design

Perugino, *Altarpiece of the Decemviri*, 1495–1496,
Pinacoteca, Room VII

concepts depicted on altarpieces in the 15th century – the Madonna in the centre of the composition, enthroned and surrounded by saints against an architectural or landscape background. The figure of the Virgin in the *Madonna and Child and saints* known as the *Altarpiece of the Decemviri* (Room VII) sits in a slightly asymmetric position (accentuating the composition's sense of depth) on a throne placed on a high base with the child on her knees. The throne is perfectly depicted in perspective, decorated with a false bas-relief which is reminiscent of ancient reliefs. The saints at the sides are not characterised by the instruments of their martyrdom but by the symbols which allude to the role they played in the Church. In the foreground on the left we can see St. Ludovic, the archbishop of Toulouse with his crosier while on the right we can see St. Lawrence dressed as an archdeacon. Behind them we can make out the two saints Herculanus and Constant (both wearing the bishop's mitre), the patron saints of the town of Perugia, where the work was to be placed. The space is defined by a Renaissance loggia which lets viewers see beyond to a landscape and rose-coloured sky. The significant advancement in this composition can be identified in the fact that the loggia does not stand in the background but, thanks to the intentional occlusion of the protruding arches, it seems to come forward into the real space on the viewer's side of the painting.

Oil painting

During the second half of the 15th century in Italy the practice of painting on canvas instead of wood panels became more widespread. Canvas was more practical and cheaper; it allowed the buyers of the paintings to move the works in their collections from one residence to another and, more importantly, it simplified the painter's job considerably. The use of canvas became so popular that it even substituted frescos for large-scale interior decorations and people came to prefer paintings on canvas affixed to walls and ceilings. The artist could paint these cycles in his studio, avoiding the tiresome scaffolding and limitations associated with the fresco painting technique, such as having to establish the "giornata" (day's work) in advance and not being able to carry out corrections on areas which had already been painted. The frame for the painting continued to be made of wood, but afterwards canvas was stretched over it. Until then canvas had been used almost exclusively for processional banners and, much earlier still, it was stuck on wood and used as an intermediate layer between the panel and the gesso preparation in panel painting. By the end of the 16th century wooden panels had been almost completely abandoned in favour of canvas.

Another important development was the implementation of oil colour in place of the tempera used in panel painting. The binding substance in oil painting was vegetable oil such as linseed or walnut. The advantages were undisputed. The range of pigments increased, the impasto was denser, the colours became brighter and the chromatic tones of the browns and the darker colours in general became deeper. All these advantageous factors accentuated the naturalistic aspect of the paintings. It is certain that the oil painting technique was first implemented in Flanders before it became popular in Italy, although it was not invented by the Flemish. It was known as early as the Middle Ages but it was not used by painters because it was incompatible with the gesso and glue preparation used on the wood panels which, being porous, became saturated with oil so the pictorial film could not adhere to the preparation. The Flemish artists hence picked up on a well-known technique, motivated by the need to create brighter paintings. The oil painting technique, however, was not exclusively used by artists until the end of the 16th century as they preferred using a mixed technique which alternated tempera and oil colour to bring together the brightness of the second with the guarantee of durability and solidity provided by the first. Consequently, when scholars talk about oil painting in the 15th century, they are referring to a mixed technique of oil and tempera. Furthermore, each artist jealously guarded his techniques as they were considered to be professional secrets – the preparation of the support, the colours and their application all involved complex procedures.

Humanism in northern Italy: Padua and Venice

In the 15th century Padua was a thriving centre for the development and diffusion of artistic innovation. This came about due to a series of historical and cultural circumstances. When the town came under Venetian control it benefited from the economical advantages provided by its connection to the rich lagoon city, but it was not bound by the traditional Byzantine and eastern cultural legacy which was so prevalent in Venice. On the contrary, Padua had already been at the centre of advanced artistic activities in the 14th century when, for example, Giotto worked in the Scrovegni Chapel. Unsurprisingly, the city then created contacts with Florence from the first half of the 15ᵗʰ century onwards, and aside from the significant role of the local University in Padua, the flourishing study of ancient civilisations also contributed to the town's artistic development. The origins of Paduan pictorial humanism can be sought amidst this backdrop. This way of thinking and creating blossomed in the studio-school of Francesco Squarcione (1397-1468), a traveller and impassioned antiquarian. Squarcione's open school produced some of the foremost rising stars of Renaissance art in northern Italy and it was here, in all likelihood, that Carlo Crivelli carried out his training (1430-1494).

The characteristic elements which can be found in the work of those who trained in the school include: a taste for linear drawing; a propensity for pathos in sorrowful facial expressions and violent gestures; a preference for sharp and broken forms; the excessive use of decoration both in the oppressive, lavishly-modelled and carved niches and shrines in which figures were usually positioned, and in the garish festoons of fruit and flowers; the addition of rare details and an antiquarian-archaeological tendency which became apparent in the depiction of rare types of marble, coral and metal. Essentially, the common link which can be found in those who learnt from Squarcione and absorbed his influence is a characteristic expressive tension.

Carlo Crivelli, *Madonna and Child*, 1482, Pinacoteca, Room VI

Giovanni Bellini, *Lamentation over the Dead Christ with St. Joseph of Arimathea, Nicodemus and Mary Magdalene*, 1471–1474, Pinacoteca, Room IX

■ Carlo Crivelli, *Madonna and Child*

The *Madonna and Child* (Room VI) by Carlo Crivelli is an emblematic example of this style, as too is the *Pietà*.

The Madonna is seated on a throne decorated with characteristic festoons of fruit, and the artist's tendency for decorative superabundance can also be seen in the precious cloak worn by the Virgin. The drawing is noticeably linear and the rhythms are broken. These enthroned Madonnas with characteristic Squarcione-esque stylistic elements were frequently represented. The signature and date of this *Madonna and Child* are engraved on the step where the Virgin's feet are resting and the buyer of the work is depicted kneeling.

In Venice, like in Florence, many commissions for works of art came from public bodies such as the government, ecclesiastical institutions and especially schools, or rather associations of a professional and charitable nature dedicated to a saint. Consequently, these schools often commissioned paintings in honour of their patron saints. The Venetian Renaissance had its own beginning in painting. The growth of Padua nearby and the work Antonello da Messina carried out in Venice led to the formation of a magnificent local school which found its high point in Giovanni Bellini (1432-1516), whose main interests were focussed on colour and light. We must not, however, place too much emphasis on the traditional difference between Florence and Venice in the pictorial field, which singles out the first of these towns as the birthplace of drawing and the second as the home of colour. All the foremost Venetian artists were primarily incredible draughtsmen, even though it is also true that the linear values which were widespread in Florence in the late 15th century (exemplified in Sandro Botticelli's work) were undervalued in favour of chromatic ideals. In Florence, colour was set above the pliable forms predisposed by drawing. In Venice, forms merged with colour and took shape thanks to it.

■ Giovanni Bellini, *Lamentation over the Dead Christ*

The *Lamentation over the Dead Christ with St. Joseph of Arimathea,*

Nicodemus and Mary Magdalene (Room IX) by Giovanni Bellini is thought to be the crowning (cymatium) of a large altarpiece which the artist painted for the Church of San Francesco (St. Francis) in Pesaro. The scene does not depict a Pietà, but rather the moment in which Christ's body is covered with oils and perfumes before it is buried. The figures represented are Joseph of Arimathea and Nicodemus along with Mary Magdalene, who is holding one of Jesus' hands in her own. The composition is compressed and the viewpoint is raised: the figures draw close to each other in an intentionally restricted space which aims to portray a concentrated sense of pain, closed in on itself and not overtly visible. This composition was in line with Bellini's poetics as he was not a painter who showed strong feelings, nor was he prone to portraying sentimentality. His figures are composed and do not ardently show their feelings, their pain is shut away inside. All the figures are looking towards Mary Magdalene's caressing gesture as she delicately oils one of Christ's stigmata. This reference leads us to St. Francis, the titular saint of the church for which the altarpiece was destined. He is depicted standing to the right of the throne in the central scene of the *Pesaro Altarpiece* illustrating the *Coronation of the Virgin*. His stigmatisation is also depicted in one of the panels of the predella, with intertwined cross-references running through the whole pictorial complex. The only spatial point of reference in the composition is the edge of the coffin with Christ's legs depicted hanging over the side. Otherwise the spatial context is undefined as the viewer looking up at the painting from below is not able to see where the scene is set and it seems to be devoid of any landscape. The only natural element is the cloudy sky whilst the unifying feature, which is also present in the altarpiece this work came from, is light, a warm late afternoon glow.

THE SIXTEENTH CENTURY

In the *Lives of the most eminent Italian architects, painters and sculptors from Cimabue to our times*, Giorgio Vasari hands down an image which would become emblematic of the "third age" or "manner", as an insurmountable stage both in the depiction of nature and the renascent ideal and classical model. The "first age" of the 14th century had given rise to an initial phase of the recovery of the image and natural space. The "second age" of the 15th century witnessed the high Renaissance, but was often suffocated by excessive rules and fixed designs. During the "third age", that is in the 16th century, the perfect equilibrium between manner and nature would be achieved; in fact his *Lives* Vasari defines the term manner as the style which would reach full command of its expressive means in the imitation of nature. The foremost artists of the "third manner" were Leonardo, Michelangelo and Raphael who, each with their own specific ability or "manner", endowed Italian civilisation with a common and unified culture and visual language, which could be understood by the whole peninsula beyond local traditions.

Raphael (1483-1520) was mainly influenced by Pietro Perugino during his training. He inherited his master's ideal and harmonious vision, and he studied the methods Perugino used to organise images and the types and positions of the figures until he completely assimilated his figurative language. Once he had learned his lessons, however, Raphael looked beyond Perugino's methods in search of more naturalness in his figures and more flexibility in his compositional rhythms. The most important contribution the artist made to the development of the mature Renaissance style was his ability to succeed in both establishing a flow of motions and looks among the figures which conferred naturalism and humanity to religious subjects and, at the same time, overcoming any residual compositional rigidity. These developments, along with the new magnificent architectural and landscape settings which blended in with the foreshortened figures in the foreground, ensured that his works became the standard for altarpieces. During the 15th century the desire to transform altarpieces with more lively scenes had already become apparent. The characteristic image of the Madonna in majesty with saints had been placed next to other scenes with a narrative quality such as the Adoration of the Child, the Baptism, the Crucifixion and the Pietà. These images, however, were always portrayed through the immobilisation of the scenes in compositions of symmetrical centrality which guaranteed their balance and harmony. The difficult part came in trying to conciliate a noble composition with the narrative liveliness which the 15th-century works were missing. Raphael freed himself from the traditional mould and was able to portray strongly dynamic and dramatic effects.

■ Raphael, *Coronation of the Virgin*

The *Coronation of the Virgin* (*Oddi Altarpiece*) (Room VIII), including the three sections of the predella conserved in the Pinacoteca depicting the *Annunciation*, the *Adoration of the Magi* and *the Presentation at the Temple*, is known as the *Oddi Altarpiece* after the name of the family who commissioned the work for their funerary chapel in Perugia. The painting, originally done on wood, remained in the chapel for which it had been conceived until it was seized by the French at the end of the 18th century and taken to

Raphael, *Coronation of the Virgin* (*Oddi Altarpiece*), 1502–1503, Pinacoteca, Room VIII

Paris where, in all probability, due to its condition upon arrival, it was transferred onto canvas. The altarpiece is narrative and the story unfolds from
the bottom to the top. The apostles rush to the Virgin Mary's coffin but they
find it empty and filled with flowers (including lilies) instead. In the next
scene, after their surprise, they contemplate the heavenly vision. The Madonna rises into the sky, body and soul, surrounded by the heads of cherubs
and angel musicians and is crowned by Christ as the Queen of the Heavens.
In this regard, only Pius XII (Pacelli, 1939-1958) proclaimed a dogma of the
Assumption into the sky of the Virgin, the first figure to rise to the heavens
in body and soul, but this creed was evidently already well established in
the hearts of devout believers in the 16th century. The structure of the altarpiece still follows a rigid layout, an aspect which demonstrates that Raphael
had not yet fully broken away from the methods of his master Perugino. A
thin layer of clouds divides the altarpiece into two clearly distinct sections,
separating the earthly event from the heavenly. We can observe, however,
some evidence of advancements and modernity. The tests carried out on
the painting give weight to the hypothesis that the panel was painted in two
different stages. The higher section with Christ crowning the Virgin was
done first, and at a later date, the artist completed the composition with
the apostles and flower-filled coffin. In the higher section the figures are
more rigid and reminiscent of Perugino's style while the positioning of the
apostles, captured in a variety of poses and foreshortened, create a more
dynamic structure in which the landscape blends in wonderfully with the
figures in the foreground. The key element of the whole altarpiece is the
empty coffin, situated in a prominent position and set diagonally in order to
accentuate the scene's sense of depth.

- Raphael, *Madonna of Foligno*

The great fame Raphael quickly acquired in Rome, following his commission to decorate the apartments in the Papal Palace, induced some ecclesiastical figures and people linked to the papal court to entrust the artist
with other high-profile commissions. This was the case with the so-called
Madonna of Foligno (Room VIII), a painting on wood transferred onto
canvas which Raphael was asked to paint by the historian Sigismondo
de' Conti, a member of an illustrious family from Foligno who, among his
various duties at the Papal Court, was also the secretary of Julius II and
prefect of the St. Peter's construction site. Although the buyer's heirs took
it to Foligno after his death, the painting was not done for the town. Sigismondo had intended to place it on the main altar of the Church of Santa
Maria in Aracoeli (St. Mary of the Altar of Heaven) in Rome, as a votive offering to thank the Virgin for having saved his house from the fall of a meteorite or a bolt of lightening. The painting is divided into two sections. In
the higher section, we can see the heavenly vision of the Virgin and Child,
seated on a throne of clouds and surrounded by angels. In the lower section we can see an earthly scene, with one of the most extraordinary representations of atmospheric landscapes of the 16th century. The buyer is
depicted on one side, kneeling in formal dress as he gives thanks while
he is presented to the Virgin by St. James dressed in a cardinal's robes.
On the other side we can make out St. John the Baptist wearing animal
skins and St. Francis. In the centre, an angel holds a sign without an inscription, on which, according to the wishes of the buyer, the reason why
the work had been done was meant to be explained. Sigismondo died before he was able to tell Raphael what to write, but the episode is fully described in the background of the painting where a meteorite or lightening

bolt can be seen as it strikes a town. The vertical structure and the division into two sections, though it can be linked to the structure of the *Oddi Altarpiece*, reveals significant new developments and modernity. Firstly, the figures are no longer isolated but communicate with each other in a network of gestures and looks, almost seeming to involve the viewer. St. John the Baptist is looking towards the viewer, indicating the Madonna. In contrast, St. Francis points towards the viewer but turns his eyes up to the sky and St. James, aside from presenting the buyer, indicates the building which has escaped from harm to highlight the reason behind the votive offering. Secondly, the landscape in the background, dotted with buildings and lovely figurines, is immersed in the rain-filled air, evoking an environment which is incredibly atmospheric. Finally, a unifying element which links the heavens and the earth is the rainbow, confirming and broadening the sense of harmony it confers on the scene.

The invention of a new, 16th-century standard for altarpieces is, to a great extent, due to the rivalry cleverly stirred up by Cardinal Giulio de' Medici, the nephew of Leo X who became Pope Clement VII, between Raphael and Sebastiano del Piombo, Michelangelo's favourite pupil. Sebastiano del Piombo painted a *Resurrection of Lazarus*, commissioned by Giulio de' Medici for Narbonne Cathedral in France, his bishop's see. The task was first entrusted to Raphael, but the artist was under pressure with other commissions and delayed starting the work. Giulio therefore offered the commission to Sebastiano, who fully devoted himself to it as he wanted to deliver a product which would bear comparison with anything Raphael could have painted. Even Michelangelo worked with him and did the preparatory drawings for the figures of Christ and Lazarus.

Raphael, *Madonna of Foligno*, ante 1512, Pinacoteca, Room VIII

- Raphael, *Transfiguration*

Annoyed by the fact that one of his commissions had been taken away
and given to someone else, Raphael tried to outdo Sebastiano and created an altarpiece, still for Giulio de' Medici, which was equal to, if not
more magnificent than the other – the *Transfiguration*. Raphael died
soon after, leaving this incredible spiritual testament. The energy he
put into it is demonstrated by the fact that it was painted almost entirely by the artist himself, instead of being entrusted to his pupils. The
composition holds two episodes which the artist connected in such a
way as to make each one exalt the other. The scene above portrays the
transfiguration on Mount Tabor or rather the appearance of Jesus in
his divine role to the prophets Moses and Elijah. The scene below is set
on earth and shows the episode of the miracle of the possessed boy in a
crowd of gesticulating and highly expressive figures. At first, Raphael's
altarpiece was meant to have portrayed the transfiguration scene on
its own. The addition of the episode of the healing of the possessed
boy can be attributed to his vying with Sebastiano del Piombo. In both
altarpieces the main theme is the power of Christ as a divine healer.
The double structure aims to emphasise the relationship between the
heavens and the earth. Above, in a dazzlingly bright sky, the figures
are positioned hieratically and symmetrically following a traditional
layout concept. Below, on a dark background, the figures stand out as
full forms, enhanced by the low light in this bold and revolutionary
composition. These masterpieces resulted in the emergence of a new,
dramatic type of 16th-century altarpiece, historically suited to an era of
strong contrasts and uncertainty. This was partly due to the schism of
Luther, which had inflicted a deep wound on the unity of the Church.

Raphael, *Transfiguration*,
c. 1515, Pinacoteca,
Room VIII

Pieter van Aelst (workshop), *Miraculous draft of fish*, c. 1519, after a cartoon by Raphael, Pinacoteca, Room VIII

The tapestries in the Sistine Chapel

Leo X wanted to link his name to a prestigious building like the Sistine Chapel and decided to decorate it with a series of precious tapestries, entrusting Raphael with the task of painting the preparatory cartoons. These designs were then sent to Flanders (now Belgium) and the tapestries were woven in Brussels in Pieter van Aelst's workshop, one of the most prestigious of the time, renowned for its high quality workmanship and materials. The subjects the Pope decided upon were the stories of St. Peter and St. Paul with episodes taken from the Acts of the Apostles. This theme was conceived to complete the design concept of the fresco decorations. The tapestries were intended to be hung on hooks around the lower section of the walls of the Sistine Chapel on special occasions. Leo X wanted this cycle to underline how the message of Jesus, thanks to the two apostles, reached Rome from Jerusalem and gave rise to the Church. Moreover, the Sistine decorative cycle as a whole aims to exalt the foremost spiritual guides of humanity on its journey: Moses in the Old Testament, Jesus in the New Testament, finishing with the Church represented by the Popes (established thanks to Peter and Paul).

The cycle dedicated to Peter and Paul started on the far wall either side of the altar where Michelangelo's *Judgement* is now situated. The

Miraculous draft of fish was the first of the *Stories of St. Peter*, which then proceeded around the right-hand wall under the frescoes of the *Stories of Christ*. The *Martyrdom of St. Stephen* was the first of the events of the life of St. Paul, which then unfolded under the frescoes of the *Stories of Moses* on the opposite wall. The *Miraculous draft of fish* is based on the well-known evangelical passage in which Jesus calls upon the first apostles Peter and his brother Andrew to be the "fishers of men". Here, the allusion made once again to the future Church is clear, represented by the small boat with Jesus as the guide. Although the tapestry weavers did not have a wide range of colours at their disposal, like, for example, a painter would have, they still were able to succeed in the arduous task of transferring the three-dimensional grandeur of the figures and the transparent effects of the water onto a weave of woollen threads.

Tapestries

The Italian word for tapestry (*arazzo*) derives in all likelihood from Arras, the northern French town which had produced them from around the 14th century onwards. Tapestries were very popular and widespread during the Middle Ages. At first they were used as ornaments and didactic tools in the cathedrals of central Europe (especially in France, Flanders and Germany), where they were hung on poles with hooks, positioned around the walls or between the naves and substituted painted scenes. These tapestries were characterised with sacred themes from the Old and New Testaments such as the edifying lives of saints. Later on, making use of their ornamental and practical qualities, tapestries became widespread among the lay nobility. They were used to decorate the rooms of castles, create moveable dividing walls and guard against the cold and humidity. As they came to be popular among wealthy individuals there was a great increase in their production and a preference arose for profane subjects which could be depicted in themed cycles such as the legend of King Arthur, knights and heroines and hunting scenes.

The most commonly used material was wool, woven by hand on a loom by the tapestry weaver according to a design provided by a painter. Consequently, there was a clear distinction between the moment the design was conceived and the making of the actual tapestry. The two tasks were entrusted respectively to the creator of the preparatory cartoon and the tapestry weaver. The weaver would use his loom to weave the warp threads (plain, sandy-coloured, vertical threads) and the weft threads (horizontal threads of various colours and textures). He would then chose the weaving material best suited to the design, as only he would know and understand the material and aesthetical traits of the threads. Weavers, therefore, were not just simple craftsmen, the executor of someone else's design; they were crucial participants in the process of transforming the design into a tapestry, creating a living scene with three-dimensional figures, expressive faces, landscapes, buildings in perspective and light and shadow. The loom was usually in a vertical position (haute lisse loom) and the weaver would sit behind it with the rear of the tapestry in front of him (the preparatory cartoon would be set up behind him). In order to check the work the weaver would have to either move round to the front of the loom or use a strategically placed mirror. As a result of both the value of the materials used (particularly with silk, gold and silver threads), and the care and attention required of the painter and the master weaver, the cost of tapestries was infinitely higher than the cost of frescoes or paintings on wood. It was for this reason that the buyers were always of a high social class and extremely wealthy.

Leonardo's St. Jerome

- Leonardo da Vinci, *St. Jerome*

Leonardo da Vinci (1452-1519) developed a modern conception of art considered as knowledge based on scientific principles. The aim of this conception was not to create a mechanical imitation of nature or a simple external reflection, it was to reproduce its internal aspects. This led Leonardo to fully investigate natural phenomena and go into anatomical science in depth. Essentially, Leonardo demanded a profound experience of reality from art, away from the abstract principles of the 15th century. This induced the artist to set his figures in atmospheric space with the subsequent study of the movement of air and light on the bodies. Hence the artist freed his figures from the rigid perspectival cage of the 15th century to

Leonardo da Vinci, *St. Jerome*, 1480,
Pinacoteca, Room IX

create a freely moving space in which the figures seemed to be enveloped by a soft and almost cloudy chiaroscuro effect, a characteristic Leonard-esque sfumato which left outlines and details undefined.

The oldest work in the 16th-century section is the painting on wood with *St. Jerome* by Leonardo da Vinci, a piece which has an unusual history. It was referred to for the first time in the 18th century in the will of the Swiss painter Angelica Kauffmann (1741-1807), who lived for some time in Rome and must have had the painting in her collection. When the art-ist died the painting was lost but luckily, it was found again, although it had been split into two parts. The first part, which formed the lower sec-tion of the work, was found a few years before its other half and it was said to been discovered being used as a lid in a junk shop. The second part, with the head of the saint, is thought to have been used as a shelf for a shoemaker's footstool. The details of these stories were probably made up, but we know for a fact that the panel was cut into two pieces, as often happened at the hands of antique dealers as they considered the single parts to be more marketable than the whole.

Leonardo left the painting in a rough draft form. The most common iconography seen in depictions of St. Jerome has two key forms: the saint represented as a penitent in the desert and the saint as a man of letters and scholar in his study. Leonardo chose to portray the saint as a penitent in a rocky landscape. St. Jerome lived in the 4th century and after a dream he had one night, he renounced the study of pagan literature, which he had admired, and withdrew into the desert to de-vote himself to the study of Hebrew and biblical texts. These studies led him to revise the Latin translations of the Bible with the Vulgate on the appointment of Pope Damasus (366-384), who is credited with promoting the transition from Greek to Latin as the liturgical language of the Church. This was a great change which can be compared to the introduction of the modern languages at the Second Vatican Council. This painting provides the opportunity to discuss the artist's main in-terests – the anatomical study of figures and landscape. The saint is de-picted half naked (his face hollow from his long abstinence from food) against rocky peaks, enveloped in an atmospheric setting with sfumato effects. We can see the characteristic attribute often seen in pictorial depictions near the saint – the crouching lion. According to tradition, the lion had a thorn in its paw which Jerome managed to remove, thus obtaining the animal's unconditional loyalty.

Venice: The other great alternative of the high Renaissance

The change which took place in art in central Italy at the beginning of the 16th century had the effect of stimulating Venetian painting during the developments of the high Renaissance style. Giorgione played a lead-ing role in the renewal of Venetian painting. Vasari identified the inno-vative stance of the painter and placed him among the founders of 'the third manner we can call modern'. Like Leonardo, Giorgione also per-ceived the need to move beyond the 15th century style. He rejected the abstract geometry linked to the earlier preparatory drawings and turned his attention to the problem of imitating nature with an experimental ap-proach similar to the one used by the Tuscan master. As Vasari wrote, 'he studied design, and was so fond of it, Nature assisting him to her utmost, and was so enamoured of the beauty of that art, that he would never introduce anything into his works which he had not drawn from life'. Giorgione therefore started working without a preparatory drawing and, for the first time, a freer style of expression was used in harmony with colour. Colour was no longer subordinate to the outlines of the objects nor complementary to their construction, the hues themselves became creators of form. This concept gave rise to soft images, formed by areas of colour without a precise outline, in which the traditional positioning of the shapes was abandoned. A whole generation of Venetian painters adhered to Giorgione's innovative breakthrough, including Titian (1490-1575), and it gave rise to the well-known contrast between Florentine drawing and Venetian colour which was visible throughout the artistic historiography of the 16th century. Even though it was schematic, this contrast effectively corresponds to the persistently discernible difference between the two pictorial traditions, where the Venetian school resolved its reference to nature in matters of vision – colour and light.

■ Titian, *Madonna dei Frari*

The large altarpiece with the *Madonna and Child with saints* known as the *Madonna dei Frari* was done for the Church of San Nicolò della Lattuga (St. Nicholas of the Lettuce) in the Lido of Venice, known as San Nicolò dei Frari (St. Nicolas of the Friars). When this work was being restored, the presence of an earlier version came to light. In the first version, at the top of the pyramid-shaped layout, the Madonna surrounded by saints is not on a separate level as she is in the final version. The current painting was actually done a lot later, when the artist had already begun experimenting considerably, and the main

Titian, *Madonna and Child with saints* ("*Madonna dei Frari*"), 1533–1535, Pinacoteca, Room X

reason behind the change was due to the iconography imposed by the buyers (the monks of San Nicolò dei Frari). The subject, therefore, was no longer a *Sacred Conversation* as it had been in the original, but the miraculous apparition of the Madonna to a group of saints or rather St. Catherine, St. Nicholas in a bishop's robe, St. Peter, St. Anthony with the lily, St. Francis and St. Sebastian. Unfortunately, the higher section of the panel was deprived of its lunette in the 19th century. This lunette held the dove of the Holy Spirit emanating divine rays which allowed the saints to contemplate the mystery. The reason for this separation was incidental and of a practical nature as the work was intended to be positioned next to Raphael's *Transfiguration* in the museum layout. The figures of the saints are gathered together in a small space known as an exedra (a covered area open on one side, used as a meeting place). The artist's signature is visible on the structure and the figures are depicted in various positions with different levels of foreshortening. The use of these modern techniques allows us to associate this work with the previously mentioned altarpieces by Raphael. Finally, the use of colour as a creator of shape and the supernatural light which shines down from above as a main feature and unifying aspect of the whole scene, together with the abovementioned layout of the figures, also allow us to count the work among the modern and revolutionary 16th-century altarpieces.

Renaissance and Baroque: A crisis of Manner

The term Mannerism is generally used to refer to the artistic phenomena which developed after Raphael's death, leading up to the beginning of the Baroque period. Inside the great classical equilibrium of the "third manner" established between Florence and Rome by the "greats" such as Leonardo, Michelangelo and Raphael and in Venice by Giorgione and Titian, the need arose for a renewed experimentalism with form and skill in the name of a desire to distort the principles of the Renaissance.

In Venice, too, the spread of the mannerist culture signalled a need for change which became apparent in the experimentation with new expressive possibilities and in the progressive modification of the traditional linguistic structures. During this period Jacopo Robusti known as Tintoretto (1519-1594) and Paolo Caliari known as Veronese (1528-1588) would devise new figurative codes. Veronese carried out his training in Verona, a suburban centre which had already felt the effects of the flow of modern thinking. Veronese's working life, however, was strongly linked to Venice as the town's political stability and ruling class (an aristocracy which was fully aware of its social and cultural role), fostered a rich artistic environment. This was partly due to a surge in building on the Venetian hinterland which had become possible thanks to the land investments made by the very same aristocracy. Veronese led the way into a temple of wordly glory, in the splendour of a secular society for whom past and present, and sacred and profane came together in a fantastic fusion. A constant on any artist's journey was therefore the equation of his painting with the ideals and the world of the Venetian aristocracy so that profane themes based on mythology and allegory, and subjects of a sacred nature had the same importance. Veronese's ability was confirmed chiefly in the field of great ceiling decorations, where a more scenographic and ostentatious style with subjects of a celebratory-allegorical nature allowed him to experiment with daring foreshortening on the figures and, in the field of colour, with bright hues and violent chromatism.

■ Veronese, *St. Helena*

In the painting of *St. Helena* (Room X) we can find some of the characteristic aspects of Paolo Veronese's painting, although it was unusual for him to portray just one figure. Helena, the mother of the Roman Emperor Constantine (306-337 AD) converted to Christianity and is said to have seen a vision of Christ's cross in a dream as a premonition of the discovery she was about to make. On a pilgrimage to the Holy Land, Helena found a piece of wood from the cross and brought some of the fragments back with her to the West. The subject matter more than the vision represents Helena's dream, as she is depicted sleeping with her head resting on her hand while a winged putto holds the cross before her. The compositional layout is solid and monumental, characterised by a decorative interest evident in the care which has been taken over the fabrics of the dress with their bright colours and heavy folds, and the background. Helena appears to be a very secular figure: flaunting attributes of sovereignty such as the gold crown, the rich dress and the purple cloak. We could compare her to a heroine from Greco-Roman mythology or to an allegorical image.

Furthermore, Veronese often used a free and secular interpretation of religious themes, a habit which even led to a censorial intervention by the Inquisition and culminated in a trial against the artist. After the Council of Trent, the religious authorities kept an eye on sacred painting to make sure it conformed to customary iconography and doctrine. Veronese, however, dared to go back to ideas based on the evangelical episodes and transformed them into ostentatious and spectacular representations of the Venetian nobility being entertained, an approach which did not go down well with the Counter-Reformation.

Veronese,
St. Helena, c. 1525,
Pinacoteca,
Room X

■ Federico Barocci, *Rest on the flight into Egypt*

The Catholic Church was intent on redefining its own role and doctrinal systems at the Council of Trent, after damaging its hope of reaching a reconciliation with the protestants.

Although it did not manage to formulate a set of rules which established norms for artistic activity, the Council still produced important consequences in the figurative field. In view of its sophisticated and intellectual nature, the mannerist language revealed itself to be unsuited to the new artistic requirements of the Counter-Reformation (aimed at divulging in clear and persuasive terms the principles of orthodox Catholicism) formulated during the Council of Trent. This stance soon led to the necessity of inspecting the congruency of the sacred images being produced with the themes of faith they were meant to expound. The new tendency, marked by a strong and severe line, culminated in the theoretical and actual censorship of Michelangelo's *Last Judgement*, with the work being used to set an example to others. The premises for judging works of art were therefore defined and based mainly on devotional value, relegating the artist's expressive freedom to the background. Federico Zuccari became the official representative of this tendency. The time Federico Barocci (1535–1612) spent in Rome was fundamental in his training. He came into contact with Federico Zuccari and worked with him, assimilating the state of contemporary artistic tendencies. Barocci became interested in religious orders and brotherhoods, interpreting the new religious ideals of comprehensibility and simplicity in works of art. Finally, he studied the great masters of the Renaissance, favouring Raphael and taking on his ideals.

In the *Rest on the flight into Egypt* by Barocci we can see the expression of the ideals of simplicity and immediacy capable of exciting devotion in the hearts of the faithful. The subject depicts the moment

Federico Barocci, *Rest on the flight into Egypt*, 1570–1573, Pinacoteca, Room XI

the sacred family rests during their journey to Egypt, which Joseph and the Virgin Mary were forced to make to save Jesus from the massacre of the innocents ordered by King Herod. Scenes from everyday life had become popular at that point and Barocci reinterpreted the traditional iconography of the sacred family resting from an angle of domestic simplicity. In the centre of the composition the Virgin is drawing water, while Joseph is behind her as he offers Jesus a small branch with some cherries in a loving and spontaneous gesture. The presence of the straw hat, the flask of water and the bag of food all contribute to creating an atmosphere of everyday life and familiarity that many people could relate to, while the cherries, like the other red fruit, red flowers and the coral are symbols linked to Christ foreshadowing his Passion and project the life of the son of God into a dimension of exceptionality. The artist has a great ability to use colour, infusing his works with Venetian emphasis in his own way. The colour is seen as vehicle of light which creates shapes and makes them evanescent at the same time.

THE SEVENTEENTH CENTURY

The opposition to Mannerism:
The Carracci family and Caravaggio

At the end of the 16th century figurative culture had not yet been permeated by mannerist concepts which heightened the principles of form and symbolism of classical Renaissance art. This sophisticated, intellectual language, based on learning and aimed, therefore, at a restricted cultural circle, could not avoid going against the Church's wishes. In order to be able to formulate a policy for sacred images, intended as a medium of popular devotion, the Catholic authorities called for a simple and clear figurative language. Consequently, as early as the mid-16th century the counter-reformist Church's perseverance in controlling sacred figures became more rigorous. Ideological criticism turned into aesthetical and stylistic criticism, and the premises were set down for surmounting Mannerism. There were two artists from northern Italy, however, Annibale Carracci and Michelangelo Merisi da Caravaggio, who initiated a profound figurative renewal in Rome at the end of the 16th century. They opposed mannerism in the name of a common desire to go back to the truth of objects and move closer to nature. A recovery of Renaissance concepts ensued, which defined the imitation of nature as the essential foundation of art.

■ Caravaggio, *Deposition*

Michelangelo Merisi, known as Caravaggio (1573-1610), did not want to take anything for granted and consequently he did not want to recognise any master, except nature and life. After more than two centuries of venerating antiquity, in a revolutionary move, Caravaggio refused to study it, contesting the authority of the past and the codified aesthetical norms. His cognitive experience, drawn from life, led to a harsh vision of reality portrayed with shocking vividness. The immediate result of the new aesthetical concept was the artist's reinterpretation of traditional subjects and his adoption of new expressive elements. Firstly, he carried out an intense overhaul of religious iconography: a realistic vision of history pitched against an ideal vision. Secondly, the new aesthetic inevitably involved the adoption of new expressive elements: emphasis on colour, light and shadow became fundamental elements inherent to pictorial progress. Light acquired an unprecedented structural role and almost became a third element next to drawing and colour, a revolutionary event comparable to the discovery of perspective in the 15th century.

The altarpiece of the *Deposition* (Room XII) was commissioned from Caravaggio for a chapel in the Church of Santa Maria in Vallicella (St. Mary in Vallicella) in Rome and although we can identify the artist's new way of dealing with sacred themes, this was one of the very few public works which aroused unanimous approval. As regards the subject, the work is not a burial, because the main figures are not portrayed in motion; it is not an actual deposition as the body of Christ is not being lowered into the tomb but laid on a stone slab; and in spite of the presence of the Virgin Mary, it is not a Pietà, given the number of and type of the figures present. The moment represented here is that of the deposition of the body of Christ onto the oiling stone, the tombstone which would be used to seal the chapel. The positioning of the figures in the composition is unusual and can be identified as the first tangible innovation. The body of Christ is supported by St. John and Nicodemus, while the Virgin Mary, Mary Magdalene and one of the pious women behind them are depicted in a pyramidal layout which comes to a point with the raised arms of the pious woman, her face distraught and turned up to the sky. The stone in the foreground forms the ideal base to support and develop the whole group of figures and can be interpreted from a symbolic point of view, given that

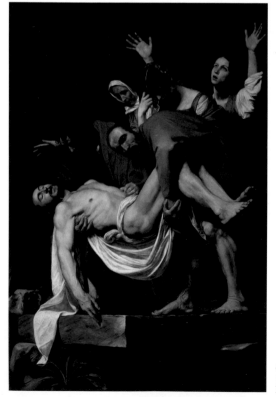

Caravaggio, *Deposition*, 1602–1604, Pinacoteca, Room XII

Christ is referred to in the Sacred Scriptures as the cornerstone on which the Church would be built. The artist's approach to the sacred theme is revolutionary: a realistic vision of history pitched against an ideal vision where life is introduced into the history of art. The Madonna's face is that of an old woman with her forehead furrowed with wrinkles, a result of her age and her suffering; Mary Magdalene's clothing and hairstyle is typical of the members of the lower classes in Rome at the beginning of the 17th century; and the muscles on Nicodemus' legs are protruding with the strain. The main aspect above all others is the light-dark contrast which creates volume and infinity in space. In particular, although the light confers three-dimensionality on the figures and makes them appear real, it does not deepen the space because the darkness, as a negative element which is opposed to light, fills the background. The figures therefore emerge from the shadows in the dark and impenetrable background: the figure of Christ, however, is fully visible and defeats death.

- ■ Guido Reni, *Crucifixion of St. Peter*

In the recovery of natural reality, Annibale Carracci was less drastic than Caravaggio and accepted history as an example of past experience to bring it back into the present. He added the study of ancient art and Raphael to the direct study of nature. The Carracci brothers drew on ancient art and models from the past and passed their classicist poetics on to their direct followers – Guido Reni and Domenico Zampieri known as Domenichino. This classical tendency was supported by commissions from the papacy and the great families of the Roman aristocracy and, consequently, the disciples of the Carracci family became exponents of the official line on taste.

This need for balance between nature and classical principles was put into effect in the work of Guido Reni (1575-1642), although the artist always kept up his constant expressive exploration and his desire to compare his work to others. The *Crucifixion of St. Peter* (Room XII) by Reni is a perfect example of this way of working. When Reni received the commission for the work he looked carefully at the altarpiece of the same subject done by Caravaggio a short time previously for the Church of Santa Maria del Popolo (St. Mary of the People). The light he uses can be described as Caravaggio-esque: it gives three-dimensionality to the figures and makes them seem real, but it does not deepen the space because the darkness, as negative element, forms the background from which the figures emerge. The layout, however, is in the classical style and derives from the artist's study of Raphael and the ancient masters. The cross is set intentionally in the centre of the scene in order to create a sort of symmetrical axis around which the figures are orderly positioned. In Caravaggio's work, on the other hand, the cross is set diagonally in an intentionally asymmetric position, while it is raised up vertically by labourers as if it were any other event from a humble life. Finally, Caravaggio portrays St. Peter's facial expression full of sorrow, while Reni, in line with the ideals of equilibrium and classicism, does not make the saint's face fully visible, almost as though he wants to respect his suffering.

Guido Reni, *Crucifixion of St. Peter*, 1605, Pinacoteca, Room XII

■ Domenichino, *Communion of St. Jerome*

Domenico Zampieri known as Domenichino (1581-1641) worked with Monsignor Agucchi in the theoretical definition of classicism. The fulcrum of his artistic conception was the rigor of drawing and the need for principles of order and clarity in the composition of the scene. The *Communion of St. Jerome* by Domenichino was inspired, in its rare iconographical subject, by the altarpiece painted by the artist's master Agostino Carracci. Agostino and Annibale Carracci founded the *Accademia del Naturale o del Disegno* in Bologna, the second city of the Papal States. This Academy did not offer elaborate aesthetical theories, but wanted to inspire its students in the unending and personal study of the reality around them through drawing from life. Besides the references to rich methods of Venetian emphasis on colour and an emotional conception of form, they aimed to achieve a devotional style of art or rather a way of painting capable of communicating religious sentiments of a popular nature, in line with the augured renewal of the Church. This altarpiece illustrates an episode from the life of the saint. As tradition has it, he felt his approaching death and gathered his remaining strength to take communion, supported lovingly by his disciples. The centre of the composition is the host, which attracts the attention of those present and the faithful viewer in line with the principles laid down by the Church of Rome. At that time the

Church considered – and still considers – the Eucharistic mystery to be at the centre and heart of believers' lives, contrary to accusations made by the protestant world. In Agostino Carracci's altarpiece, as in that of Domenichino, we can make out programmatic elements typical of this 17th century atmosphere. The figures' gestures and expressions are depicted with a careful descriptive analysis with the aim of inviting the faithful viewers to participate intensely in St. James' last communion with devotion equal to his. The use of colour and light, according to Venetian methods, is aimed at involving and moving the viewer in line with a conception of art capable of arousing devotion and holiness. The great arch of a church, under which the event is set and organised with compositional rigour, frames a wide stretch of landscape. During the 17th century landscape painting reached complete figurative autonomy, whilst in Italy the approach to the natural world had cultural connotations linked to the classical tradition, so artists such as Annibale Carracci and Domenichino created works in which landscape became a place where a common ideal between man and nature could be fulfilled.

Domenichino,
Communion of St. Jerome,
1614, Pinacoteca,
Room XII

Patrons, collectors, dealers and connoisseurs in seventeenth-century Rome

At the same time as the official patronage bestowed by the Pope, religious orders and great, aristocratic families, a large client base grew in Rome of cultured men such as scholars, doctors, lawyers, private collectors and even foreign travellers who were interested in the world of art. Amidst this backdrop, prestigious private galleries were founded which reflected the tastes and sensibilities of the buyers, and at that point in time paintings were bought, sold and inherited more and more frequently. This gave rise to the concept of works of art as consumer goods in addition to their cultural and social value, with the resulting development of economic investment interests and profit making. The growing demand for paintings had an effect on the way the arts were protected and the traditional rapport, which involved artists being regularly employed and maintained at the house of their patron, became less common. Over time, this rendered the figure of the intermediary or professional art dealer more and more important. They personally contacted living artists, who were then becoming self-employed, so as to take the works of art and offer them to collectors. However, as there were no precedents for setting prices for valuations and commissions, as soon as artists realised what was happening, they preferred to make do without the intercession of a dealer. It was easy to come across unscrupulous characters who promoted the production of unsigned works, copies and fakes. Along with the dealers, another figure representing a higher professional level emerged – the connoisseur. One of these connoisseurs was Monsignor Giovanni Battista Agucchi, a scholar and theorist of the concept of the *ideal* in art. Being part of the higher echelons of society, these cultured men and well-known professionals had friendly relationships with the most renowned artists of the time and, as they were collectors too, they also acted as mediators in the buying and selling of paintings. Furthermore, in a revolutionary new development, painting increasingly took on the characteristics of a public cultural phenomenon. This was due to the gradual spread of exhibitions organised for religious ceremonies and moments of particular popular devotion such as the festival of *Corpus Christi* (the feast of St. Joseph), when paintings were put on display at the Pantheon and the Church of San Salvatore in Lauro (St. Salvatore at the Laurels). Artists could therefore exhibit their works and the paintings were hung on the façade of the church, in the cloisters or the inner courtyards of the surrounding houses. These exhibitions became real opportunities for the artists to make themselves known and establish a rapport with the official critics of the time, such as Giovanni Battista Agucchi, as mentioned above, and Pieto Bellori.

■ Orazio Gentileschi, *Judith and her handmaid with the head of Holofernes*

The revolution led by Caravaggio was very appealing and full of innovative effervescence, which his followers became ingenious at recreating. Naturalism was not interpreted as a flat description or unequivocal imitation of life, but as a new cognitive experience. Thanks to Caravaggio painting acquired new expressive elements and emphasis on colour. Light and shadow became fundamental elements inherent in pictorial methods. In Rome, among the artists who were capable of renewing the pictorial language in a naturalistic way, following Caravaggio's example,

Orazio Gentileschi (1563-1639) took on a particularly important role, although his forms lost the dramatic emphasis Caravaggio produced. *Judith and her handmaid with the head of Holofernes* by Gentileschi depicts the famous biblical episode of the decapitation of the Assyrian King Holofernes by the Hebrew widow Judith, who wanted to save her people from foreign domination. This subject was commonly depicted in the 17th century because of the symbolic nature of the triumph of truth over heresy, interpreted in light of the dispute between Catholic reform and the protestant ethic at that time. Caravaggio, too, put himself to the test with the same subject in his *Judith and Holofernes*. We must remember that only the pictorial representation of "history" allowed painters to obtain public commissions and thus create a name for themselves, showing that they were able to cope with themes which, at that time, were considered to be at the highest level in the hierarchy of pictorial genres. In Gentileschi's painting, however, we cannot see the same dramatic force which Caravaggio conveys in his work. Caravaggio's scene portrays the moment Judith decapitates Holofernes and reveals the physical tension in her actions as she cuts off his head, culminating in the cry etched on Holofernes' face. Gentileschi chose to represent the moment immediately afterwards and inevitably softened the tone, even though Holofernes' head still forms the perspectival axis of the composition, which is more balanced and thus classical in style. The dark background from which the figures emerge and the emphasis on their form provided by the light, shows how the artist learnt from Caravaggio, although the rendering of the preciousness of the brocades and silks, the softness of the materials and the balanced and classical composition, distances the artist from the typically Caravaggio-esque religious scenes.

Orazio Gentileschi, *Judith and her handmaid with the head of Holofernes*, 1611–1612, Pinacoteca, Room XIII

Still life

In Room XIV of the Pinacoteca we can see various subjects including some representations of flowers and fruit. The rediscovery of nature and the new need to exalt the values of imitative methods, brought about a copious influx of still life paintings. This new genre reached complete autonomy in 17th century, although its origins can be traced to Flemish and Italian painting in the second half of the 16th century. In the northern European countries, where naturalistic tendencies emerged as early as the 15th century, artists created paintings with sacred subjects with elements such as flowers, fruit, pulses, fish and birds placed in the foreground; or religious scenes were transformed into genre scenes, in which the objects possessed intrinsic value. Until scientific tendencies came to be prevalent, however, which would lead to the recognition of the aesthetical and structural value of the object itself, the first examples of still life carried allegorical meaning, particularly of vanity or *memento mori*. Between the end of the 16th century and the beginning of the 17th century, the composition of objects such as a skull, an hourglass, a burning candle and a vase of flowers proffered the theme of the transience of beauty, and of time which consumed it. Soon after, however, allegorical representations were joined by illustrative, naturalistic depictions, promoted by the prevalence of buyers with scientific and botanical interests. Floral subjects were favoured because of their extraordinary botanical variety. Artists created works which portrayed such detailed scenes of natural reality that they astonished the imagination and the visual perception of the viewer. It was Caravaggio who gave the Italian still life genre complete freedom in its development. As the artist tested himself in the mimetic process of the natural world, he conferred deep representational nobility on nature, which was already considered to be intensely meaningful in itself. He marked the genre with a new form of expression which would then be assimilated by European Italian culture and which manifested itself in the meticulous description and emphasis of forms revealed by light.

THE EIGHTEENTH CENTURY

Amidst the cosmopolitan climate which characterised the 18th century, more and more foreign travellers came to Italy, many of whom were also distinguished collectors. The biographies of artists, for example, mention how English aristocrats would visit the studios, pay extraordinary prices and invite artists from all over Italy to go and live in England. Furthermore, the tradition of the Grand Tour continued, that is to say the educational journey young European aristocrats would make, usually with the guidance of a tutor, primarily to discover Italy. More especially the artists travelled tirelessly all over Europe; the favour they met with was linked to the fact they came from a long artistic tradition and possessed considerable technical ability. It was also based, however, on their capacity to recognise new trends and tastes and to take different experiences on board which contact with the wider world could offer. The resulting effect on art was the emergence of much more freedom. Images were gradually released from celebratory and persuasive objectives which had strongly marked 17th-century art in the name of the need for autonomy. Consequently, when 18th-century artists embraced the legacy of themes and methods of tradition, like historical, mythological or religious painting, they concentrated essentially on the demonstration of their own professional ability, becoming real "experts of image".

Furthermore, the spread of minor genres such as landscape, genre scenes and still life constituted a more consummate manifestation of the new climate, characterised by a new objective approach to the visual stimuli which came to be seen as the most open, enlightened path of 18th-century art. The words of Ludovico Antonio Muratori are emblematic: 'On one hand, poetry paints and represents truth as it is, or even as it should or could be, on the other hand it paints it directly with the aim of painting, imitating and translating with this beloved image, filling another person's imagination with beautiful, strange and wonderful images' (*Della perfetta poesia* [On perfect Italian poetry], 1706).

■ Pompeo Batoni, *St. John Nepomucene in adoration of the Virgin and Child*

Pompeo Batoni (1708-1787) established himself at the forefront of the Roman scene and remained there as its undisputed adjudicator for a considerable period of time. He championed a return to the sources of 17th-century classicism, which would gather new strength during the impassioned rediscovery of the ancient and in the subsequent theoretical words of Winckelmann, the first representative of the neoclassical movement. In his writings the central themes were Renaissance classicism and the great painting of the 17th century by Annibale Carracci, Domenichino and Guido Reni. At the same time, as a man of his time, he linked these classicistic tendencies to a new, completely 18th-century taste for beautiful painting: graciously composed and balanced in

Pompeo Batoni, *St. John Nepomucene in adoration of the Virgin and Child*, Pinacoteca, Room XV

the organisation of the expressive means and yet vibrant in its rich and precious brush strokes. He also tackled sacred and profane themes, distinguishing himself as a portraitist and becoming sought after by the most illustrious foreign clientele, especially the English. The painting of *St. John Nepomucene in adoration of the Virgin and Child* constitutes a model in itself for altarpieces, revealing the artist's ability in depicting religious scenes as well as other genres. St. John Nepomucene, the patron of Bohemia, was a priest and preacher at the court of King Wenceslas in the 14th century. He died as a martyr when he was thrown into the waters of the Vltava River and drowned. The composition is laid out on a diagonal axis following an ascending motion which differs distinctly from the symmetrical frontal design of sacred altarpieces. St. John is depicted in adoration of the Child who is revealed to him in an area closed off by architectural structures which spread over the edges of the painting.

■ Pompeo Batoni, *Portrait of Pius VI*

Batoni heralded a form of portraiture typical of the Enlightenment, which preferred the subject to be positioned in an elegant and seemingly casual pose against a background of landscapes and fragments of the ancient, in line with the antiquarian passions of the European aristocracy. His fame was mainly due to his great ability to portray facial features and to capture people's personalities. Even Pius VI (Braschi, 1775-1789), who completed the Pius-Clementine Museum (the first collection of Greco-Roman art in the Vatican) and founded the first Vatican Pinacoteca, wanted to have his portrait painted by Batoni as soon as he had been elected.

Pompeo Batoni, *Portrait of Pius VI*, Pinacoteca, Room XV.

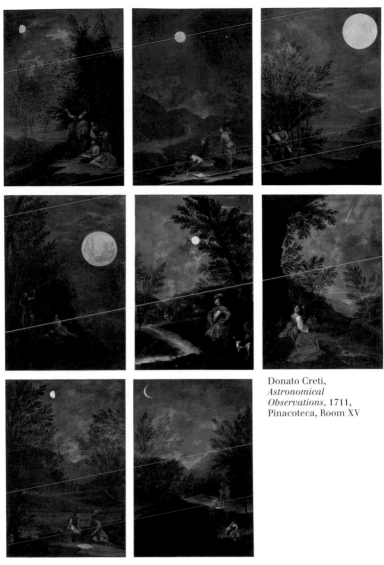

Donato Creti,
*Astronomical
Observations*, 1711,
Pinacoteca, Room XV

■ Donato Creti, *Astronomical Observations*

This journey comes to an end with an example of the renewed scientific interests typical of the Age of Enlightenment, which demonstrate how artists as well as scientists embraced the new aspirations. An absolute advancement can be seen in the astronomical subject of the small paintings of the *Astronomical Observations* (Room XV) by Donato Creti (1671-1749) portraying the *Sun*, the *Moon*, *Jupiter*, *Saturn*, *Venus*, *Mars*, *Mercury* and the *Comet*. The series shows the then known solar system as if seen through a telescope. The representation of the heavenly bodies supports the notions of the time: the small figures busy observing with telescopes and various optical instruments become lost in the vastness of the celestial landscape, once again, demonstrating the full autonomy the landscape genre had reached. Nature was no longer a background in which to set the events of history, but an opportunity for the study of the natural world enclosed in the enormity and complexity of the cosmos. The Church proved itself to be well up to date in its desire to deepen its knowledge of the universe and its laws through scientific investigation. Gregory XIII (Boncompagni, 1572-1586), the Pope who commissioned the Gallery of Maps, had the Tower of the Winds built to hold a sundial and an anemometer (wind gauge), and then invited astronomers and mathematicians to work out the changes which needed to be made to the calendar. From then on, the Church has never ceased to show its interest and give its support to astronomical research. As a result of these developments, Leo XIII (Pecci, 1878-1903) founded the Observatory on the Vatican hills behind St. Peter's Basilica, partly to counteract the accusations aimed at the Church over the centuries of it being opposed to scientific progress.

- ■ Wenzel Peter, *Adam and Eve in the Garden of Eden*

Let us finish with the serene image of the painting portraying *Adam and Eve in the Garden of Eden* by Wenzel Peter (1745-1829), an Austrian painter working in Rome, which forms a sort of zoological and botanical catalogue of the Old and New Continents executed with great scientific precision. The temporal reference in the scene is clear: the painter has not depicted the two main characters in an atemporal setting, but in the moment immediately before Adam accepts the prohibited fruit given to him by Eve. After this fateful moment nothing will ever be the same again. Here, we can stand in contemplation of the perfect peace which is about to be shattered.

Wenzel Peter, *Adam and Eve in the Garden of Eden*,
Pinacoteca, Room XVI

Indexes

INDEX OF ARTISTS

printed by Tipografia Vaticana

Reprint										Year										
1	2	3	4	5	6	7	8	9	10	2010	2011	2012	2013	2014	2015	2016	2017	2018	2019	2020